SQUARE DEAL DENIED

by

E. A. GIBBINS

M.C.I.T.

Published by
Leisure Products
11 Bedford Grove
Alsager
Stoke on Trent ST7 2SR

This book is dedicated to Irene for her encouragement
and to my parents.

I wish to thank those who assisted my research:
the Public Record Office, House of Lords Record Office,
Chartered Institute of Transport Library, Keele University
and public libraries at
Alsager, Birmingham, Crewe, Ellesmere Port,
Hanley, Liverpool, Manchester, Widnes

I am especially grateful to those, whose computer expertise
has been invaluable in enabling me to bring this work to a conclusion -
Julian, Simon, Sara, Andy, John and Brian

Published January 1998

ISBN 0-9521039-3-1

TO EVERY MEMBER OF THE PUBLIC

Remember the Railways are
ESSENTIAL in PEACE and VITAL in WAR

Their financial position is grave.
They are playing their part well now.
Can they go on doing it?

YES - If they have a fair share
NO - If they are bound while their competitors are free

Road carriers, Canal carriers, Coastwise carriers are free to quote without restriction whatever charges are appropriate in each case. Railways alone are restricted. WHY?

Red Tape is tough: Old prejudices die hard : It is hard to shake off the dead hand of restriction. But it must be shaken off, if the Railways are to survive and play their part.

The need for action is urgent, it must not be deferred until it is too late.
A short Act of Parliament is required this Session to meet a crying national need.

Support the claim of the Railways for Equality and

A SQUARE DEAL NOW

Issued by the Railway Companies Association

One of the "Square Deal" campaign advertisements published in November 1938.

The Author

In 1946, Ted Gibbins followed his father into the service of the London, Midland & Scottish Railway Co. He began as a junior and ended as a Chief Officer with British Rail. His 40 year career took him to three Regions and to BR Headquarters in London, serving in several Operating and General Management positions, before taking early retirement.

His first book, "Blueprints for Bankruptcy", was published in 1993, with a second edition in November 1995 (ISBN 0-9521039-2-3). Drawing from Public Records, it reveals how Government policies on charges, closures, investment and competition finally brought Railways to bankruptcy. No other industry in the private or public sector, was subject to such interference and restriction. Ministers criticised British Rail for being unprofitable, when their own legislation specifically directed that it should not make a profit! Governments went further and enforced policies which ensured that BR could only make losses. In return Ministers offered interest bearing loans! No other industry, however skilled its managers could have avoided bankruptcy in such a situation.

He exposed the role of the Transport Tribunal - a Court of Law, which decided fares and charges for 20 years, with occasional interference by Ministers to make matters worse, and revealed its destructive effect on rail finances. Hitherto, little had been written about this important body. Its deliberations delayed price increases and changes for 12 years! Railway charges trailed the RPI for 34 consecutive years, not merely because of the delay caused by the Tribunal, but also because it reduced BR proposals on virtually every occasion. Despite this loss of income, they were expected to fund modernisation.

The role of the rail users Watchdogs is highlighted, revealing 'U' turns, commercial unreality and some incomprehensible complaints statistics. No other industry accepts that standard of service be judged on the basis which these watchdogs pursued.. As rail mileage and business declined, so their activities expanded. Unreliable equipment from the private sector, other industrial failures and public actions assisted BR's downfall.

The book was reviewed three times for varying interest groups:-

The Railway Magazine - July 1996

This book is an immensely thorough study of the industry, written by a totally committed professional railwayman. The publisher deserves our thanks for this timely and efficient work.

Chartered Institute of Transport - Proceedings, 1996

This is a healthy revision of the original, through the release of, or access to more Government & British Rail papers, partly because the book now covers much of the traumatic period leading up to BR's privatisation. Many chapters have been greatly expanded. The style is uncompromising and forthright. There is a very welcome index and a list of sources. A remarkable collation of arguments which run contrary to the conventional wisdom. It does not deserve to be neglected.

Railway & Canal Historical Society Journal - July 1997

An ammunition store of missiles to hurl at Government's policy throughout the 20th century and, in particular, today. Reveals that Government has deliberately placed obstacles before the railways and has given every possible opportunity to road haulage. Those opposed to privatisation will find much useful material to support their case. It points to a new aspect of British railway history. A comprehensive index. Paperback - well bound, does not fall apart with use.

PREFACE

In researching Public Records for my book "Blueprints for Bankruptcy" - the record of Government's ruinous policies towards British Rail - I began to uncover large quantities of, hitherto, unpublished material on the pre-war campaign by privately owned railways for a "Square Deal". In that book I made references to the "Square Deal" and other pre-nationalisation developments, to set the background. This new book presents a fuller picture of events leading up to, and surrounding the "Square Deal" campaign.

Many may be aware of a "30 year rule", which enables Government to withhold papers for a minimum of 30 years, some for 100 years. There is often no indication of what is withheld until it is released - many are simply listed as "Correspondence & Papers" for a particular year or years. The researcher is confused on discovering that the years in question overlap so that several files contain papers for a particular year. On accessing them, there may be nothing of relevance. Some file titles give no clue to their link with items sought - e.g. none are titled "Square Deal", although enclosed papers are so titled. There was no direct reference to the "Stedeford Committee", whereas files on other Reports clearly refer to the Chairman's name.

Files on the abolition of the iniquitous Railway Passenger Duty, [tax] in 1929 were closed until 1986; that on the rejected demand for a "Square Deal" [equality with road transport] until 1990; that on requisitioning in 1939 of wagons owned by non Railway companies until 1991, [but released in 1972]; those on railway wartime sequestration in 1939 to dates varying between 1991 and 1999. That on 1939-45 War Damage compensation to railways was still labelled: "Closed to 2000" when I saw it in 1992, having apparently been released "early". Papers of the 1946 Charges Consultative Committee, arising from its Public Inquiry into rates and charges, and confidential recommendations to the Minister of Transport were endorsed "Closed to 1997", when I saw them in 1995. The 1961 "Stedeford Report", commissioned by Government, into BR finances and organisation was kept secret, until 1991. None show Governments, of any political persuasion, favourably, in relation to railway viability. None were prejudicial to State Security. The conclusion one reaches, is that those concerned hoped that by the time these politically embarrassing papers were released, there would be no public interest in them.

Of some reports, there is no trace. Likewise, there is no trace of some Memos or letters which are referred to in available files.

Ted Gibbins

CONTENTS

INTRODUCTION

Those who have heard of the "Square Deal" campaign : railways equality with road transport, believe it was initiated in 1938, but it was first sought in 1921. Their proposals for achieving it changed, because of Government inertia on initial concepts. It was not until 1938 that Sir Ralph Wedgwood of the LNER called for their long running campaign to be given that snappy title. It suited the book of those with the power to implement an overdue change, and who accepted that existing legislation was inequitable, to regard it as a purely 1938 campaign, because they were able to plead the imminence of War for their prevarication.

There were five window dressing Inquiries in response to Railways' pleas: in 1921, 1928, 1932, 1935 and 1939. In aggregate they occupied over seven years, and had the effect of kicking the problem into touch to avoid the political risks which may be involved in repealing immoral, but electorally popular, legislation.

PRO file MT6/2876 reveals that Government had no intention of giving the freedom sought by the Railways, nor the pale substitute proposed by the Inquiry which it set up and totally discounts popular belief of these last 60 years, that it was only a War which blocked anti-rail legislation from being repealed. Public Records reveal duplicitous conduct by pre-war Ministers and Civil Servants in their dealings with the private railway companies. Quite unambiguously, they were not prepared to concede to railways, the same legislative and commercial freedom, which was enjoyed by road transport operators.

Government files contain memoranda and papers which clearly indicate that Ministers and their senior Civil Servants accepted that the source of the decline in rail freight was the railway rates system forced on railways under the 1921 Act, coupled with the retention of anti-rail legislation dating back to 1845. They acknowledged that the iniquitous rates system, and a convoluted Rebates Fund, were designed to protect and subsidise UK industry and agriculture - at railway expense.

As War became inevitable [measures to prepare railways for war were in hand for years], Ministers and Civil Servants played "pass the parcel". In May 1939, the MoT told the Cabinet that "It does not seem possible to accept that railways should be put on the same footing as other transport". Had there been no war, Government's prevarication must have led to railway insolvency in the 1940's. A rumour that Lord Stamp threatened voluntary liquidation of the LMS would have become a reality. Government would have had to concede equality, replace railway subsidies to heavy industry by State subsidies or nationalise railways.

Government moved quickly enough to pass complex Defence Laws but were paralysed by this crisis. They soon confirmed that Railways would play a vital part in evacuation, moving 100,000 persons per hour from London, on top of industrial and war traffic, and millions travelling to work by train to factories and elsewhere. Railways moved 1.3m evacuees in the first four days of September 1939. Four weeks before War was declared,

Government passed the 50 page BOAC Act, which did not control their charges! The Railways' just claim required a one page Act setting out a short list of repeals..

There was never any prospect that an industry, so disparate as road haulage would establish a common rates system to facilitate co-oordination, which Government claimed it sought, and frequently reiterated, as an excuse for inertia. When the same political party returned to power in 1951, they promptly ditched their oft proclaimed policy.

War did not preclude action because the Cabinet busied itself with post war plans long before they knew that the war could be won. A post war national health plan was developed and more Civil Service leave considered. A Railway Charges Act could have been passed in early 1939 or prepared for implementation at the end of the war for this problem would not disappear but could only get worse.

Government was thinking ahead about the need for post-war exports to repay huge debts and pay for a welfare state. Ensuring Railways did not continue to lose traffic due to inequitable legislation would have released road vehicles for export and killed two birds with one stone. Railway freedom to decide their own prices in line with the rest of industry, competitors and suppliers, would have been just, and enabled them to adjust charges, up or down, at will to remain solvent. Instead, Government controlled charges for a further two years after the War and enacted legislation that nationalised Railways must devise Charges Schemes, still subject to a Court of Law to control monopoly powers lost 29 years earlier! This, despite evidence of pre-war diversion of traffic to road, and a major post-war expansion of road transport.

Although transport nationalisation was planned, there would be more competing road vehicles on the road than before the war. Heads firmly in 19th century sand, the BTC was told to prepare passenger and freight Charges Schemes, for rail, road, canal and docks, and submit, them within two years, for consideration, by a Court of Law - whose predecessor, under the same Chairman, took seven years to produce one freight scheme!

It has been claimed, that railways were only too pleased to be taken over in the 1939-45 War, by Government in exchange for a fixed Rental, because of fears of insolvency. Public Records show that to be untrue. Ministers and Civil Servants expressed surprise at railway confidence of higher wartime traffic levels, despite the fact that contemporary Government documents clearly showed that substantial traffic increases on railways were seen as inevitable. Their disparate attitude to railways in war, compared to other industry and transport ensured post-war insolvency.

Some statutory, but no political, equality between rail and road transport, came in 1962. It was too late. The subsequent demise of heavy industry, on which the Government's rates system had made railways dependent, dragged railways down. Commercial equality with shipping came in 1980. There is still no equality in safety, infrastructure and bridge costs, working hours and maintenance, in all of which road transport lags behind.

ABBREVIATIONS

ABCC	Association of British Chambers of Commerce
AGM	Annual General Meeting
ARP	Air Raid Precautions
BEF	British Expeditionary Force [The Army sent to France in 1914]
BI&SF	British Iron & Steel Federation
BOAC	British Overseas Airways Corporation
BoT	Board of Trade [Responsible for railways before 1919]
BR	British Railways [A subsidiary of the BTC]
BRB	British Railways Board [Created in 1962]
BRF	British Road Federation
BRS	British Road Services [A subsidiary of the BTC]
BTC	British Transport Commission [created in 1948, abolished in 1962]
CBI	Confederation of British Industry
CC	County Council
C&D	Collection and Delivery
Cd	Command Paper [1900-18]
CGM	Chief General Manager
Cmd	Command Paper [1919-56]
Cmnd	Command Paper [1956-]
Col.	Colonel
col.	column (in Hansard)
CSO	Central Statistical Office
cwts	Hundredweights [one twentieth of a ton].
d	penny (pre 1971 coinage; 1d = 0.44p)
DoT	Department of Transport [set up by an Act of 1919]
DoWT	Department of War Transport [1941-46]
EEC	European Economic Community
eohp	Except otherwise herein provided (Used in GCM - see page 77).
EPT	Excess Profits Tax (A wartime tax)
ft	feet [one foot = approximately 30.5cm]
FBI	Federation of British Industry
GCM	General Classification of Merchandise
GCR	Great Central Railway
GM	General Manager
GNR	Great Northern Railway
GWR	Great Western Railway
Govt	Government
HoL	House of Lords
HM	His Majesty's [Forces]
HT	High tension
KC	Kings Counsel
LCC	London County Council
LGOC	London General Omnibus Company
LMS	London Midland & Scottish Railway

LNER	London & North Eastern Railway
LNWR	London & North Western Railway
LPTB	London Passenger Transport Board
LSWR	London & South Western Railway
Lt. Col.	Lieutenant Colonel
LYR	Lancashire & Yorkshire Railway
m	millions
MoT	Minister of Transport [set up by an Act of 1919]
MoWT	Minister of War Transport [1941-46]
MP	Member of Parliament
MSC	Manchester Ship Canal
NBR	North British Railway
NER	North Eastern Railway
NFU	National Farmers Union
pa	per annum
Para.	Paragraph
POW	Private Owner Wagon [not owned by railway companies]
PRO	Public Record Office
PS	Parliamentary Secretary
PSV	Public Service Vehicle
RAC	Rates Advisory Committee [Set up by the Ministry of Transport Act, 1919]
RCA	Railway Companies Association
R&CC	Railway & Canal Commission
RCT	Royal Commission on Transport
REC	Railway Executive Committee [Wartime Group of Railway Managers]
RFR	Railway Freight Rebates
Rly	Railway
RPI	Retail Price Index
RRT	Railway Rates Tribunal [a Court of Law]
RSNT	Railway Staff National Tribunal [Independent Arbitration body]
RTC	Regional Transport Commissioner [for wartime road transport]
s	shilling [pre 1971 coin = 5p]: written as 1/- or 1s
Sec.	Section [of an Act of Parliament]
SER	South Eastern Railway
SR	Southern Railway
TAC	Transport Advisory Council
TCCT	Traders Co-ordinating Committee on Transport
TGWU	Transport & General Workers Union
TUC	Trades Union Congress
vol.	volume [of Hansard, a book, or other publication]
WPI	Wholesale Price Index
WW II	World War II [1939-45]

THE PRINCIPAL PARTICIPANTS

Balfour-Browne, J.H., KC : Chairman 1921 Committee on Railways' Road Powers
Barnes, Albert : Minister of Transport 1945-51.
Barnes, Major H., MP : Member of Colwyn Committee.
Blee, David : Member, Railway Executive, 1948-53
Birtchnell, C.A. : DoT/DoWT, Assistant Secretary, Traffic Section.
Bruce-Thomas, Wm, KC, : President RRT 1921-47, & Transport Tribunal 1948-50.
Browett, Sir Leonard : Permanent Secretary, DoT/DoWT 1939-43.
Burgin, Leslie : Minister of Transport, 1937-39.
Butterworth, Sir Alexander, : General Manager, NER.
Churchill, W.S. : Chancellor, 1924-9, Prime Minister 1940-45, 1951-55
Clarke, H.T. : DoT/DoWT, Rates & Charges Officer, Secretarial Section.
Colwyn, Lord : Chairman of Departmental Committee, 1920.
Dickson, D. : DoT/DoWT, Staff Officer [Statistics], Secretarial Section.
Geddes, Sir Eric: The first Minister of Transport : 1919-21.
Gore-Browne, Sir Francis KC, : Chairman, RAC.
Graham, Wm. MP, : Member of Colwyn Committee.
Griffith-Boscawen, Sir A.S.T. : Chairman, RCT; Chairman, TAC.
Hambro, Sir Charles : Chairman, GWR.
Hill, R.H. : Principal Assistant Secretary, DoT, Deputy Director General, DoWT 1941-47
Hind, W.M. : DoT/DoWT, Finance Officer, Public Utilities Section.
Holland-Martin, R. : Chairman, SR until 1944.
Hopkins : Treasury, Second Secretary.
Hurcomb, Sir Cyril : Director General of Ministry of Shipping 1941, & MoWT 1943-45,
Keenlyside, F.H. : DoT/DoWT, Private Secretary to Permanent Secretary.
Leathers, Lord: Minister of Transport : 1941-45 & 1951-53
Llewellin, Col. J.J. : Parliamentary Secretary to MoWT
Matthews, Sir Ronald : Chairman, LNER.
Milne, Sir, James : General Manager, GWR.
Moore-Brabazon, Lt.Col. J.T.C. : Minister of Transport 1940-41 [Later, Lord Brabazon]
Newton, Sir Charles : Chief General Manager, LNER from 1939.
Noel-Baker, F.J. : Parliamentary Secretary to the MoWT
Page, S.J. : DoT/DoWT,Assistant Secretary, Public Utilities Section.
Robinson, A.T.V. : DoT/DoWT, Deputy Secretary.
Royden, Sir T. [later Lord] : Chairman, LMS 1941-47.
Salter, Sir A. : Chairman Road-Rail Conference, 1932.
Stamp, Sir J. [later Lord] : Chairman & President, LMS until 1941.
Stedman, G.F. : DoT/DoWT, Assistant Secretary, Secretarial Section.
Sturgess, A.B. : DoT/DoWT, Finance Officer, Public Utilities Section
Walker, Sir Herbert : General Manager, LSWR, Chairman REC 1914-19.
Wallace, Captain Euan : Minister of Transport 1939-40
Wedgwood, Sir Ralph: CGM, LNER until 1939, Chairman REC 1939-41.
Weir, Lord : Chairman of 1929-31 Committee on Electrification of Railways
Wilson, Sir Henry. : Treasury, Permanent Secretary.
Wood, Sir Wm : Vice President, LMS, President from 1941.

MAIN SOURCES

Blee Papers	PRO : AN6/10
Cabinet Minutes & Papers	PRO : CAB [see also below]
Charges Review, 1946	PRO : MT6/2704, closed to 1997*
Colwyn Committee	PRO : MT6/3134, closed to 1971; Cmd 1228
Command Papers	34 Papers examined are shown in text by their N^{os}
Manchester Ship Canal	
Board & Other Minutes	County Record Office, Manchester
Directors Reports	Manchester Central Library, F.386.M9
Marshall Plan	PRO : MT6/2830, closed to 1999*
Midland Railway AGM's	PRO : RAIL491/12
"Paying their way" - legal view	Butterworths' Annotated Legislative Service Supplements 49 [Page 51], 50 [Page 108]
Parliament Debates & Answers	Hansard, volume and columns shown #
Railway bridges	PRO : MT39/671, MT39/929, closed to 1981
Railways - finance & future	PRO : MT47/275 closed to 1996*
Railway Passenger Duty	PRO: MT47/128, closed to 1986
Special Advisory Group [Stedeford Committee]	PRO : MT124/361, MT124/547, MT132/80-88 closed to 1991
Square Deal	
Cabinet	PRO : CAB60 [38], CAB18 [39], CAB24/286
DoT	PRO : MT6/2876, closed to 1990
LMS	PRO : RAIL424/27, includes some RCA copies
RCA	"Clear the Lines", "Railway Crisis", "Coming of Age"
TAC 1937 Report	PRO : Cabinet Minutes 1938, CAB23/92, CAB24/274
Transport Bill, 1952	PRO : MT62/138, closed to 1983
War compensation paid	PRO : MT47/263, closed to 2000*
Wartime control	
Cabinet	PRO : CAB65/18, CAB66/17
DoT	PRO : MT6/2604, MT47276, 277, 278 closed to 1991-2; MT47/279, closed to 1999*
LMS	PRO : RAIL424/15, RAIL424/16. RAIL424/18
Other	Cmd 6168; Cmd 6314
Wartime control revenue	Keesings Contemporary Archives
Wartime requisition of POW's	PRO : MT6/2611, closed to 1991
Wartime traffic & statistics	1914-18 : Pratt; 1939-45 : Bell, RCA, Savage [see Bibliography]; both wars : Command Papers
Weir Report on electrification	PRO : MT6/3335, closed to 1986
1952 Bill [for 1953 Act]	PRO : MT62/138

* Released earlier than originally specified, as I saw them from 1992 onwards.

References to Hansard are to the House of Commons unless shown as HoL [Lords].

OTHER SOURCES

Bibliography

In the text, references to a source from an author is shown by naming the author, and the page concerned. Where more than one book by an Author is quoted in the text, it is shown as Barnett[1] or Barnett[2].

Albert, W. : The Turnpike System in England, 1663-1840
Aldcroft[1], D.H. : British Transport History 1870-1970[1]
Aldcroft[2], D.H. : British Transport since 1914[2]
Anderson, D. : Coal
Barker & Gerhold : The Rise & Rise of Road Transport, 1700-1990
Barnett[1], Correlli : The Audit of War[1]
Barnett[2], Correlli : The Sword Bearers[2]
Bell : History of BR during War 1939-45
Bonavia[1] M.R. : The Four Great Railways[1]
Bonavia[2] M.R. : Railway Policy between the Wars[2]
Bullock, A. : Life and Times of Ernest Bevin
Burton, A. : Great Days of Canals
Cairncross, A : British Economy since 1945
Chester, Sir N. : Nationalisation of British Industry
Court, W.H.B. : History of the Second War - Coal
Deighton, Len : Blood, Sweat & Tears in the Darkest Hours of the 2nd World War
Elliot, Sir John : On & Off the Rails
Fiennes, G.F. : Fiennes on Rails
Ford - A Breviate of Parliamentary Papers
Grinling, C.H. : The History of the GNR
Goodspeed, D.J. : Ludendorff
Hadfield : British Canals
Hamilton, J.A.B., : British Railways in World War 1 [The "Great War"]
Henshaw, D. : The Great Railway Conspiracy
Hindle, B.P. : Roads, Trails & Their Interpretations
Keesing : Keesings Contemporary Archives
Klapper, C.F. : The Golden Age of Buses
"Manifold" : North Staffordshire Railway
Nock, O.S. : A History of the LMS
Paget-Tomlinson, E : History of Canals & River Navigations
Perkin, H. : The Age of the Railway
Plowden, Wm. : Motoring and Politics
Pole, Felix : Felix Pole, My Book.
Pratt, E.A. : British Railways and the Great War
Ransom, P.J.G. : The Archaeology of the Transport Revolution 1750-1850
Rogers, H.C.B. :Turnpike to Iron Road
Royle, T : The Kitchener Enigma
Sanderson, H.F. : Railway Commercial Practice, vol 2.

Savage, C.I. : Inland Transport in World War 2
Sherrington, R.C.H. : Economics of Rail Transport in Great Britain, vol. 2
Smith D.N. : The Railway & Its passengers
Supple, Barry : The History of the British Coal Industry, 1913-46
Sutton, Richard : Motor Mania
Taylor, A.J.P. : English History, 1914-1945
Williams, H. : Stage Coaches in Wales

The following are referred to by title:-
British Railways in Peace and War by GWR, LMS, LNER, SR
British Transport Commission Annual Report & Accounts, [shown as BTC Report]
"Blueprints for Bankruptcy", 2nd edition, E.A. Gibbins
"Clear the Lines" - RCA Publication
"Coming of Age" - RCA Publication
"Fair Play for Railways" - RCA Publication
"Peoples Year Book" - Co-operative Wholesale Society
"Railway Crisis" - RCA Publication
Statistical Digest of World War II
Statistics of the British Empire in the Great War
"Transport Goes to War", published by the Ministry of Information,
"Your Concern" - published by Railway Stockholders

Newspapers & Journals
References to
"Commercial Motor", show the date.
"Economist" show the date and the page number.
"Financial News", show the date.
"Modern Transport", show the date.
"The Times" show the date and the page and column number.

NOTES

[ ] - Used where the text enclosed was in the document concerned, or a related document. Also used, generally at the end of the text, to show the source.
( ) - Used to enclose text from documents or statements unrelated to the preceding text - the source being shown. Unattributed text are the author's views & comments. Also used, usually at the end of a paragraph to cross refer to another chapter or page in this book.

Page - with a capital 'P' and a number, refers to a page in the Report or Source concerned.
page - with a small 'p' and a number, cross refers to another page in this book.

Where italics are used, they are the author's.

PART I

THE BACKGROUND

The Government's Committee recommended that the Government should repudiate Agreements, to which they had become parties, and to treat these documents as scraps of paper.

[Chairman of Midland Railway at 1920 AGM]

Chapter 1 PRE RAILWAY TRANSPORT

Before the advent of railways, goods transport was largely water based. Before the advent of canals, it was by means of coastal vessels or natural inland waterways. Goods carried by coastal vessels were subject to damage by sea water or infestation, and in wartime, vessels were vulnerable to attack by enemy vessels. In addition to using rivers to reach ports, goods were conveyed by river between towns. Delays were experienced in winter, during periods of drought and when rivers were in flood. To reach ports and rivers, goods were conveyed by pack horse or cart over inferior routes. All transport added significantly to costs.

Improved River Navigation

In 1532, responsibility for maintaining rivers lay with the King's Commissioners. Between 1539 and 1700 numerous Acts of Parliament were passed to grant powers to improve navigation on rivers and improve harbour facilities. These often attracted opposition from towns and businesses which feared a loss of involvement in through traffic, and hence of profits. [Albert, Pages 11 & 12].

Owners of improved river navigations could price at will - until carriers on the Thames objected, when legislation was enacted to protect them. The Loughborough Navigation produced a return of 140%. [Albert, Pages 7 & 194]

Road maintenance

From 1555, road maintenance was, by law, carried out by local men who had to devote four days pa to the task, "roads", such as they were, being mainly for local traffic. A local "surveyor" was responsible for seeing each man performed the required number of days, which was later increased to six days. "Surveyors" were not qualified as we understand them today. Many "roads" were usable only by packhorse. Inadequate transport limited potential markets and increased prices. Rising industrial output taxed the existing means of water transport and seriously worsened the condition of "roads", especially those leading to ports or rivers.

As traffic increased, parishes were unable to cope with increased maintenance. This led to the concept of Turnpike roads, whereby the users of roads could be charged for their use of roads and the funds devoted to maintaining and improving them. Turnpike Trusts were established by Act of Parliament which specified the tolls which could be charged. The earliest Turnpike was in 1663. [Albert, Page 17].

As more were developed, there was opposition by users and from owners of other turnpikes who may lose their own traffic. The top surface of the better Turnpike roads consisted of small stones, which were progressively crushed by coach and waggon wheels, thereby compressing the surface.

By 1706 the Turnpike system embraced all main roads - 22,000 miles; 100,000 miles of secondary and minor roads remained the responsibility of parishes. There was little overall improvement - if some roads were better, others were noticeably worse. Many users were critical of turnpikes - due to the frequency of having to stop to pay tolls at gatehouses, and to the condition of surfaces, some of which were not as good as users considered they had a right to expect for their tolls. [Rogers, Page 26].

Trusts were profitable, with returns which usually exceeded those from other available investments. By the end of the 18th century, new development had passed its peak, although measures to improve existing turnpikes continued. [Albert, Page 114 & Appendix C].

The original idea of turnpikes was that a Trust would borrow money, needed to repair a road, against security of future tolls, and when the income had paid off the debt, the road would revert to the parish, so Trusts were set up for a limited period, usually 21 years. In practice they seldom, if ever, succeeded in paying off debts, and were renewed by Parliament as a matter of course. After the 1870's, Parliament ceased to renew Turnpike Acts, and Trusts were gradually extinguished. [Ransom Pages 22 & 195].

RCT 3rd Report Cmd 3751 1930, Para 24: Between 1760 and 1774, over 450 Turnpike Acts were passed. Between 1785 and 1809, 1062 Acts were passed. Para 25: Turnpikes were never popular, and were a source of resentment. Para 29: A nation of horse lovers and users marked its aversion to the use of roads by steam carriages by placing every obstacle, notably excessive road tolls in the way of its development. Para 33: In the mid 19th century, Parliament embarked on a policy of disturnpiking, reverting the liability to parishes. In 1888, liability was transferred to the newly formed County Councils. In 1909, a Roads Board was created with an income which averaged £1m pa for five years.

A Commission of Inquiry in 1843 was told that in Swansea they cannot go 100 yards from their doors without paying a toll. Even a short journey could involve passing from the ambit of one trust to another. Users referred to exhorbitant tolls demanded, whilst many glaring defects persisted. In 1835, before railways came to Wales, visitors found roads in a bad and insecure state. [Williams, Page 72].

Road Authorities led the campaign against the mechanisation of road vehicles fearing the motorised vehicle would increase damage to the highway surface. Support was lent by lovers of horses, public house landlords and breweries and all who made a living from horse hauled stage coaches.

Cars travelled faster and as they became more numerous, they began to destroy road surfaces which had been built for the much slower coaches and wagons. To make things worse, buses weighing up to 7 tons, soon appeared. [Hindle, Page 138].

Canals

There were earlier canals, but the "canal age" began with a 1759 Act empowering the Duke of Bridgewater to construct a canal from Worsley to join the River Irwell, which was navigable. Between 1761 and 1830 over 4,700 miles of canal were constructed in England and Wales.

Early canals were given generous toll maxima until the 1790's when they were seen to be profitable. Tolls were reduced by the advent of railways. [Paget-Tomlinson, Page 18].

The Trent & Mersey canal, which opened in 1777 was paying 75% dividend in 1825, and 32% in 1838. ["Manifold", Page 13].

A Royal Commission was set up in 1906 to report on the waterway system in the British Isles. It made four Reports, the last in 1910, [Cmd 4979]. It identified problems inherent in narrow canals and low bridges, and produced the first comprehensive statistics. It stated that the most profitable canals companies were also carriers, and that on average, there was a lock every 1.25 miles. The Commission advocated national ownership as the only prospect of modernisation. Many undertakings enjoyed extremely high returns.

Although canal company tolls were controlled by Parliamentary Acts, those of carriers were not. [Modern Transport, 2nd December, 1939]

Railways forced down canal rates - volume on the Grand Junction Canal increased from 0.9m tons in 1838 to 1.1m tons in 1858, but receipts fell from £0.15m to £0.07m in the same period. [Ransom, Page 195].

The advent of railways reduced the price of coal in London, led to the sinking of new coal mines, the development of new markets, and the opening of new iron ore fields. [Grinling, Pages 103, 238, 288 & 370].

There is much evidence to show that railway expansion was a consequence of price, capacity and year round availability, rather than a "desire for speed" as suggested in the "Rise & Rise of Road Transport". [Barker & Gerhold, Page 34].

Consequential Influence on Rail Legislation

Turnpikes and Canals were subject to statutory control as to rates which could be charged. These were largely based on a crude form of "Classification" by value of the goods conveyed - a principle carried forward, enlarged and made even more restrictive with railways. Developments in these various pre-railways forms of transport overlapped. The profits made by them obviously influenced Parliament in controlling railways, which were initially seen as another public "highway" on which users would be free to pass along subject to paying statutorily controlled tolls.

MONOPOLY PERIOD - Pre 1914

rcised close control of a wide range of business and sharp contrast to Government attitudes to industry, of Parliament was necessary before a company could re trains could begin to run. Only one in twenty r Concern"].

ment & Construction

en nationally beneficial, over which Governments in respect of route selection. Hence, the UK ended ome strategically disadvantageous routes. Other vantages of railways and ensured that routes were c value. It is usually pleaded that this happened but the policies continued in respect of subsequent had initiated wiser policies. Moreover, even self longer term possibilities, because he insisted that all were laid to a standard gauge, even when they were again, Parliament blocked proposed direct routes".

mission on Transport, [Cmd 3751] stated:- Page 16: due to heavy capital expenditure, extremely high pect of depreciation - real or fancied. Opposition in rt from the natural line to one which involved world's first railway tunnel). This is merely one e 17: Stations often had to be constructed at centre of towns, [due to local opposition]. The remunerative or higher charges ensue. Excessive Government. Page 18: During the past 100 years, with the regulation of railways.

nt that the cost of building railways per mile, was - £26,000, USA: £14,000. [Hansard vol. 130, col. 2453].

lway to open without notice to the Board of Trade. c. 10: Companies to provide and maintain lineside r fencing costs even 150 years later. Fencing off a landowner's responsibility to prevent trespass or roads. When new roads are constructed which the Highway Authority erects boundary fences - ity of the landowner. A farmer is compensated for through a railway fence whereas, on a road, he is 4, in Walker & Lancashire CC v BRB, BR was *ed line*).

Construction of Future Railways Act 1844, Sec. 13: Compelled railways to permit laying of electric telegraph lines along railway routes if required by Government. (No payment was mentioned).

Railway Consolidated Clauses Act 1863. Replaced previous Consolidation Acts covering construction, working agreements, amalgamations, etc. (Other businesses could amalgamate at will, but not railways).

Lands Clauses Consolidation Act 1865 : Differences as to compensation to be settled by Arbitration.

Regulation of Railways Act 1868: Statutory requirements as to accounts to be rendered by companies to the Board of Trade and shareholders. Specifies the format of Accounts.

Abandonment of Railways Acts 1850 & 1869 required approval of Railway Commissioners and Parliament before closure.

Regulation of Railways Act 1873 Sec. 17: Railway companies which own canals must maintain them for use by independent carriers or others. Commissioners to sanction agreements between companies and canals and determine disposals.

Railways [Private Sidings] Act 1904: Reasonable facilities under the 1854 Act shall include reasonable facilities for the junction of private sidings or private branch railways. (It obliged railways to provide reasonable facilities for anyone wishing to have private sidings. Repealed in 1962 after BR pointed out that many private sidings had been used only for traffic at uneconomic charges).

Railway Companies [Returns & Accounts] Act, 1911: Amends previous Acts and introduces provision for Depreciation Funds. (The statistics demanded by the Board of Trade would amaze today's critics of Brussels' bureaucracy. Even 80 years later, BR had to publish statistics and furnish others to the MoT which eclipse those applying to other industry. Franchisees publish far less data in their Accounts).

"The process of Parliamentary Committees entailed £0.5m of GNR funds on preliminary expenses". [Grinling, Page 72].

Statutory Control of Railway Charges

Each "Enabling" Act authorising the building of a railway contained a schedule of rates and charges, based on a crude classification of the value of goods. An Amendment Act in 1850 was required to empower the GNR to increase charges. [Grinling, Page 97].

When a railway company was incorporated by statute, the Act contained a schedule of commodities and specified the maximum rate per ton which may be charged for each class. Railways were free to charge at will ***up to the maximum***. By 1888, there were 900 Acts giving powers of charging. The first public railway to be opened for public use was the Surrey Iron Railway. In 1803, Parliament approved its charging powers on a basis of classification with tolls varying between three and six pence per ton [1p to 2.5p]. [Cmd 1098].

Railways [Conveyance of Mails] Act 1838 - Railways must carry mails, not as common carriers, but as a statutory obligation.

Construction of Future Railways Act 1844, Sec. 6: Companies to provide one cheap train each way, daily on weekdays, - "at moderate fares", "in carriages protected from the weather" and to call at every station, maximum fare 1d per mile. Sec. 10: If a company runs trains on Sundays, it must make provision for such similar trains on Sundays.

Railway Clauses Consolidation Act 1845, Sec 90: All users must pay the same charges in like circumstances - the first prohibition of Undue Preference to users.

Railway & Canal Act 1854, Sec. 2: No company shall make or give any undue preference or advantage to or in favour of any particular person or company or traffic. Sec. 3: Companies must afford all reasonable facilities for receiving and forwarding traffic. (These conditions were never imposed on road transport. Any industry could give undue preference to whomsoever it wished. Those supplying rails were not obliged to charge the same price to each railway company).

A Royal Commission inquired into railway charges in 1865. They did not believe it expedient, even if practicable, to adopt legislation to abolish freedom railway companies enjoyed of charging what they desired within their maximum rates. [Sherrington, Chapter 4].

Regulation of Railways Act 1873, Sec. 1: Commissioners to be appointed to administer the Acts of 1854 and 1873. Powers of arbitration could be exercised at the instance of parties or on reference from the Board of Trade, which had to authorise the hearing of complaints by the public & others. Sec. 12: Commissioners to decide through rates. Sec. 14: Obliged railway companies to publish rates & keep them available for public inspection at stations. Sec. 27: Complaints, on request to be heard in open court. Sec. 37: This Act to continue in force for 5 years.

"The creation of this Tribunal [Railway Commissioners] to regulate railways was in the nature of an experiment". [Times, 11th December 1877, 3d].

Cheap Trains Act 1883, compelled railways to charge third class passengers 1d per mile, on one train each way, per day, throughout the system, and exempted such reduced fares from Duty. (see page 18).

Post Office [Parcels] Act 1882 and Conveyance of Mails Act 1893 provided for arbitration on differences on the amount to be paid by the Post Office to Railways to be referred to the Railway & Canal Commissioners for a binding decision. (No arbitration was enacted on sums paid by railways to anyone).

Railway & Canal Traffic Act 1888 called for a unified Classification and revision of rates by means of Provisional Orders to be subsequently approved by Parliament.

Sec. 2: Established the new Railway & Canal Commission, [A Law Court], to deal with disputes by traders about charges - replacing the Railway Commission, as the 1873 Act provisions had expired. Powers of arbitration could be exercised at the instance of either party or on reference from the Board of Trade which had to authorise the hearing of complaints by public and traders.

Sec. 10: Gave Commissioners jurisdiction over tolls, rates or charges for merchandise traffic if any question arises.

Sec. 11: Reasonable facilities to be provided.

Sec. 24 : Companies to submit revised Classification of Merchandise & Rates within six months of the Act. Excludes mineral traffic or war stores.

Sec. 27: No Undue preference.

Sec. 33: Classification of Merchandise to be open for inspection at stations & depots.

Parliament did not define "Undue Preference", but left the R&CC to decide in each case. (Cmd 3751, Para 58).

In 1891/2, Parliament imposed uniform classification of merchandise in eight classes. Railways were free to vary within the specified maxima.

The Railway Rates & Charges Order Confirmation Acts, 1891/2 - there were 35 Orders - confirmed the new classification covering all UK railways - adopting a uniform classification of merchandise in eight classes : A, B, C and 1-5. (It was displaced by the 1921 Act). No provision was made to alter maximum rates, no restriction was placed on the quotation of rates below maxima and the Act did not deal with passenger fares. A number of Private Acts were passed in connection with this Order in respect of different railway companies.

Following the 1888 and 1891/2 Acts, Railways submitted a revised classification of merchandise and a revised schedule of maximum freight charges, there were 4,000 objections. New rates came into operation on 1st January 1893. Railway companies raised all rates to the maximum. Under the 1894 Act any member of the public could challenge as unreasonable any increase in railway freight charges made since 1892 and rates were pegged at 1892 levels. [Perkin Page 285]. (see 1894 Act, below).

"The BoT published new uniform Classification and Schedules and invited criticism from traders, Needless to say criticism came freely. The BoT decided to open a public inquiry, which lasted 85 sittings. This was followed by a Hearing by a Joint Committee of both Houses which took 48 days. The reason for using maximum rates was that railways did not have enough time to implement new changes in the time limit allowed - this led to a new Act. The GNR Chairman told the AGM: "It is remarkable that during the whole outcry, not a word of protest has been uttered by traders to the reductions that have been made. In business, increased cost of production is met by increasing prices. Railways are restricted by the charges embodied in their powers. Endeavours by Scottish railways to increase rates were blocked by the unjust 1894 Traffic Act". By 1900, the price of coal was more than double the price of a few years back. [Grinling, Pages 404,412,445 & 446].

In the 1926 coal strike, foreign coal cost the GWR £1m, unlike gas, electricity or municipalities, railways could not raise charges to cover. [Pole, Page 227].

1894 Railway & Canal Traffic Act, Sec. 1: Where a railway company has since 31st December 1892 increased [or hereafter increases] any rate or charge - if any complaint is made that it is unreasonable - it shall lie on the company to prove it is not unreasonable. It shall not be sufficient to show that the rate is within any limit fixed by an Act of Parliament. The Railway & Canal Commission have jurisdiction to hear or determine any complaint and can award costs. (Any application would be heard in public. Due to the high incidence of joint passenger and freight costs, proving an increase in freight costs was virtually impossible. No other industry has faced a similar control of prices).

Replying to the MoT request for views on new rates on 30th March 1920, the RCA said the "hybrid system was established by Parliament in 1894 in a moment of public tension, viz standard charges, without liberty to change them. [Cmd 682].

The 1911 strike came at a time when Government became alarmed by German naval activity in the "Agadir incident" - and feared that the Royal Navy's essential coal supplies could be blocked. Troops were mobilised to guard key installations against war, not take over railways, as some historians suggested. Government gave companies "peremptory instructions" to settle immediately. Only 40% of GWR staff were on strike and, but for Government panic, "the strike would have been beaten". Union membership increased as a result. [Pole, Page 106].

The RAC Report, Cmd 1098, stated that during the 1911 railway strike, Government promised, that if railway companies made concessions to the men, an Act would be passed allowing increases to cover higher labour costs which were otherwise difficult to recover due to the 1894 Act.

The Bill was opposed in Parliament and did not become law until 1913.

Railway & Canal Traffic Act, 1913, Sec. 1: To amend the 1894 Act with respect to increases of rates to meet a rise in costs due to improved labour conditions since 19th August 1911. Commissioners could authorise a consequential rate increase if they were satisfied by the facts.

As a result, from 1st July railways increased rates, mainly exceptional rates, by 4%. However, they were not successful in achieving the benefit therefrom. "Even to this day - seven years later - it [the 4% increase] has not become fully operative. It has been disputed by traders and judgement has not yet been delivered in the law case, which was required to settle the dispute. Conditions which lead to accounts being unsettled for seven years are intolerable". [Midland Railway AGM 1920].

The root cause of railway difficulty was the statutory limitation of fares & freight charges. [Perkin, Page 305].

Arguably, when there was no competition, some of these Acts were justified. But, as more competing railways were built, the need for protection diminished. In the 1920's road hauliers ruthlessly exploited the Acts to capture railway traffic, and those self same Acts prevented railways from retaliating or protecting their position.

Statutory Control of Profits

Dividends were controlled by Parliament in the Act which authorised the building of a railway, e.g., Liverpool & Manchester Railway Act 1826, Sec. 128: When a dividend on shares exceeds 10%, statutory maximum tonnage rates were to be reduced in the following year by 5% for each 1% paid in dividend in excess of 10% This limited dividends, not profits, and was amended by a Public Act to limit profits

Construction of Future Railways Act 1844, Sec. 1: If after 21 years from passing this Act, profits shall exceed 10%, the Treasury may revise the scale of tolls and fix a new scale. (Canal profits of 32-75% were not uncommon, waterway profits of 140% were reached - see pages 10 & 12). Sec. 2: Empowered the State to purchase a Railway at a cost of 25 years profits based on the average of the preceding three years.

Railway critics often refer to the railway lobby - Directors in Parliament. "In 1910, there were 74 directors in the House of Lords, and 42 in the Commons. However, it was a mistake to assume they would all vote in favour of railways on a controversial matter. Many were also directors of shipping, industry or commerce concerns as well, and their major interest might be opposed to railway interests". "What motivated people to become directors, initially, was to protect their investment. But the ironfounders, canal owners and shipping magnates who filled railway boardrooms did so to make sure the railway company on which they depended was run efficiently, and not too profitably. The NER Board was supposed to think of the trader first, and the railway interest came second". [Robbins, Page 89 & 87].

Railway Directors with Iron & Steel interests would have objected to rates increases. [Bonavia[2], Page 66].

Safety

Regulation of Railways Act 1868 : Engineers must certify each six months that track, structures and rolling stock are maintained in good condition.

Regulation of Railways Act 1871 gave the Board of Trade powers to appoint Inspectors and direct enquiries into accidents. (Their thoroughness and powers are unmatched in the road industry 125 years later. In aircraft accidents, there seems to be no public allocation of blame of individuals, in contrast to railways).

Regulation of Railways Act 1889, Sec. 1 : Railways to adopt block signalling and fit continuous brakes on passenger trains. Sec. 4: Must submit returns on overtime worked.

Railway Regulation Act 1893: Amended the law in respect to hours of railway servants. If a complaint was made, the Board of Trade was empowered to inquire if hours were excessive or rest intervals between turns of duty were insufficient. Fines of £100 per day could be imposed for a continuing default to a R&CC decision. (Action on roads tended to be 40-70 years behind rail, and, even then, less severe).

Railway Employment [Prevention of Accidents] Act 1900, Sec. 1: BoT has powers to make rules regarding dangerous operations.

Additional Taxation : Railway Passenger Duty.

Under an 1832 Act which amended the rate of Duty on Stage Carriages and Horses for Hire, railway companies were required to pay a half penny per mile per four passengers carried. In 1842, a further Passenger Duty Act, changed the tax to 5% on gross passenger receipts. It was further amended under the Construction of Future Railways Act 1844, which called upon companies to provide trains at fares not exceeding one penny per mile calling at every station. Sec. 9: No Tax to be paid on fares not exceeding 1d per mile by any such cheap train.

It has been claimed by various authors that the Cheap Trains Act 1883 set Workmen's fares at low levels as a quid pro quo for Government reducing the Railway Passenger Duty. Hence these fares could not be increased unless Passenger Duty was re-imposed at original levels. That was not the case. The 1883 Act addressed an anomaly which arose when some companies reduced 3rd class standard fares to one penny per mile. As these applied to all trains, including express trains, not calling at every station, these fares were not exempt from the Duty. The 1883 Act ended this anomaly. In addition, the Act specified that in return for running Workmen's trains in areas certified by the BoT to be of urban character - over 100,000 population, Duty on fares exceeding one penny per mile, would be reduced from 5% to 2% . Failure to run such trains would lead to the ending of the 2% concession in such areas.

Sec. 2 After the commencement of this Act, the duties now payable will be:-

[1] Fares not exceeding 1d per mile will be exempt.

[2] In return for running workmen's trains, Duty to be reduced from 5% to 2% on fares over 1d per mile between railway stations within the same Urban District, [subject to certification by the BoT that the area has over 100,000 population].

Sec. 3 [3] Provided for the resumption of [the higher rate of] duty in the event of failure to provide sufficient workmen's trains and accommodation.

In July 1920, the President of the Board of Trade, who had personally drafted the 1883 Act, told the RAC [Cmd 857] that the change in Duty was not a bargain for Workmen's fares. An 1876 Select Committee was told by the Board's Permanent Secretary : "It was undesirable to maintain Duty longer than necessary from a fiscal point of view and he recommended that until finances of the State should warrant abolition of the tax, it should be restricted to fares over 1d per mile". The Chancellor made the change in his Budget on 5th April - the Act was passed on 20th August. The RAC said that the Act envisaged lifting the tax back to 5% on urban fares if insufficient trains were run between 6.0pm and 8.0am for workmen. The Chancellor reduced Duty in urban areas "as a fair arrangement to meet omnibus competition". [Railway Gazette, 19th April 1929].

Duty rose from £153,000 in 1842 to £0.5m in 1868. [Smith, Page 34].

Objections to the Passenger Duty

In 1874, a meeting was held by Railway Directors and shareholders to form an Association for the repeal of Passenger Duty. Duty was levied at 5% on gross receipts, and as the cost of working was 50%, it amounted to a 10% [tax] on net receipts of passengers. The tax had often been denounced. The District Railway Company said it was 78% on their 3rd class traffic. Mr. S. Laing, MP, said that he had attempted last session to have the Duty removed. [Times 24th February, 7e].

A month later, a deputation met the Chancellor, and drew attention to the taxing of 3rd class workmen's travel because they carried tools. This was not intended by the Cheap Trains Act [1844]. The Chancellor argued the need for the tax for the General Exchequer and asked if it was taken off passengers on what other railway traffic it should it go. The representatives said they did not seek that, but sought an end to the tax altogether. [Times 18th March, 7f].

The "Cheap Trains Act" was the Construction of Future Railways Act. (see page 14).

A later meeting referred to the Duty as an obnoxious tax. [Times 9th September, 5f].

In 1877, a deputation from London Trades Council representing every branch of industry met the Chancellor to ask for the abolition of Duty on fares below 1d per mile. A Commons Committee of Inquiry had recommended repeal of Duty on urban & suburban traffic on fares amounting to, and, under 9d, [4p]. Thirty years earlier, Government sought to help the working class by exempting Duty if trains complied with certain conditions. After a time, it was found conditions were onerous limiting the advantages of working classes rather than increasing them. [Times 12th February, 6c].

Two weeks later, a deputation representing railways, trade unionists, and the public met the Chancellor and asked him to grant, "until the state of the revenue will permit a total abolition of the Passenger Duty, the following three recommendations:

1. exempt all fares not exceeding 1d per mile;
2. to apply to weekly and season tickets;
3. in urban & suburban districts all fares not exceeding 9d to be exempted.

They pointed out that the Tax had been taken off all horses including tramways. Fifty three railways which had paid no dividends were paying Duty. One person pointed out that the London General Omnibus Company [LGOC] paid 12% Dividend and used roads made good from rates paid by railways. The Chancellor referred to the Cheap Trains Act 1844. He argued that railways had paid the tax from the beginning so they knew it was there. He said that the Exchequer needed the revenue. [Times 23rd February, 8a].

He did not explain why it did not still apply to horse drawn passenger transport, such as the LGOC for the same historical reasons.

Fare increases imposed by Government during the 1914-18 War raised 3rd Class above one penny per mile, and by Government Order, the Duty was to be on fares which were above one penny per mile before the War.

The Railway Passenger Duty Act 1917, suspended separate accounts in respect of passenger duty and making separate payments for the period of Control. This was an administrative change, because Government was skimming out all profits above 1913 levels, whilst its traffic was carried free of charge. If railways profits fell below 1913 levels, Government had to make up the difference, hence it was nonsense to take the Duty with one hand, if they would have to pay it back with the other.

Over a period of 60 years, railways had pressed the Government to abolish the Railway Passenger Duty. In 1928, they approached Churchill, Chancellor of the Exchequer, but he initially rejected their request. The Railway Companies appealed to the Royal Commission on Transport to support their claim for an end to Passenger Duty. It was repealed in the 1929 Finance Act, before the Royal Commission submitted its first Report, but, was subject to conditions. (see page 88).

Railways in Wartime

Having not contributed to costs of building, development or construction of railways, but compelling promoters to fight every inch of their way through Parliament, and be forced to pay out huge sums to reduce opposition, and buy land, Government acted at an early stage to use railways on its own terms.

Only 12 years after the first passenger railway opened, the Better Regulation of Railways Act 1842 provided for Conveyance of Troops - Sec. 20: Railways shall convey Military, Marine & Police Forces [& baggage, stores, arms & ammunition], at prices to be settled between Secretary at [sic] War and the Railway Company concerned.

The charge agreed was 1d or 1.125d per mile. The War Office found the fraction inconvenient, and told a Select Committee so. They recommended 1d per mile for other ranks, 2d per mile for officers. [PRO file AN80/18]

Construction of Future Railways Act 1844, Sec. 12: [Amends the 1842 Act on Fares for the Military]: Provide for Military, Marine and Police Forces at fares not exceeding 2d per mile for Officers in First Class, and 1d per mile for others in 3rd class - also for wives and children. (The concept of agreeing charges had ended).

Regulation of Forces Act 1871, Sec. 16: Secretary of State may empower any person to take possession of Railways for one week only, renewable on a weekly basis. Compensation for loss or injury to be agreed between both parties. In the event of difference, compensation to be settled by arbitration - as provided in the Land Clauses Consolidation Act 1865. (Government ignored this - see page 32).

The 1871 Act was doubtless inspired by the conduct of the 1870 Franco-Prussian War, when both sides made extensive use of railways to move troops, guns, munitions and other stores. It is evident that the availability of this relatively new form of transport was hugely beneficial to swift redeployment and the successful prosecution of the war.

Militia Act 1882 Sec. 28 [2]: All Acts concerning railways applying to Regular Forces will apply to Militia Reserves.

Cheap Trains Act 1883, Sec. 6 provided for military movements at reduced rates - up to 150 personnel at 75% ordinary fare; if more than 150, the balance at 50% of the ordinary fare. The 75% rate applied to families entitled to travel at public expense. [The Royal Navy obtained powers for the cheap fares under this Act].

National Defence Act 1888 Sec. 4 [1]: Military traffic to be given priority whenever an Order for the embodiment of militia is in force - Sec. 4 [6]: Reasonable remuneration paid by Parliament to a Railway Company, such as may be agreed upon, or, in default of agreement, by arbitration.

Parliament passed several Acts between 1842 and 1888 to enable Government to use or take over railways and specified how little it would pay for military travel in peace and war. Acts which required them to pay fully to take over railways in wartime, with, in the event of disagreement, independent arbitration, were replaced by dictating "next to nothing" terms in two World Wars. (see pages 35, 133 & 138).

Arrangements for the take-over of railways started in 1911. Railways, and Railway owned canals, [but not other canals], were taken over on 4th August 1914, under the 1871 Act and told they should consider that the [Statutory] weekly Order would be renewed until advised to the contrary. [Pratt, Pages 1162-65].

Government implemented the provisions of the 1871 Regulation of Forces Act, rather than the 1888 National Defence Act because the latter - which only required precedence for military traffic could cause civil needs to suffer. [PRO : MT6/3134].

Trains carrying the BEF to Southampton for embarkation to France, arrived at 12 minute intervals, which the Daily News said was "A wonderful achievement. When medals are distributed, railway workers should certainly receive them". Some 69,000 troops, 21,000 horses plus over 2,000 horse drawn vehicles, 166 guns and thousands of tons of stores were involved in this embarkation. [Pratt, Page 116].

The Railway Executive Committee [REC].

The REC was formed in 1912, in anticipation of war. Its members selected by Government were General Managers of the principal railways: GCR, GNR, GWR, LNWR, LSWR, LYR, Midland and NER. They invited the NBR to be a member, but they declined, and were replaced by the Caledonian. Government said the President of the Board of Trade [BoT] would be the independent Chairman, but railways would select an acting Chairman to preside over meetings. The first "Acting Chairman" was Sir Frank Ree of the LNWR. On his death in April 1914, Sir Herbert Walker, LSWR, became Chairman, and another LNWR nominee joined to replace Ree. Later, the SER General Manager joined them. The President of the BoT would be called on to solve a conflict of military and civil needs, should the REC be unable to do so. It was never necessary for him to be called in for this purpose. [PRO : MT6/3134].

The President of the Board of Trade did not attend a single meeting. [Pole, Page 50].

The REC ceased to function from 31st December, 1919.

Statutory Compensation

The 1871 Act required Railways to be paid full compensation, agreed by them and the Secretary of State, or failing agreement, by arbitration, under the Land Clauses Consolidation Act 1865. In August 1914, Government proposed compensation based on comparing aggregate net receipts for all companies with the corresponding period of the previous year to be determined, in default of agreement, by the Railway & Canal Commission. This clearly meant 1913, not that each ensuing year would be compared with the previous year, since the War was forecast to be over by Christmas. "It was anticipated that the possession would only last a few months". [Cmd 1132, Para 4].

In fact, the Secretary for War, secretly told the Cabinet that the War would last 3 years. [Royle, Page 258]. (Doubtless, this influenced the Government in its subsequent cavalier actions).

A "Special Agreement" modified the Act, which required Government to treat each railway individually. As the Act stood, it could have led to some making increased profits resulting from diversion of traffic from other lines, whilst "losing" companies would have had to be compensated. Consequently, Government stood to pay less for sequestration. [PRO : MT6/3134].

On 3rd August 1914 the REC told the Board of Trade they would recommend companies should accept this Special Agreement On 6th August, the Government then added a codicil : "Provided that, if net receipts for the first half of 1914 are less than for the first half of 1913, the ascertained deficiency to be reduced proportionately". This was agreed on 8th August. Government did not say when compensation would be paid. [Pratt, Pages 99 & 101].

On 16th September, the Government announced that "Compensation will cover all special services, such as those in connection with military and naval transport rendered to Government by the railways and it will therefore be unnecessary to make any payments in respect of such transport". [Hamilton, Page 45].

On 14th April 1915, the Board of Trade further modified the Agreement. "It has now been agreed that this reduction [from comparing 1914 with 1913], will not be made, but that 25% of the war bonus granted to railway employees who come within the railway conciliation scheme shall be borne by the railway companies not by the Government". [Hamilton, Page 45].

The bonus was a "temporary" wage increase, which politicians assumed could be withdrawn at the end of the war, when they imagined inflation would vanish. The principle was adopted in the 1939-45 war, and likewise "consolidated" into wage rates at the end of the war. In no industry did wage rates revert to pre-war levels.

By this time, Government must have realised that the prospect of total revenue falling below 1913 levels was zero. In effect, Government did not have to pay their 75% up front, whilst net revenue exceeded the 1913 level - which it did, in aggregate, throughout the war. They paid little or nothing. The "bonus" was authorised by Government to compensate for inflation arising from a War which Government had initiated, and which historians have revealed could have been ended 18 months earlier than it did. Similar retrospective arbitrary action was repeated in World War II. Government's share of the bonus would be recouped as a consequence of not paying for any military traffic and by picking up net receipts in excess of the 1913 figure.

The Agreement was conceived as a short term one. But, as months wore on, some companies began to find themselves in difficulty. Ordinary revenue (discouraged by Government) had dropped. They were carrying more for Government, but not getting paid. Eventually, Government agreed to pay in monthly instalments. [Hamilton, Page 45].

In August 1915, when it was realised that a long war would produce large costs, and may cause friction with Government, the Treasury allowed railways to report costs due to arrears of maintenance which could not be carried out due to labour and material shortages, and resulting from the use of railway workshops to manufacture munitions. [Pratt, Page 1021].

In September 1916, Government decided to retain control for two years after War ended, (which would reduce Government costs during demobilisation). Railway solicitors said an extension was not possible under the 1871 Act. Fresh legislation was required. This came ten months after the War, which itself should, legally, have marked the expiry of Control. The Ministry of Transport Act 1919, provided for Control to remain with Government for two years after that Act. (see page 39).

Government Measures to reduce Passenger traffic

To release resources for freight, particularly war traffic, in January 1915, passenger services were reduced to deal with coal and war traffic. All excursion and reduced fares were withdrawn, except HM Forces. However, civilian passenger traffic increased. [Pratt, Pages 128 & 130].

In 1916-17, Government closed 400 stations to passenger, but not freight traffic. In January 1917 they imposed a 50% fare increase [excluding Season, Workmen and Traders Seasons, which were regarded as essential travel], to curtail civilian travel - not to increase revenue. Passengers switched from Ordinary to season tickets, as air raids caused people to move from London and commute from safer towns. The net decrease in passengers was not more than 7%. [Pratt, Page 149].

In 1917, to release rolling stock, locomotives and drivers to France, passenger trains were withdrawn, fares increased, lines closed, speeds reduced [permitting heavier trains] and Sunday trains reduced. In addition, some lines were closed to release rails to send to France to enable military railways to be laid. Railway companies were also required to release staff to join HM Forces, or to operate railways in war zones. [Pratt, Page 145].

By 1918, passengers carried by the larger companies were up on January and February 1917 by between 14% and 43%. [Hamilton, Page 154].

In 1918, more stations were closed, and trains withdrawn to further reduce civilian travel. In May, to reduce travel by 40%, Government restrictions were placed on season tickets, including no refunds, fares increased by 10% for up to 12 miles and 20% over 12 miles. No season ticket would be issued for over 12 miles, or less than six months except to an existing season ticket holder. Traders Season fares were increased by 20%, eligibility was lifted from £300 pa of freight business to £500 pa per ticket, and the minimum distance raised from 30 to 50 miles. Railways had to be given powers to refuse to issue seasons in accordance with this Government edict. [Pratt, Page 159].

Restrictions on passenger travel and other allied changes were issued in the name of the REC, but in accordance with Government instructions. The public blamed railway management for the ensuing inconvenience.

Loss of Income

In 1915, Railways had to suspend most reduced fares to cut civilian travel. Apart from the suspension of cheap tickets, no fares increase took place until 1917, - and that was to discourage travel - despite ever rising costs fuelled by material costs and wages comparable with those in other industry. [Pratt, Page 153].

British working classes were in receipt of unexpectedly higher wages and were inclined to travel extensively. [Hamilton, Page 154].

Moreover, munitions workers and others were given free and cheap travel. (see page 26).

In 1916, passenger traffic, apart from military, was in excess of the record year of 1913. Partly due to workers travelling to munitions factories, and those on Government business. (Either at pre-war fares or free of charge). Passenger travel in 1918 was higher than 1917, excluding free on warrants. [Pratt, Pages 137 & 153].

Between 1913 & 1919, passenger travel increased by 19%, and goods by 5%, apart from the still considerable Government demands. [Hamilton, Page 191].

Government kept rail freight rates at 1913 levels until 1920, whilst coastwise shipping rates rose 200% and canal charges increased, [Pratt, Pages 282 & 743], causing more diversion to railways, which were then overwhelmed with traffic, (carried free of charge due to the terms of sequestration). Government would not increase freight rates despite pleas by the REC that railway charges, in common with those in other industries, should rise to reflect increased costs. [Bonavia[1], Page 10].

Coastwise shipping conveyed an average of 21.9m tons in 1910-14 and 10.2m tons in 1919. Canals, including railway owned, carried 34m tons in 1913, and only 21.7m tons in 1919. The balance of canal and coastwise traffic, some 24m tons, (plus war traffic went by rail - effectively free of charge). [Cmd 1098].

Railway Docks profits of £0.5m in 1913 fell under Government control to a loss of £2.1m by 1919, despite the most intensive activity. [Pratt, Page 1136].

Government secured a good bargain, having only to guarantee 1913 receipts in return for free transport of men and materials on an unprecedented scale. In addition, they used railway workshops to produce, at cost price, a vast amount of munitions and equipment. (For detailed statistics - see Pratt).

The RCA said that in the 1914-18 War, the railways carried in 1918, 50% more traffic than in 1913. ["Clear the Lines!, Page 53"].

The records of the Midland Railway show traffic, excluding Government and military, increasing throughout the war: -

1915: Railways busier than ever before. Trucks underload for long periods. Compared to the record year of 1913, invoiced merchandise freight was up 8%.

1916: Merchandise freight was up 0.7% on 1915. Passenger revenue had increased.

1917: "Some traffic which passed last year for payment, is now being treated as Government traffic and travelling free". Government and military traffic amounted to nearly 4m tons plus thousands of men and horses and many special trains. [Midland Railway AGM's in 1916, 1917 & 1918].

1918: Ran 18,000 special trains conveying 2.4m men, 175,000 horses and 25,000 tons of baggage. [Midland Railway AGM 1919].

In 1936, the Chancellor was asked what was the total paid by the Exchequer for transport of forces, munitions and all impedimenta of war, to railway companies by Government during the Great War 1914-19, and was told: Under the Railway Agreement, no charge was made for conveyance of Government traffic. [Hansard vol. 310 col. 2958].

Free & Reduced Rate Government Travel

Throughout the period of Government control - August 1914 to August 1921 - HM Forces duty and main leave travel was on warrants, amounting in 1917 to 28.52m journeys, and other Government to 1.12m. Free transport was conceded to all allied forces for similar travel. The 50% fare increase did not apply to HM Forces or Allied Forces travelling at their own expense for short leave breaks - their fares remained at pre-war levels. In 1917, 22.2m reduced rate vouchers were used by HM Forces on leave at their own expense. [Pratt, Page 180].

Relatives of wounded in hospital were given free warrants by Police on behalf of the War Office or Admiralty. In September 1917, the War Office and Treasury agreed that nurses from any establishment involved in war wounded should get a half fare voucher every six months. Between September and December 1917 41,000 vouchers were issued. Media Reports show that this freebie - at railway expense - which was increasing their post-war deficit - continued until 1920. This free travel included military hospitals in UK and France. [Times 3rd April 1920, 2c].

The Ministry of Munitions was authorised to issue 20,000 half fare vouchers each week to 80,000 married workers working away from home. By June 1917, issues were less than 6,000 per week. The War Office and Admiralty were given a share so that the whole allocation, totalling 1m pa, could be used. The Ministry of Munitions was authorised to issue an extra 40,000 for August Bank Holiday 1917, and 60,000 at Christmas. In December 1917, 138,000 Munitions workers were given reduced fare vouchers when the public was being asked not to travel. The Ministry issued 80,000 extra vouchers for Easter 1918, 102,000 in March, and 80,000 at Whitsun, whilst the public had again been asked to forgo holidays. The REC protested to the Board of Trade when the 80,000 vouchers were requested for Easter 1918, which led to reductions in issues from June 1918. (The war was nearly over). Vouchers were intended for married men only, but were extended to everyone and not limited to travel home. They were UK's best paid workers. Use of warrants and new concessions were expanded by Government. A Ministry of National Service pamphlet March 1918: "Provided there is no unforeseen change, you will get a free railway warrant to travel home at any general holiday, or generally observed trade holiday". [Pratt, Pages 172-174 & 180]. (see also reference to Scapa Flow on page 27).

Voluntary war workers paid Ordinary fares, including the 50% increase, and were considered unpatriotic for travelling. A Government Department ticket was introduced in March 1918. In six months to November 30th 1918, 1.4m were issued by Departments [excluding Military], plus 0.54m warrants exchanged for tickets at booking offices; a total of 1.94m. This compared with 1.2m for the whole of 1917. In March 1918 alone, military reduced rate and free travel totalled 5.2m warrants. A Select Committee Report in 1918 said: There is reason to think the number of warrants issued by Government Departments is excessive. [Pratt, Page 174 & 180].

If 1.94m and 5.2m were typical, the annual total would be about 133m journeys.

"The President of the Board of Trade made hardly any practical proposals for bringing about a reduction in travel. Increases of 50% in fares have not affected bookings. Parliament should pay more attention to the growing and widespread abuse of traffic on warrants. One result of State Control is the vast numbers of people constantly travelling on warrants which would not bear close investigation. It is not only a matter of military warrants, although the Army is responsible for a reprehensible amount of unnecessary passenger traffic. The Ministry of Munitions is most careless in its use of railways and the way its staff exercise their privileges with regard to passenger traffic ought to be carefully examined. [Times 9th May 1918, Page 7b].

Inflating free travel whilst discouraging public passenger traffic was harmful in the short and long term to railways, because the public became alienated and began to make more use of buses.

Select Committee 3rd Report [1918 Session]: "Whether railways are returned to their owners or retained in public ownership...". (An ominous warning, which was secretly voiced during the 1939-45 War - see page 129).

Pre-war army strength of 733,000 rose to 8.97m, of whom 2m were wounded, and most of these travelled in special railway trains to hospitals. Between the end of the war in November 1918 and May 1920, 4m troops were demobilised, all would travel by rail, free of charge, most making at least two journeys in the UK - to a depot, not necessarily near to home, and then home. All military travel tended to be over much longer distances than civilian travel. [Statistics of the British Empire in the Great War].

Free Freight Traffic

By 1916, the volume of ammunition manufactured in the UK was some eleven times greater than the first part of the war, and was all transported by rail.
["Statistics of the British Empire in the Great War"].

On 19th May 1919, The BoT was asked if it was aware that 35m tons which used to be carried by coastwise was now on railways. (This would be without gain to railways and was in addition to war traffic). [Hansard vol. 116, col. 5].

The pre-war strength of 25,000 army horses rose to 165,000 in 10 days. At the end of the war, there were 791,000. [Statistics of the British Empire in the Great War]. All went by rail.

Before the War, the First Sea Lord had the "inspiration" to base the Home Fleet at Scapa Flow in the Orkneys, over 500 miles as the crow flies from the principal source of the most essential of supplies - good steam coal, which they insisted must be from South Wales. It was 16 times as far from the coalfields as Portsmouth, the historical base of the fleet. 13,631 trains of Admiralty coal ran from South Wales : August 1914 - December 1918 with 0.54m wagons. All stores, ammunition and, of course, personnel were involved in correspondingly longer journeys. [Pratt, Page 491].

The cost of transporting peacetime needs was substantially greater, the cost of transporting much higher wartime needs was, by sleight of hand, zero. Government must have seen that the sequestration of railways was the only way to pursue the naval war.

Reduced resources

Serious wagon detention by the military and industry created artificial shortages. Thousands stood for over 24 hours, some up to 10 months waiting to be unloaded. Much Government traffic was loaded for journeys as little as 2 miles or less. Excessive mileage was incurred by redirected wagons, some travelling five times the distance required, some contained as little as 41 lbs weight. One munitions factory was taking an average of over three weeks to unload wagons. [Pratt, Page 301-324].

Railway trucks are kept under load by the military for indefinite periods.
[Midland Railway AGM 1915].

On railway advice Government did not take over the POW's but introduced a Back Loading Order on 16th March 1917 empowering railways to load back when empty at a maximum of 1/- [5p] per day. Of 626,000 POW's, only 20-30% were usable for general merchandise. From March 1917 to February 1919 they were used on approximately 280,000 occasions. With the intensive workload, locos should have been getting more maintenance, but were getting less due to a shortage of materials and labour, and because workshops were turned over to munitions. [Pratt, Page 691, 718, 731].

This increased the number of locos out of service awaiting or undergoing repairs. The backlog of loco repairs by the end of the war was 20%. By June 1919, the main line railways had fewer locos fit for service than in 1913, but traffic was higher. In June 1919, sixteen principal railways had 6% fewer locos fit for service than in 1913, to handle more traffic. [Hamilton, Page 191].

The heavy character of trains caused rapid wear and tear of the permanent way, causing further deceleration of trains and reduced line capacity. [Savage, Page 40].

The lack of adequate materials in the war resulted in minimum attention to maintenance and repairs. By 1919, railways needed a complete overhaul. The permanent way was sadly in need of attention, there was a great shortage of locomotives and rolling stock - most in use was overdue for repairs. [Cmd 3751, Paras 66 & 67].

After the First War, maintenance was so far in arrears that it was a barrier to development for a decade after control ceased in 1922. [Modern Transport 17th February 1940].

Overseas Demands

Government demanded locomotives, rolling stock, track and skilled men from railways for use overseas, which contributed to winning the war, rather than the puny motor vehicle, which some propagandists for the motor industry tried to claim.

It is pertinent to note that Ludendorff, the German military leader said: "There comes a time when locos are more important than guns". [Savage, Page 637].

In many ways, it was a railway war. [Goodspeed, Page 219].

Railway construction, maintenance and operation was carried out in war zones by British railway companies, using experienced railway staff. [Pratt, Page 611-641].

The War Office told the REC in June 1916: Up to 200 locos should be earmarked for despatch to the Continent! Railway companies and POW owners were asked to provide 1,500 wagons. About 50% of the UK fleet were POW's, but they were unsuitable, so the burden fell solely on the railway companies. [Pratt, Page 644].

In December 1916, REC undertook to provide 20,000 wagons for use abroad, on the understanding that they would obtain an equivalent number from the private wagon companies. The Army wanted only standard railway company wagons. Railway companies had sent 20,403 wagons abroad by November 1917, and needed replacement at home for increased traffic. [Pratt, Page 708].

Early in 1918 railways were called on to supply a further 10,000 wagons and obtain replacement by a levy on collieries, through the Coal Controller, Guy Calthrop GM of the LNWR, who had been seconded to this Government role, without charge. Demands later increased: 516 locomotives, 29,704 wagons and 388 coaches were sent overseas. [Hamilton - Pages 162 & 191].

"In the First War, Railways sent 184,000 men abroad, [one third of the work-force], 675 locomotives, 30,000 wagons, materials for 2,300 miles standard gauge, and 1300 miles narrow gauge track for use in or behind the front line in France. Railways provided £126m worth of free services to Government. By 1918, all rolling stock and permanent-way was run down". [Perkin, Page 306].

Seven months after the war ended, Parliament was told that 570 locos and 29,648 wagons were sent abroad by railway companies. Of these 458 locos and 29,398 wagons were no longer required and will be returned as quickly as transport facilities permit. [Hansard vol. 116 col. 2277].

By June 1919 only a small percentage of 31,000 wagons sent abroad had been returned. Out of 20,000 POW's promised to them in replacement, they received 10,000. By 1921,

458 locos, 28,943 wagons and 382 carriages had been returned but a large proportion were unfit for further use. During the war railway companies had to build 49 ambulance trains. [Pratt, Pages 200,207].

Two months later, it was announced that 15,371 wagons had been returned from overseas; 14,304 still remain. [Hansard vol. 126, col. 1514].

Meanwhile, road transport was being helped to resume normal activity and to expand rapidly due to Government disposing of tens of thousands of lorries - some brand new and unused, at knock down prices. (see page 53).

Government requisitioned 126 railway vessels, guaranteed 1913 revenue, covered all war risks, and undertook to refund the cost of restoring vessels to the same condition, fair wear and tear excepted, as when taken over. "The financial arrangement was an exceptionally good one - for the Government. The compensation paid in no way compared with the abnormal profits made by vessels running in connection with such railway services as could still be carried on, nor was it adequate". [Pratt, Page 380].

"Generally speaking, rolling stock is on loan, and the War Department is only liable for putting it into good repair on its return or for the payment of its value if it is not returned". [PRO : MT6/3120].

Rolling stock was not returned in good order. [Pratt, Page 664].

Government had up to seven years use of rolling stock, in the worst conditions, free of charge. Nor did they recompense its depreciated value, perhaps equal to 10-14 years.

"Dock warehouses are bursting with imports which cannot be moved due to a shortage of trucks. We need someone to insist that trucks will be returned from abroad". [Times, 22nd August 1919, 10f].

It is, as the saying goes, an ill wind which does no one any good, (or words to that effect). In this case, railways' ill wind did the road industry, ready and waiting with cheap ex Army lorries, a great deal of good.

The war had been over two years before the bulk of the wagons - 28,671 - had been returned, many requiring repairs. This Ministerial statement indicated that 29,792 wagons had been sent overseas during the war. [Hansard vol. 133, col. 1526].

Increased labour costs

Rail wages had increased throughout the war by Government direction. Between 1913 and 1920 the cost rose 240%. On the eve of the 1919 General Election, with a suggestion of some political significance, Government, in direct negotiations with unions conceded an eight hour day and wage rises against the wishes of the railway companies. Agreements between Government and unions covered overtime and night duty enhancements. The RCA opposed the eight hour day. [Pratt, Page 783].

Sir Herbert Walker [REC Chairman], said: it was perhaps the most wicked thing that had ever been perpetrated on a community. Railways had been under the REC, but was fettered in every possible way by Government. He believed that 8 hours work per day was enough, although he didn't practice it. It put signalmen at a rural box, with a few minutes work per hour, on the same plane as London termini. It was economically unsound and wholly unjustifiable, cost 76,000 more men and an additional £13m pa. Government also guaranteed a week's wages. As a direct result, during the miner's strike [October -

November 1920], railways had to pay £0.15m wages for time not worked. In 1913 the wage bill was £47m; in 1921, it was £173m. (An increase of 268%).
[Times, 2nd June 1921, 7e & Pratt, Page 783].

Increased, standardised wages and the eight hour day put rural railway services at risk. Wages in Scotland were lower and hours longer. An example was given of a level crossing keeper who had to be replaced by three, total wages were up 830% on pre-war. Likewise, one signalman replaced by two cost 700% more. The wages bill of the railways is greater than they can bear. These conditions were due to Government action during the Control period against the advice of railway management. [Cmd 1098, Pages 22 & 27].

Manufacture of Armaments

Railway workshops were used to manufacture armaments. Whereas lorries built for war use had a civilian use when the war ended, guns, tanks, ships, etc built in railway workshops did not. Railways suffered because rolling stock and assets were not maintained, but were under considerably greater strain.

The Government terms for manufacture were :-

> Work done for Government - Materials and labour charged at cost, plus usual workshop expenses as applying to various shops, and supervision at 12%. No interest will be chargeable for advance payments. Payments by the Ministry of Munitions to the end of 1919 was £10.2m. The War Office paid £6.3m, including £2.8m for conversion of ambulance trains. The Government gained by the fact that this work was done virtually at cost price, unlike in factories. The value of this work alone to the country was incalculable. [Pratt, Pages 592 & 607].

Special demands

In 1914, fearing invasion, Government set up a camp with troops ready to send anywhere. Railways had to provide 70 trains for use at short notice. They stood idle for two years. [Pratt, Page 801].

"We have to keep trains ready for the troops". [Midland Railway AGM, 1915].

Compensation

When it came to paying out, railways found that a Government in wartime and one in the post war era were two very different kinds of animal. [Hamilton, Page 48].

Railway net revenue from August 1914 to the end of 1918 was £213.2m, compared to £196.2m pa guaranteed, leaving a Government gain of £17m. The estimated value of services rendered by railways to Government free of charge for the same period was £112m. Services rendered to Government by other railway businesses, apart from rail conveyance was £10-15m. The total gain acknowledged by Government was £146m. [Cmd 402]. In view of their subsequent attitude, this was, doubtless, an under-estimate.

If rail prices had increased, as those for other industries increased - see pages 37 & 38 - net railway profit would have been greater, but would still not have compensated for free Government travel and traffic. The loss of revenue from civilian traffic, due to Government restrictions, much of which went to foster road transport growth, was not computed. Almost certainly underestimated, was the value of free travel, due to poor Government records on the issue of vouchers; and including that by Armed Forces - 12-13 times as large as peacetime, and aggravated by the scale of wounded returned to the UK. Increased materials were carried for the military from clothing [up to 32 times more] to weapons, ammunition and horses. About 11 times as much ammunition was produced in 1916 as pre-war. [Statistics in the Great War].

The value of business other than rail conveyance, included manufacture of munitions in railway workshops and the deployment of railway assets and staff abroad, and was almost certainly underestimated at £10-15m.

Colwyn Committee

On 24th June 1920, the MoT told Parliament that railways were trying to claim large sums to which they were not entitled. Rumours circulated that Railways were claiming £200-400m, but they said no claim had been calculated. [Pratt, Page 1144].

Some or all of the reports emanated from the Ministry, which was trying to justify its existence. [Times, 14th February 1921, 11b].

In September 1920, the MoT set up a Departmental Committee under Lord Colwyn, to look into compensation and payments which were due to Railways under the 1871 Act. [Hansard vol. 133, col. 1342].

Its' remit was to inquire and report on:-

1. The nature and terms of Agreements made between Government and railways relating to the possession by Government of the undertakings of the companies.
2. The possible extent of the outstanding liabilities of the State thereunder, according to the interpretation which may placed upon such Agreements.
3. Whether, with due regard to costs, any further steps should be taken to secure that the interests of the State in reference to such Agreements are adequately safeguarded.

The Committee consisted of Lord Colwyn, five MP's, one Treasury official, and the President of the FBI. As the FBI objected in 1919 to Government investigating costs of production of Government contracts he was an inappropriate choice to be investigating allegations that railways were claiming more than their due, and trying to secure a return on assets which would have been substantially less than other industry. (see page 38).

Colwyn's companies were probably members of the FBI. (see page 34 & 38).

The MoT said the Committee would meet in private. "The Railway Agreements involve questions affecting hundreds of millions of pounds and must result eventually in a contest of negotiation between railways and the MoT". It sat in private for seventeen days - behind closed doors. [Hansard vol. 133, col. 153].

Seventeen days to consider a complex issue, covering seven years of sequestration.

Although the Committee was constituted with his own men, which should have ensured that it arrived at the pre-determined conclusion, he prevented them from seeing everything of relevance, lest they may misguidedly arrive at the wrong conclusion. Internal Memo 8th November 1920 : The MoT has laid down that the Committee are entitled to see original correspondence, but not Departmental minutes. [PRO : MT6/3134].

Despite extensive searches and unstinting help by PRO staff, these minutes cannot be found. One can only speculate on their content, but it is fair to conclude that disclosure would not have helped, indeed could have embarrassed, the Government. It may be that the railways were aware of the content, even though they had no copy. However, the exclusion of Railway representatives from the proceedings ensured that they could not let a cat out of the bag.

"The constitution of the Committee was open to criticism, Government had their representatives, the railways didn't. There was no opportunity for cross examination of witnesses. By meeting behind closed doors, railways were unable to know the charges against them nor were they furnished with particulars of those charges or asked to refute or confirm them. The Committee recommended that Government should repudiate a considerable number of the Agreements to which - after seeking advice from two of the most eminent financial experts in the country, and obtaining the consent of the Treasury hereto - they had become parties, and to treat these documents as scraps of paper". [Chairman of Midland Railway, AGM, 1920].

The appointment of the Colwyn Committee was an attempt to justify his [MoT] superfluous Department. There was no need or justification for it. He claimed to have found accounting discrepancies. They had been discovered and pointed out by Railway Accountants. [Modern Transport, 19th January 1921]. (see also Times, pages 34-35).

"The only purpose of the Committee seems to have been for it to say 'ditto' to the Minister. Its report was couched in obscure language, but the aim was evidently to make it as difficult as possible for the railway companies to substantiate their claims". [Hamilton, Page 201].

The post-war deficit arose because Government increased wages without the slightest regard as to whether receipts would cover that cost. Had railways been allowed to increase charges pro rata with the higher prices levied by producers of every conceivable commodity, there would be no railway deficit today. Subsequent increases were two years behind time. [Modern Transport, 22nd January 1921].

There was no need for the Committee, the 1871 Regulation of Forces Act provided that railways taken over should be paid full compensation - agreed between railways and Secretary of State or failing agreement, by arbitration under the Land Clauses [Consolidation] Act 1865. The purpose of the Committee was clearly to enable Government to avoid paying a legal and honourable debt in full. (see pages 20 & 21).

Colwyn Report [Cmd 1132], 8th February 1921.

Chapter 1. Para 1: This Committee is not competent to express legal data [having said interpretation is a matter of law], and made no attempt to deal with legal interpretations. The Committee said "they did not sit as a judicial body"; as the interpretation of agreements is a matter of law, they disavowed any intention of expressing opinions. Their recommendations "must not be regarded as the result of and investigation from a legal standpoint". Para 3: "It would be a matter of regret if the spirit of mutual trust and fair dealing which had characterised the negotiation of the agreements and their application were to give way to ***a tenacious insistence on documentary rights***.

(In effect, this was to preserve an unwarranted and immoral financial gain for Government, whose "fair dealing" was characterised by its profligate use of free and cheap travel, traffic transferred to rail free of charge from coastwise shipping and canals, rail assets transferred to war zones, manufacturing munitions at cost when industry was making huge profits and by other miserly measures).

The Report referred to a number of Agreements made after the initial Agreement in 1914, including Maintenance arrears, Abnormal wear & tear, Replenishment of pre-war stores and Interest on capital.

(The Committee claimed that "Agreements" were not Agreements - then argued against a tenacious insistence on rights, which could not be rights if the Agreements were invalid. Abandonment of documentary rights meant that Agreements should be retrospectively ignored, by inference, to the advantage of Government).

Chapter 2. Para 2: Had railways not been under Government Control since the War, they would have lost revenue due to the railway strike, coal strike and trade depression. The Report claims that 1913 was a favourable year.

(They assumed charges remaining at 1913 levels, Government not paying rail charges for its wartime traffic, or for millions of demobilised men, 125,000 horses, and millions of greatcoats handed to and conveyed by railways. It ignores munitions manufactured at cost, which were not covered by the 1871 Act. It ignores that Government arbitrarily conceded an 8 hour day and a guaranteed week to railway staff, which cost £13m pa, guaranteed a week's wages, and inflated costs on rural lines to an extent which prejudiced viability, all of which changes would not have been made by railway management - see page 29. They overlooked that 1913 results improved because Government had belatedly authorised rate increases to compensate for increased costs which Government had forced on railways in 1911. They overlooked the prospect that, in the absence of war, railway profits, which had increased since 1907, would have continued an upward trend. They ignored the fact that, due to Government Control, other civilian business was lost to road).

Page 22: Companies contend railways should be returned to their owners in the same condition as taken over. We cannot find Government has admitted such an obligation. (So much for their "fair dealing").

The Report says the amount of deferred work on permanent way was greater than rolling stock. (Post-war repair figures for rolling stock were much higher than pre-war).

Chapter 5: Railway companies were unable to furnish at present an estimate of claims they may put forward at the end of possession. The Committee estimated that the railways claim may total £150m:- maintenance arrears £90m, abnormal wear & tear £40m, replacement of stores £20m - but noted that the Companies may put forward other claims. (Government had admitted to a gain of £146m - see page 30).

Chapter 7: "Further steps necessary to safeguard the Interests of Government". (A pointer to bias, which would not have occurred with the arbitration set out in legislation).

Appendices included 148 pages of Letters and Documents between Government & Railways relating to Agreements, and written evidence and opinion expressed by witnesses.

"The method by which the Secretary to the Committee has been permitted to print critical and highly controversial memoranda of his own as Appendices constitutes a departure from the procedures of Departmental Committees for which there is no precedent". (Times, 14th February 1921, 10d).

Recommendations included :-

1. Charges for maintenance in excess of 1913 should not be allowed. (i.e. railways not having profited, like the rest of industry, from the vastly increased activity, should pick up the tab for ensuing higher maintenance costs).

2. Discontinue current payments on account of maintenance, other than renewals.

5. Claims for Abnormal Wear & Tear to be justified:-

[a] As being due to Government Control and user of the undertaking.

[b] That Abnormal Wear & Tear is not offset by reduced maintenance expenditure elsewhere.

[c] Amounts received are insufficient.

Evidently, "mutual trust" would not be displayed by the Government.

Two members favoured cancelling the Agreements and reverting to the provisions of the 1871 Act. That would have benefited railways and was dismissed by the MoT. (see page 35).

Graham stated: Within a comparatively short time, the Committee had to apply their minds to a mass of Agreements between Railways & Government. He claimed that the 1871 Act was ambiguous (if so, that was Government's fault).

Barnes stated : The Act included limiting words which excluded the allowance or compensation for what could be attributed to war circumstances as distinct from the effects of Government Control. Railway companies insisted on the deletion of these words and Government ***gave way***. (see the Midland Railway comments on page 32).

Barnes had a mirror image. The Government had imposed limiting words in the "Special Agreement" to reduce the sums they would have had to pay under the Act. (see page 22).

"The Committee suggests a few very stupid and innocent Treasury officials were outwitted by a group of subtle, supremely able railway managers. Our opinion is that Treasury officials can match any number of railway managers. Arrangements for Control had been in hand since 1911". [Times, 14th February 1921, 10d].

It is improbable that any other industry would have forgone "documentary rights". No other industry, including those of which Lord Colwyn was a Director - coal, cotton or rubber - was treated so shabbily. Neither was the Manchester Ship Canal, of which he later became a Director. (see below & page 38).

The coal industry in particular was accused of profiteering at the country's expense and even of jeopardising the war effort. Other unnamed profiteering industries were criticised in Parliament. [Times, 1916, 23rd November, 6g & 27th November, 9b]. (see also pages 37-38).

Suspicions hinted at by Sir Alex Butterworth that the MoT dominated the proceedings of the Colwyn Committee were strengthened by the absence from the Report of many points which tell in favour of railways. The Committee made no mention of the 300% increase in prices since 1913 which increases the cost of abnormal wear & tear, whereas the Agreement provided for only 113% increase in prices. Exaggerated statements of the contents of the Report have been circulated. Clearly the object was to create in the public mind an atmosphere of prejudice against railways. Some, if not all of the statements emanated from the MoT. We are not persuaded that the Committee should ever have been appointed. Geddes sought to justify his Ministry by denouncing Agreements between railways and Government. He claimed to have discovered a flaw in the Metropolitan District Railway accounts, but this is absurd - Government were told of it by the railway companies before the Ministry of Transport existed. The Colwyn proposals are not just or acceptable and should be set aside. [Times 14th February 1921, 10d, 11b].

No one except the MoT knows why the Colwyn Committee was appointed and its admission that it had to ignore the legal position of the parties indicates that its origin was more political than financial. During the war, the Prime Minister admitted that the Government had had the best of the bargain with the railways, for the latter carried an unprecedented volume of traffic and yet were prevented from obtaining any benefit therefrom. [Times 15th February 1921, 17d].

We cannot recall any precedent for the proposals of the Colwyn Committee to treat the Agreement as scraps of paper. [Times 23rd February 1921, 17a]

The Prime Minister made a mistake in creating a huge Department to fit a "super-man". If the MoT had not forced his way into control, the Treasury and the railways would have settled long ago. We are glad to believe the grandiose Ministry will soon disappear. [Times Leader, 4th March 1921, 13d].

In June 1921, the House debated the Compensation. The MoT said he would pay £51m in satisfaction of all claims under the Agreements, further explanation showed it was £60m less tax and then Government gave themselves extended credit - half to be paid December 1921, half in December 1922 - four years after the War ended. Geddes could not explain how the £51m was made up. [Hansard vol. 142, col. 2001].

One MP pointed out that 50% of the Compensation shall be treated as income - whether it is spent as income or not and will be subject to Income Tax. He described the provisions in the Act as penal. [Hansard vol. 142, col. 682]

Geddes told Parliament that there was no obligation to put railways back into its pre-war position. Asked if the 1871 Act had been repealed, he replied that "it was not necessary to go into that". [Modern Transport 4th June 1921] .

An MP who was a member of the Colwyn Committee [Barnes] could not believe that workshops could not carry out railway repairs as well as munitions. (By definition, he was assuming that pre-war profit motivated railways carried uneconomic surplus capacity in their workshops). [Hansard vol. 142 col. 1376].

Sir F. Banbury MP: It is untrue to say that railways agreed to £60m, it was agreed by one Chairman and two or three GM's. Colwyn was a hostile Committee and they said £150m compensation was due, with a possible further £50m. GNR workshops repaired 4.25m 18 pounder shells at half the price charged at Woolwich factory and manufactured 124,000 shells at less than two thirds the Woolwich price. He challenged Major Entwistle [who defended Geddes] - If we entered into a bargain and it turned out to his advantage and not mine, what would he say if I said: 'As the bargain has resulted in your favour and not mine is he going to abide by his strict legal rights?' The State made a very good bargain, maintenance fell behind due to workshops being employed on munitions. [Hansard vol. 142, cols. 1376 & 1381]

Mr Marriott, MP: "Not only were railways carrying free all Government traffic during the war, they placed all workshops at the disposal of Government without drawing a farthing in profit. They produced [munitions] in railway workshops at cost. In accepting £60m, railways are debarred from proceeding under Statutes. Government retain the right to prosecute claims under the law. Never before has there been a case of heads I win, tails you lose". [Hansard vol. 142, col. 1381].

It was an unwarranted and immoral additional gain for Government and less than its own Committee's estimate of £150-200m. They surely erred Government's favour. Why did railways accept this miserly sum? In December 1918, Churchill said their policy was based on nationalisation. The Midland Railway Chairman told the 1920 AGM : "Whether railways are destined to become the property of the State ......". The companies also feared threatened MoT powers set out in the Bill for Railway reorganisation. (see pages 45 & 46).

A Labour Party Bill for Nationalisation valued the railway companies at 30% less than pre-war. [Railway Gazette, vol. 34, Page 569, 15th April 1921].

The MoT declined to accept the [judicial] decision of the R&CC for the immediate payment to the North British Railway of £0.43m for expenditure on maintenance which Government had, in general terms, accepted responsibility. An additional sum for £0.5m for the first five months of this year has been deducted. [Times Supplement 16th July 1921, 345].

An internal Memo to the MoT drew attention to a statement by the Home Secretary in the House when the 1919 MoT Act was debated, that "arrangements made in August 1914 were not exhaustive as regards railways' rights to compensation". The MoT was advised, by his Civil Servants, that they need not be held to such a statement. [PRO : MT49/58].

If Government had paid for its traffic, receipts would have been £112m greater* - exceeding by £17m, compensation paid up to the end of 1918 [i.e., the "Guarantee" of 1913 profits]. Expenditure increased by £56m between 1913 and 1918 due to the large increase in war traffic. There was a great increase in materials and labour cost.
[Times Supplement 15th January 1921, 417].

(* £112m is based on charges being unchanged throughout the period of Control, when costs had doubled. The amount is clearly grossly under estimated).

Two weeks later, the Times Leader asked : Are railways to be left financially derelict after having been brought to this position by muddle headed State interference? The stumbling block is the grandiose Ministry created not to meet a public need, but to gratify the overweening ambition of Sir Eric Geddes. [Times 29th January 1921, 11b].

The chaos which Government brought into the transport system of the country can only be described as an industrial tragedy of serious magnitude. Government Control destroyed the railway system as a commercial undertaking, converting what was a profitable business into a heavy burden on the community. [Times Supplement 16th July, 1921, 345].

Seven years of Government Control reduced railways from relatively prosperous commercial concerns to a precarious financial position. [Bonavia[1], Page 10].

The principal road transport journal stated : "We know that it took many years to renovate the railways after 1918". [Commercial Motor, 30th March 1940, Page 158].

Gratitude - no substitute for cash

There were many letters, speeches and media reports of gratitude and appreciation of railways' wartime efforts from military leaders : Kitchener, French, Haig & Robertson; the President of the Board of Trade; MoT; Select Committee and others. (Gratitude is cheap!).

In 1920, the MoT said that the Cabinet is profoundly impressed with [the need] ...... to remove handicaps under which they [railways] are suffering. [Hansard vol. 130, col. 2455].

Ensuing years, produced no evidence of these words being turned into actions.

A Memo to the MoT on 4th February 1921, stated: The bulk of the claim is due to the railways whose right to the money cannot be challenged. [PRO: MT49/57 - closed to 1972!].

Sir Herbert Walker wrote : "The end of military occupation of railways found the commercial revenue of those undertakings virtually destroyed. [Pratt, Page 1159].

Treatment of other industry

Why did Government sequestrate railways but not other industries? Coal was crucial to the war - for the Navy, shipping, industry, electricity, gas, canals, railways and domestic use. Miners would have responded more to State control than to the much hated owners, with whom Government was also unhappy. Government would gain from railway control, moving vast quantities of men and goods without payment. Had they taken over coal mines and held prices static, as with railways, they would have had to pay subsidies. Powers enacted in November 1916 to control collieries were ineffective. "The prosperity of coal owners has increased, and dividends are higher". [Times, 21st August 1916, 3b]

Miners believed owners were making undue wartime profits and were anxious to conceal it. At the start of the war, miners offered not to ask for rises during war if owners undertook not to raise prices. It was not accepted and prices began to move upwards. Lord Rhondda said that Government should have taken all the extra profits of coal-owners and ship-owners". [Times 23rd November 1916, 6a]

Coal owners are quarrelling with their men over the division of excessive profits which both are extracting from the public. The demand by the miners for an independent audit of the costs of production was said [by the owners] to be unreasonable and unprecedented. Government had interfered a year ago because owners had so mismanaged their industry as to imperil the war. [Times 27th November 1916, 9b].

Between 1913 & 1916, average profit per ton doubled - aggregate profits [on a smaller tonnage] rose over 50%. In May 1917, miners complained to the Prime Minister of shameful profiteering. During the war, capital and reserves doubled. [Supple, Pages 92, 100]

The price of railway coal, at the pithead, increased by 132% in 1919 compared to 1913, steel tyres were 400% up. [Pole, Page 223].

Felix Pole pointed out that coal was only cut for five hours in 24, and coal owners were asking railways, which work 24 hours for a rate cut! [Times 15th January 1926, 10d].

Canals could have been helpful in moving bulk materials but were not taken over until late in the war. On 4th August 1914, Government took over railways and their canals - 1,268 miles. As costs had increased, canal carriers increased charges - they had no statutory limitations. [Savage, Page 7].

As rail rates were frozen, this led to transfers from canals to overloaded railways. In December 1916, Sir Herbert Walker, Acting Chairman, REC, wrote to the Minister of Munitions: "There is need to make better use of canals to relieve railways". On 1st March 1917, Government took over the remaining canals. Canal companies - those who owned canals rather than barges, although some canal owners were also carriers - were guaranteed 1913 profits. The aim was to prevent further transfer of traffic to railways, but tonnage continued to fall. Control of canal companies ended 31st August 1920. Control of railways continued until 15th August 1921. Control of independent canals from 1917 to 1920 cost the Treasury £3m in compensation [Savage Page 82].

Manchester Ship Canal Directors' Reports for 1914-19, during which railway freight rates were frozen at 1913 levels by Government, show the Canal Company increased rates and charges on eight occasions, and twice imposed a surcharge over and above the through rail freight rate to and from the rest of the UK. The average revenue surplus of for 1914-19 inclusive was £182.5m compared to £34.7m in 1913 - a staggering 425% increase! The railways were pegged at their 1913 net revenue figure of about £50m. 1918 Report: As Government have not increased railway freight rates, to defray the increased war cost of working, the Canal Company's proportion out of railway rates on import & export traffic [to and from the rest of the UK on the main line system] have not been increased. To meet to some extent, the increased expenditure a surcharge was put in force by the MSC as from September 1918. On certain other rail borne traffic the MSC have been able to obtain increased receipts to cover war costs. The surcharge on rail traffic, was further increased in October 1919. (Lord Colwyn, who later became a Director of the MSC, which had its own railway network serving local businesses, had not compared the profits of this transport business with main line railways).

Rail freight rates had been frozen by Government. Munitions produced by industry were on cost plus contracts, whilst railways supplied them at cost.

On 24th February 1919, Lt. Col. Sir John Hope MP asked Government "Is it not in the public interest to punish firms who endangered soldiers' and sailors' lives and obtained fraudulent profits at the nation's expense?". The Minister of Munitions said a black list existed, but it would not be released to the public. [Hansard vol. 112, cols. 966, 1361].

Despite extensive research, I cannot find this list in the Record Office. Black Lists exist of foreign companies, but not of UK companies. Ministry records refer to Munitions files destroyed under the 1877 Public Record Office Act.

In a Memo 19th March, 1919, John Mann wrote to the Deputy Munitions Minister "You will remember the effort made by the FBI to get Government to abandon its right to investigate costs during the war and prevent its continuance in peacetime. The bitterness of the opposition is a measure of its importance". [PRO : MUN7/136]. The President of the FBI was a member of the Colwyn Committee. (see page 31)

In 1920, Sir Leo Chiozza Money, wartime PS to the Minister of Shipping, wrote that prodigious shipping profits during the war, contributed in no small measure to the high cost of commodities. In 1917, only a half of available ships had been requisitioned, the other half was earning extravagant profits The industry failed to rise to the emergency. As soon as the Armistice arrived, Government set shipping free to increase profits at consumers' expense. Products hitherto carried in requisitioned ships were charged, after decontrol, at over double the former freight rates. [People's Year Book, 1920, Page 205].

In 1919, the Midland Railway Chairman said that railways were the only industry not to pay higher dividends during the war. [Midland Railway AGM].

Railway dividends were held at 6%, whilst breweries were 10%, Iron & Steel: 9-12%, other large businesses 7-11%. [Pole. Page 223].

Colliery profits were more impressive. The Fife Coal Co paid 35% dividend in 1916, compared to 32-50% before the war [Anderson, Page 22].

In April 1941, the Chancellor said that increased production required by war would not become the means of enrichment **as it did in the last war.** [Hansard vol. 370, col. 297]

Chapter 4 POST WAR DEVELOPMENTS

Coastwise Shipping Traffic

Government held rail freight rates at the 1913 level throughout the war, whilst coastwise shipping rates doubled. Consignees sought to avoid higher charges and so railways were overwhelmed with traffic. They had no legal power to refuse traffic. To protect and restore coastwise shipping, the Cabinet decided on 4th July, 1919 to refund the difference between sea and rail rates to reverse the sea-to-rail transfer. On 20th August 1919 the Board of Trade ordered railways not to carry traffic by rail, which was imported or for export, if it could be carried by coastwise shipping. The Treasury paid the REC who then paid the traders. Government did not pay for railway or shipping staff involved nor for their accommodation. The subsidy was withdrawn in June 1920. The total diverted to sea between August 1919 and June 1920 was 1.3m tons, the total subsidy was £0.48m. [Pratt, Pages 281-7]. (The BoT thus contravened the 1854 Act).

Ministry of Transport Act 1919

On 26th February 1919, without the consultation promised with the RCA, Government brought out a Bill to establish a Ministry of Ways & Communications [later renamed Transport], with draconian powers over railways. Sec. 3 of the Act gave powers to continue to control railways for a further two years from passing the Act [on 15th August], including powers over rates & charges [subject to reference to the Rates Advisory Committee]. Sec. 3: Charges to be applicable for 18 months after expiration of Government powers. It gave enhanced rights to traders to complain to the Railway & Canal Commissioners under Railway & Canal Acts 1854 - 1913 in respect of undue preference and undue disadvantage. Sec. 13: It will be lawful for the MoT to purchase POW's. Sec. 21: Created a Rates Advisory Committee. (see page 40).

Demobilisation

As mentioned on page 23, Government had decided it would retain control of railways for two years after the War. A major benefit was to enable Government to deal with the task of demobilising millions of men from HM Forces at zero transport cost. The Plan, when it was revealed, called for railways to convey 280,000 demobilised soldiers per week. 4m demobilised soldiers were told to hand in their greatcoats at a railway stations in exchange for £1 which railways were to advance and recover later! This amounted to £280,000 per week. Many stations did not have enough to pay wages inflated by Government directed increases. Railways were advanced £200,000 by the Treasury, [less than one week's outlay]. The Post Office - wholly Government owned - had refused to handle the task! Railways were required to deal with 125,000 horses - 12,500 per week returned from abroad for sale in the UK. Most of the horses were moved more than once within the UK. More special trains were required. [Hamilton, Pages 188-9].

Surplus war materials, including motor vehicles, armoured vehicles, munitions, guns and stores were returned to the UK and conveyed by rail to depots, including some created by Government for the handling of motor vehicles. Being still under Government control, no money changed hands for these huge tasks. (see page 54).

Post War Financial Reviews

Sec. 21 of the 1919 Act set up a Rates Advisory Committee [RAC] under Francis Gore-Brown, KC, together with representatives of agriculture, labour, railway, trade and one other. (Railways were a minority in deciding their own charges). Taking 1914 as 100, by May, 1920, the Cost of Living Index had risen to 241. This seriously inflated Railways' costs but, their charges had hardly moved. On 27th October 1919, the MoT asked the RAC to consider a number of rates issues:-

1. The best means of achieving a railway revenue increase of £45m.

2. [a] Increasing present charges of detention of railway trucks & sheets before or after conveyance;

[b] Decreasing the free time allowed for loading & unloading;

[c] Increasing the charge for internal use.

3. The desirability of terminating or modifying railway practice of rendering some services free or at nominal charge.

The Committee opted to deal separately with these matters, and produced six Reports.

Report on Wagon Demurrage, 1919 [Cmd 526]

They concluded wagon detention is excessive, is increasing and should be diminished. Substantial increases in charges are justified by the value of wagons. They proposed no change in free time, but recommended increased demurrage and internal user charges. The MoT implemented their recommendations from 1st January. (Internal user charges were for railway wagons used inside industrial sidings).

Interim Report on Rates for Goods, Minerals & Merchandise, 1919 [Cmd 525]

There was no Public Inquiry because of the need for speed. The Report dealt with item 1 of their Remit, increased by the MoT on December 10th by £5m [to total £50m]. They reported that the need for extra revenue was too urgent to permit of detailed examination of charges or a Public Inquiry, and advocated an Interim increase. They said there should be a general rise of goods rates of 25-60%, but 100% for Returned Empties, and smaller increases (as ever) for agriculture:-

Class A [coal] 25%, Class A [Other] 30%, Class B 40%, Classes 1-5 60%, all plus flat rate increases. There should also be flat rate increases of 3d (1p) to 9d (4p) per ton to meet terminal cost rises. These imposed a higher percentage on higher value goods and increased short distance rates more than long distance. Charges for Post Office traffic to increase by up to 60%. This Interim increase should apply from 15th January 1920. They forecast a yield of £49.6m.

They "could not deal at present with coastwise losses due to low rail rates".

There was no logic in varying the percentage increases for different classes of traffic - it made some vulnerable to newly emerging road transport.

Views of Industry, Agriculture & Others, March 1920 [Cmd 682]

On 6th February, the MoT asked the Central Chamber of Agriculture, Mining Association, Association of British Chambers of Commerce, FBI, Mansion House

Association and RCA for comments on his remit to the RAC. He said that, hitherto, railways have been free to adjust within statutory maxima. His questionnaire asked :

- Whether maxima should be fixed as in the past, with liberty for railways to increase such rates up to the maxima or a new scale imposed by the MoT,
- Whether there should be a new Tribunal,
- Should the number of Classes be increased or decreased,
- Whether lower rates should be charged for export goods.

(It was akin to asking turkeys to vote against Christmas).

Only the FBI favoured a new Tribunal but envisaged something simple and said railways should be put on a sound commercial working basis unfettered by the State, except for protection against secret inter railway agreements, but that variations should be justified before a Tribunal! They recommended lower rates to assist exports.

Railways were given no protection against secret inter manufacturer agreements - as Blee pointed out to the ABCC in 1951 when he spoke of the secret price rings which were abundantly apparent whenever we [BR] went out to tender. [PRO : AN6/10].

All, except railways, favoured retention of maxima as in the pre-war system. Mining interests called also for "some restrictions on increases". The Mansion House Association called for a new Classification.

The RCA drew attention to the huge task of revision experienced in 1889. They felt that the standard maxima might be abolished and some simple machinery set up to enable rates to be varied from time to time as circumstances require, or freedom given to vary within maxima. They called for a change which provided for a fair return on capital.

On 11th May, the RAC began a Public Inquiry on freight rates. On 6th July they began a new Public Inquiry into workmen's fares, still at pre-war levels and considered unremunerative. On 7th July the MoT gave them a new remit, to take precedence. As the estimated deficit from 1st April 1920, was £54.5m pa [including £2.2m for Ireland], and it was Government policy that railways should be self supporting, (they had been until sequestrated in 1914), they were asked:-

- to consider and advise what increase should be made in Fares & Charges, to yield by June 1921 [later extended to July], the deficit which began to accrue from 1st April.

The MoT emphasised the importance of fair maintenance of coastwise traffic, and, asked:

- what increases should be made in exceptional charges in consequence of water competition. (In effect to what level, rail rates should be enforcibly increased to reduce the ability of railways to undercut coastwise shipping, but thereby increasing the scope for road competition!).
- to what extent charges at railway company docks should be increased. (to facilitate competition by non railway owned docks).
- to consider what increases should be made in charges for Season Tickets, Workmen & other fares below Ordinary which were subject of an earlier reference on 5th May.

Interim Revision of Rates, Fares & Charges, 1920 [Cmd 857]

The RAC held an Inquiry for three days on Seasons, Workmen's and Traders Seasons and eight days on the general subject, between 6th and 23rd July. They pointed out that three months of the deficiency period had elapsed before reference was issued to them.

They stated that, after the increase in Ordinary fares in 1917, Ordinary fare revenue rose only 12.9%, whilst unaffected Seasons rose 25.5% and Workmen's 28.8%. Overall there was a drop of 14.8% in revenue. In 1919, Ordinary revenue rose by 78.6%, Seasons by 86.8% and Workmen's by 21.2%. Neither Seasons nor Workmen's fares were at standard or common levels.

Their Report stated that, in 1913, the percentage split of passenger to goods was 46.09% : 53.91%; and in the first four months of 1920, 43.8% : 56.2%. Railways said 40% of the increase should be drawn from passenger and 60% from freight. This would increase fares by 100% over pre-war, which the RAC opposed, because "they thought it would seriously impair receipts".

This ignored the view of the professionals who would lose profits if they were wrong. It ignored a 241% increase in materials prices - which no one took steps to reduce, and railway wages increased by Government - during and after the war. (see page 29).

Representatives of Season Ticket holders claimed that Seasons were part of living costs and should not increase at all! (Taken to its logical conclusion, food, clothing and many other items should still be at 1913 levels today. One suspects that they only wanted one item to remain static).

The RAC did not agree - there was no case to throw the burden elsewhere and recommended a 50% increase over Season rates in force before May 1918. Traders Seasons to be not more than 20% below standard Seasons for Traders having £1,000 traffic pa by a particular railway company. The RAC proposed to increase Ordinary fares by $16^2/_3$% [= 75% above pre-war]. Workmen's fares, which were unduly low, were to increase to levels which would not exceed 200% of the existing fares. Objectors claimed that Workmen's fares were at low levels as a quid pro quo for Government amending the Railway Passenger Duty under the Cheap Trains Act 1883 and could not be increased unless Passenger Duty was re-imposed. (They were wrong - see page 19).

What seemed to escape the minds of such bodies was that the objective was to increase profit, not passenger volume - the two are not synonymous. If railways had been free to determine fares and a 100% increase reduced profits, they would have been free to readjust fares - up or down - to maximise net profit, exactly as applied to other industries.

Government approved the proposals on 28th July operative from 6th August except workmen's fares which were from 1st September. There was a protest in Parliament but the changes went ahead.

Under these proposals, freight rates were raised by more than railways recommended, making them more vulnerable to unfair road competition.

Interim Revision of Charges : Goods, July 1920 [Cmd 886]

Three months of the deficiency period had elapsed before reference was issued to the RAC. The time necessary to implement after RAC recommendations would be about one month - the Railway & Canal Traffic Act 1888 required railways to give 14 days notice of freight rate increases. The RAC concluded that the earliest date for implementation was 1st September. The deficit to be made good by July 1921 would be £66m pa. The fares increase would produce £17m, leaving £49m pa from goods traffic. To obtain this in eleven months was equivalent to £53.5m pa.

Railways proposed increases over present rates on traffic by passenger train, some of which had been unchanged during the war: -

varying, over 1913, from 100% for Mails to 200% for Returned Empties.

and proposed increases over pre-war rates for traffic by goods train of :-

200% on returned empties; 150% on smalls; 103% on coal; 100% on other traffic. Rates for these classes of traffic were subject to an interim increase from 15th January 1920. In that revision, the percentage increases were on a graduated scale 25-60%, whereas present proposals were uniform. In effect, these restored pre-war relativities.

The RAC said that increases are not objectionable to traders (compared to 240% increases in the cost of living, this is unsurprising), and recommended railway proposals except for returned empties which should be not more than 100% and certain agricultural products should be not more than 50%. (Agriculture favoured again). To "compensate", they recommended an increase in the flat rate element on Class C goods (making them even more vulnerable to road competition)

The RAC dismissed claims by the LCC for assistance to solve housing problems through cheaper fares, and the Ministry of Labour for concessions to juvenile employees [to subsidise low wages].

The RAC stated: "Upon the question whether, when railway rates have been increased by the general percentage recommended, coastwise steamers will be able to attract a fair share of traffic at rates which will enable them to continue to compete, we have come to the conclusion, upon the evidence that they will not be able to do so. We are, therefore, of opinion that it is desirable with a view to securing the continuance of the coasting trade that if rail rates can be shown to have been reduced to meet water competition they should be restored to a normal amount, but we regret that we cannot see in what manner this can be done at present".

47 Docks owned by railways should have charges raised by 150% above pre-war producing £1.2m, and coal tipping charges increased similarly to produce £1.3m. A Railway Docks profit of £0.5m in 1913 had changed, under control of the Board of Trade to a loss of £2.1m by 1919, (despite the most intensive activity).

The RAC pointed out that the increase on January 14th had produced £43m pa. These recommendations would increase this to £47.5m - based on 1919 traffic levels. However there had been a 10% increase in goods traffic, which would add £4.4m giving a total of £51.9m. The RAC said that since Goods rates have been more severely dealt with than passenger fares, they will have a special claim to be readjusted in the future.

The RAC created the situation by rejecting railways' proposals on the proportionate split between passenger and freight. They did not acknowledge that readjustment would mean passengers paying more and a reversion to railways' proposed split. (see page 42).

On 1st September, a uniform increase of 100% was made over rates for mineral, merchandise and livestock in force on 14th January, (still at pre-war levels). This new increase was substituted for the average of 50% imposed from 15th January.

Interim Review of Fares below Ordinary & Services rendered free or at nominal charges, November 1920 [Cmd 1148]

On 14th September the RAC turned to these deferred subjects, for which they had "had ***insufficient time before the holidays***!". The remit was:-

1. What increase should be made in fares lower than Ordinary fares. (Season and workmen's fares had been dealt with).
2. The desirability of terminating or modifying the railway practice of rendering free or nominal charge services.

A new series of public inquiries occupied seven days between 14th September & 7th October. The railway view was that concessions should be given where they were justified commercially, and others dropped, except for shipwrecked mariners which were long standing concessions and cost little. The RAC recommended that the concessions should continue and that, in addition, cheap tickets should be introduced for the "Empire Parliamentary Association", and the concession relating to "parties of poor children" should be extended to all children attending elementary schools. (Road passenger transport was not similarly directed).

Some freight services, dating back many years, were performed free or at nominal charges and included free movement for short distances over railway owned canals, free clerical services for redirected or returned goods and free shunting in private sidings. The RAC supported most of the proposals to charge for these services.

Revision of Railway Rates & Charges, December 1920 [Cmd 1098]

Remit [Given to the RAC on 6th February] To advise and report on:-

1. The principles which should govern fixing of tolls, rates, and charges for the carriage of merchandise by freight and passenger train.
2. Classification of Merchandise and rates thereon.
3. Rates for Parcels and Perishable traffic.

A 41 day Public Inquiry began on 11th May. They said there was a consensus for a new Tribunal, (but see Cmd 682 - page 41 - which shows only one body was in favour). For 1919, (after labour cost increases caused by Government), gross expenditure was £187.1m, gross receipts £199.9m. Government had to pay £35.7m to make up to pre-war revenue, (as a result of their policy of freezing charges at the 1913 level). To rectify the shortfall, rates were increased by an average of 50% in January 1920 to secure £50m. Costs of materials and wages rose in 1920, requiring a further increase in fares from 6th August to 75% above pre-war - and goods from 1st September to average 112% over pre-war. (This compared to increases in costs of materials of 200% & wages of 250%).

The RAC recommended, inter alia :-

- A new Classification to be fixed by the RAC or a new Tribunal. Railways should prepare tables of merchandises divided into classes [probably 21], published for objections to be made.
- Exceptional Rates could not be abolished, but should, as far as possible, be incorporated into Standard Rates, [fixed rates rather than maxima]. Exceptional Rates not used for 12 months should be abolished.

• New Conditions of Carriage should be decided by the RAC or the new Tribunal, and provide for Company's Risk and Owner's Risk rates.
• Railways to produce rates for consideration. The Tribunal to set rates so as to give a fair rate of profit. Traders may claim that higher rates are due to poor management (higher industrial and retail prices were always due to circumstances beyond their control).
• Railways should be prohibited from charging above new maxima, but may apply to the Tribunal for authority to increase.
• Exceptional Rates may be increased, but traders may appeal to the Tribunal.
• Local Conferences should be established consisting of Railways & Traders.

The RAC said that as rates have to yield a definite net revenue, they must be fixed, not maxima, and determined by an independent Tribunal.

This was nonsense. Railways could have reverted to the pre-war control under the 1894 Act. It did not need a new Tribunal, which created "jobs for the boys". The previous body - the R&CC - continued to exist. Government would not accept their theory was flawed, even when it became evident that fixed rates did not produce the statutory net revenue. (see pages 74 & 104).

This phobia with complex rates structures controlled by a Court of Law was wholly unnecessary. If it was deemed essential, that railways, unlike any other business, should have profits limited, the 1844 Act, (see page 17), made such provision. Politicians could alter the 10% to any figure which seemed electorally advantageous, until in due time, it became obvious to even the most obtuse brain, that railways no longer enjoyed a monopoly, and the risk was, not too high a profit, but one too low to service the capital. It will be noted that the RAC said "to yield a definite net revenue". During World War II, politicians said Standard Net Revenue was not a statutory obligation. (see Chapter 12).

Future Organisation of Transport

The 1920 Railways Bill [Cmd 787] was introduced to the House of Commons on 11th May 1921 and set out Government's intention to amalgamate 120 Railway Companies into seven [later amended to four] Groups, thereby propping up railways in rural areas. It was intended that Scotland would be one Group, which Scottish interests opposed as it would be weak and urged linking with English Groups. They were to be established on a basis of operating economy, and direct competition was, as far as possible, to be eliminated. (In that respect the ensuing Act failed, because it left a multiplicity of Joint lines and lines penetrating into areas of other Groups). The Classification of merchandise was to be prepared by the RAC which would continue to exist to complete this task. Instructions as to the basis on which the classification was to be carried out were to be included in the Act. Railway groups would submit to the Rates Tribunal (RRT), by 31st December 1921, a schedule of standard charges (which would have to follow Classification).

Existing Exceptional Rates [rates below statutory Standard Rates] were to cease, and the introduction of new ones prevented until 14 days after being reported to the MoT, by which time any traffic would have been lost! [In the 1921 Act, this was amended so that the MoT could refer them to the Tribunal which had powers to modify, review, vary or cancel Exceptional Rates, especially if competing with coastwise shipping or canals!].

The RRT would consider objections and would then appoint a day [Appointed Day] for implementation. The RRT to report a limit beyond which an increase in charges would be unlawful without reference to Parliament. On and from the appointed day Standard charges would be the only permitted charges with no variation up or down, except for Special rates and certain Exceptional Charges (which must be below the Standard - maximum - charges).

The Bill planned for rates to be such, that railways would secure a net revenue equivalent to pre-war, and with due care and economy would improve on pre-war returns. Charges would be fixed in the first instance so as to be sufficient with efficient and economical working & management [in the opinion of the RRT] to yield the equivalent 1913 Net Revenue of constituent companies with certain sums on capital expenditure on some classes of expenditure which had not become remunerative in 1913. Should the RRT find Net Revenue in excess of "Standard Revenue" they may modify rates in subsequent years to reduce net revenue of a company by 80%. If Standard Revenue was not achieved, standard charges and exceptional rates may be raised provided the limit fixed for merchandise rates is not exceeded.

The Bill referred to the State "extending the Charter of the companies", entitling Government to share in surplus revenue to assist backward districts and develop light railways. The RCA stated that maximum charge scales were not "Charters" but restrictions upon charging powers which, in the absence of such scales, would be limited only by their reasonableness (even this limit did not apply to other industry). Railways had never operated under Charter. [Pratt, Pages 138-44].

The MoT was to have power to compel railways to spend capital on services, facilities and extensions which he might consider necessary. The Bill proposed that there be no capital expenditure without Government sanction and no capital raised except on methods approved by Government, which would order how depreciation and renewal funds of the groups were to be built up. Railways objected to powers to tell them to construct whatever lines he might himself regard as necessary, and to direct on running powers, pooling of receipts, common user of rolling stock and manufacturing plant. The RCA said the powers were oppressive and not required.

The Bill envisaged workers on the Boards, to which railway companies objected. Within six months of the Act railways must submit new Terms & Conditions of Carriage for the RRT to consider. The Act was to be implemented in August 1921. [The proposed speed of this legislation met with much criticism].

Chambers of Commerce opposed developments by a Government Department which would lead to political pressure to build and extend railways not justified on economic grounds. They said the proposals possessed many of the defects of nationalisation without ensuring the responsibility of the State would attach thereto. The London Chambers of Commerce said the proposal amounted to nationalisation minus the name. The FBI was critical, as was the media. The powers were dropped.

DoT Memo, 10th September 1925 : One of the objects of Grouping was to provide reasonable services - the burden of non paying portions would be borne by the more profitable portions. Scotland & Wales in particular were protected. The original grouping envisaged Scottish railways as a separate group, but it was realised they would be financially vulnerable. [PRO : MT6/3464]

The policy was undermined by creaming-off of traffic to road, but Government did not act to protect rural areas from the future inevitable loss of rail services when profits decreased leaving little scope to support rural services. (see page 72).

Railways Act 1921

Merged 120 railways into four main line companies and set up the Railway Rates Tribunal - a Court of Law - to decide all rates not merely maxima as hitherto. The Act promised profits no less, nor greater than 1913 with no provision for inflation.

Sec. 10 & Sec. 21: Expenses & Remuneration of the Amalgamation and Rates Tribunals to be recovered from Railways. (State interference paid by the victims!).
Sec. 30: Standard charges - railways to submit a schedule to the Tribunal by 31st December 1922. (The Act was dated 19th August 1921).
Sec. 32: From the appointed day no variation to be allowed up or down from Standard Rates, except for Exceptional Rates, (which must be below Standard).
Sec. 35: If railways or traders request that Standard charges be modified, the Tribunal will decide.
Secs. 36-40 deal with Exceptional Rates. (These were very time consuming for staff when charging up).

Government set up a Central Wages Board to decide railway wages, hours, etc referred to it, or on appeal to a National Wages Board. The concept of sectional councils was introduced by Government. Government went from one extreme to the other - from encouraging competition to virtually abolishing it by grouping.

Mr. Marriott, MP, wrote: "The weakness of the Act is that the State will continue to call the tune, the proprietors must pay the piper". [Times, 22nd July 1921, 6a].

Felix Pole said that the railways could operate without classification or schedules of rates - these are to benefit users. The obligation to refund 80% of surplus net receipts was a one sided clause. Railways cannot impeach traders for contributing to inefficiency by detention of wagons and poor loads in 10 ton wagons. A Trader was allowed 2-4 days to unload then charged 3/- per day. In a recent court case involving delay to a lorry, he said £1 per day was claimed. [Pole, Pages 224/225].

On 1st January 1923, the new Railway Groups reduced the level of fares from 75% above pre-war to 50% above pre-war. They introduced, as far as practicable, a standard basis for all ordinary passenger fares of 1.5d per mile for 3rd Class, 2.5d for 1st Class. As a result of the decision of the RRT, these fares became "Standard" for the four Groups as from 1st January 1928. A standard scale for season tickets which had previously been within the discretion of each company was laid down by the RRT. They also prescribed a scale for workmen's tickets which hitherto had been governed by special Statutory provisions or ordered by the Board of Trade under the 1883 Cheap Trains Act.

Railways had been merging to form bigger systems, but had had to secure Parliamentary approval. It is ironic, that, having blocked a merger of the GNR, GER and GCR as recently as 1909, the Government should embark on mergers on a more substantial scale. It demonstrates only too clearly the limited vision of politicians. The effect of this myopia was to have a disastrous effect on railways. Their blinkered thinking was clearly demonstrated during the 1938 submissions by railways. (see page 104).

Enforced mergers of coal, shipbuilding, steel and the motor industry may have made them competitive with the rest of the world, and avoided the need for them to be subsidised by low rail rates.

An attempt was made under the Coal Mines Act 1930, to amalgamate collieries into large units but was frustrated by opposition by the industry. [Chester, Page 10].

A Problem Deferred

In 1918, Government proposed the common use of non railway owned wagons [POW's], which Railways opposed due to limitations of use and the cost to the country for which there would be no return. In 1919 Government enacted powers to buy up POW's but "it was too costly and owners might buy more". They considered prohibiting new building but both ideas were dropped. The reason advanced by Government for not buying up these wagons, was that there were "powerful interests". They tried to force the pre-war main line railway companies - the "Big Four" to buy them up in 1929, but they declined. Eventually, when railways were nationalised, Government directed them to buy them out. (see pages 39, 87, 154 & 176).

An Alternative Deferred.

Churchill recommended Nationalisation in 1918. In 1947, the Labour Government was really implementing that policy, which, in 1930, the RCT implied was necessary to achieve the policy of co-ordination between road and rail, which Governments between the Wars claimed to seek. (see page 81).

PART II

THE PROBLEM

There must be either like publication of rates or like freedom to quote rates. Hauliers must give up the freedom of road quotations or the ***railway fetters must go.***

[Robinson, Deputy Secretary, DoT MT47/275].
[Secret Internal Memo]

GROWTH OF ROAD COMPETITION

Railway promoters had to obtain an Act of Parliament before buying land to construct and operate a railway. They were fiercely opposed by landowners, politicians and other forms of transport. They were built with £1.2 billion capital by private enterprise without any financial aid by the State. [Times 1st October 1928, 11d]

A 1904 GWR Bill included powers to operate buses. The Postmaster General inserted a clause requiring them to carry mails. The GWR deleted references to buses. In contrast, others who wished to operate motor transport were not required to obtain Acts to commence operations, nor make provision for carrying mails and no one could legally object to their activities before 1930. [Pole, Page 94].

Early mechanical transport

Steam powered road transport began around 1827. Trailing loads were low, and coal consumption high. There were strong objections to steam coaches by coach proprietors and ordinary people. [Rogers, Page 62].

The 1865 Locomotives on Highways Act - aimed at the only form of mechanical road transport : steam powered, which had boiler explosions on public roads - was passed 20 years before the car was invented and 55 years before lorries were capable of competing with rail. It was aimed at protecting horses - Sec. 3: At least three persons will be employed to drive & conduct such locomotives. One person shall precede the locomotive on foot, carry a red flag to warn riders and drivers of horse drawn carriages of the approach of locomotives, signal the driver of the locomotive to stop & assist horses or horse drawn vehicles to pass the locomotive. (They thought this onerous, but railways had to provide, fencing and manned level crossing gates to separate steam from animals).

The Highways & Locomotives Act 1878, Sec. 29: The paragraph numbered "Secondly" of Sec. 3 of the 1865 Act is repealed and the following substituted:- "Secondly, one of such persons, while the locomotive is in motion, shall precede, by at least 20 yards, on foot and shall, in case of need, assist horses and carriages drawn by horses in passing". (This repealed the requirement for a red flag).

The Locomotives on Highways Act 1896, Sec. 1: Acts mentioned in the Schedule restricting the use of locomotives on highways shall not apply to a vehicle propelled by mechanical power if under 3 tons unladen weight, and not used for drawing more than one vehicle of 4 tons unladen weight and is so constructed that no smoke or visible vapour is emitted - such vehicles will be referred to as light locomotives. Sec. 4: Maximum speed of 14 mph. Schedule: the 1868 Act, Sec. 3 of the 1861 Act and Sec. 5 of the 1865 Act, were repealed and replaced by new conditions relating to weight and dimensions.

The road lobby alleged that the 'red flag' Act was instigated by the 'rail lobby'. Fears expressed in the House of Commons that the Bill to repeal the 'Red Flag' Law would "ruin the horse breeding industry", suggest the vast "horse lobby" was the architect. Concern was also expressed regarding the great injury the vehicles would do to the road. With regard to bridges, it was said by supporters of the Bill, that they must be made to carry the weight. (No mention was made as to who should pay for bridge improvements). [Commons Debate, 30th June 1896, cols 444 & 445).

The "rail lobby" could not persuade Government to concede equality with road haulage! The first car was made in the UK in 1895, the red flag was repealed in 1878. Railways had no cause to fear ponderously slow traction engines, nor the puny motor car. Not even the most ardent advocate of the early motor car could have foreseen its future.

Some historians claim that motor car development was held up by the Red Flag Act and weight limits. I can find no evidence to substantiate this. Restrictions arose due to the weight of steam powered vehicles which damaged road surfaces and bridges. Germany, where the car was invented, had the same speed limit. Logically, weight limits should have inspired UK minds to invent a lighter vehicle, reducing damage to roads and bridges and acceptable to those responsible for road maintenance. It was left to foreign brains to do so, and probably rankles to those obsessed with the belief that the most inventive minds were always British.

Speed restrictions were intended to avoid damage to roads, designed for horse drawn vehicles with wheels which compacted surfaces, but were often flouted. (see page 61).

Speeding vehicles caused uplift of material from surfaces . [Lay, Page 148].

After a car went by, it took a long time for dust to settle and all surrounding greenery, and bushes would be covered with a film of dust. You knew there was a car a mile ahead by all the dust flying. [Sutton, Page 32].

Instead of unconstructively criticising road authorities for being prevented from travelling at speeds in excess of those which could be braked within safe distances, and avoiding road damage and dust nuisance, logical and inventive minds would have taken a leaf from the book of railway builders and created their own roads. Road lobbyists looked for others to pay for roads whilst they contributed nothing.

The Royal Commission on Motor Cars 1906, [Cd 3080], Para 43: Motor vehicles travelling at speeds above 10 mph increase the dust problem. Para 61: The problem can be alleviated by applying tar to road surfaces - an 18 foot road cost £40-50 per mile to treat. (122,000 miles would cost of £5.5m!). The 1903 Act established a 20 mph speed limit, but, Local Government Boards could impose 10 mph. They recommended abolishing the 20 mph limit, but a 12 mph should apply at dangerous locations.

Government subsidies

No long distance transport worth mentioning of passenger or goods traffic was done by road in 1913-14. [Savage, Page 36]. (This counters claims by the road lobby of a thriving road transport industry before the Great War).

Early in the century, the War Office began to consider the possible value of motor vehicles. In 1908, they offered a subsidy to steam, driven vehicles. [Dunbar, Page 12].

In 1911, pending the development of specifications for standardised types, they introduced the Provisional Scheme which gave a subsidy to owners of petrol powered motor vehicles. A War Office Memo contains conditions governing subsidies of £8-12 on enrolment. [Times, 27th September, 8c].

The Main Subsidy Scheme for petrol driven privately owned motor lorries required them to conform to certain specifications and then they would be subsidised for three years from the date of acceptance at the following rates:-

Purchase premium of £50 paid in six equal half yearly instalments, first payment six months from acceptance. A further purchase premium of £10 will be paid in respect of each motor lorry which is provided with a body of an approved type for carriage of meat slung from the roof - six equal half yearly payments. An annual subsidy of £20 per motor lorry will be paid half yearly, first payment six months from acceptance. Owners of subsidised lorries will then receive £110 [without the special body] over three years. The condition of the right to purchase by the War Department will also be given. [Times 1912, 15th August, 3f].

Trials were arranged for vehicles to qualify for subsidies. The War Office will purchase qualifying vehicles from manufacturers who can supply 30 vehicles pa to one owner :- Class A: 3 tons at £800, Class B: 1.5 tons at £700. [Times 14th November, 8f].

The Subsidy scheme was changed in 1914 :-

[a] From 1st April, the initial payment will be of £30 per lorry to purchasers of subsidy type lorries on acceptance of a vehicle for enrolment;

[b] Balance of £80 in six half yearly instalments in arrears, first to be six months after acceptance. Additional £10 for a vehicle modified for meat to be slung from the roof, six half yearly instalments in arrears. [Times April 4th, 3d].

In return, owners agreed to hand the vehicle to the Government on demand, in the event of war. In August 1914, Government "called up" these vehicles and paid the owners, the price of a new vehicle, less 15% for each year it had been in use. Manufacturers were advertising small vans at £215 and 3 ton lorries from £575.

War Office specifications led to improved, more reliable vehicles and were beneficial to the trade. A letter from manufacturers, Thorneycroft in "Commercial Motor", 19th June 1913: said the War Office requirements "were worth working to".

The Army Act gave the Government powers to requisition motor vehicles anyway. This scheme gave a kick start to the infant motor industry, which was producing hundreds of different vehicle types with no attempt at standardisation of parts or design. (In contrast, Railways were not offered similar terms for "calling up" 0.75 million wagons, 23,000 locos and 73,000 coaches when Government sequestrated railways. Nor offered a subsidy in 1912 to build rolling stock. Nor were they offered subsidies to build wagons, locomotives and coaches Government would demand for use abroad and at home. Nor for tanks, armoured vehicles, planes and vessels to be built in railway workshops for zero profit. Railways were paid for the use of their assets and their manpower out of their own revenue!).

Government did not sequestrate every available motor vehicle because newspapers and journals carried advertisements : "If your horse has been requisitioned, why not buy a motor van?" - and, referring to priority for military traffic: [Commercial Motor, 1914]

No Railways?
Safeguard your business by running the world's best lorry.

Obviously, once companies had invested in motor vehicles, due to Government Control of railways they would maximise their use, to the long term disadvantage of railways.

Further Government Subsidy & Favouritism

Competition for freight traffic by road transport began in earnest after the First World War, when the Army sold off at knockdown prices, thousands of vehicles.

DoT Internal Memo on 15th October 1940, Para 3: Few dreamed of the keen competition [from a new road transport industry] after the First War, at first, by means of cheap Army lorries. [PRO : MT47/275].

Their scope for competition was facilitated by decisions of the Rates Advisory Committee which placed higher value goods, at very high rates, and by reducing the proportion of railway costs to be covered by passenger traffic, increased the burden of railway costs to be borne by freight traffic. (see page 42).

Parliament was told that there were 16,931 road vehicles at Kempton Park at the Armistice [11th November 1918] and 13,177 now, and that the cost of land and railways, to service the site was £1,700 pa. The War Office has notified a large number of vehicles to the Disposal Board for sale. [Times 6th May 1919, 16b].

A public sale of 30,000 lorries, many of which were brand new, unused, to be sold without reserve, opened two week later. [Times, 24th May, 266c].

Four weeks later the Times reported that there were 150 steam tractors & lorries at Kempton all new, intended for France, but not sent - to be sold without reserve. A site at Cippenham [Slough], held 80,000 vehicles belonging to the War Office. They hoped to clear these in three years. [Times 19th June, 7c and 12th August, 14c respectively].

Kempton Park was the receiving point for new vehicles. Cippenham was a vast depot for repairing vehicles. Both were sited near railways to facilitate rail transits.

In October 1919, a UK syndicate bought 9,000 USA Army lorries in Europe to ship to the UK. Ministers asked if import could be blocked to avoid the "disastrous effect on our motor industry", but were told it could not be done. [PRO: MUN4/6764].

Parliament was told, on 19th February 1919, that one dealer bought nine lorries at a Government auction as one lot, and without leaving, sold four for the price paid for nine. [Hansard, vol. 112, col. 945].

By 1st March 1920, 17,806 lorries had been sold for £7.24m. The number under the control of the Ministry of Munitions was 15,394. On the same day, Parliament was told of 916 lorries sold for £0.35m for shipping back to the UK; and of 666 lorries in Cologne sold for £400 each to a UK company which would have responsibility to ship them to the UK. [Hansard, vol. 126 cols. 66, 67, 270 & 922].

MP's said ex-servicemen wanted to buy the 80,000 lorries which were available under hire purchase. They were told that the Disposal Board had sold all surplus mechanical transport vehicles. [Hansard vol. 127, col. 1372].

Two months later, the Times reported that, at the first sale at Slough, lorries in running order fetched £420 - £682. [Times 20th May 1920, 11c]. This compared with post war vehicles being advertised for about £1,000.

On 21st April 1920, Mr Croft MP, referred to 3,700 lorries at Cologne and to an offer for 1,626 lorries at £375 each on 12th February and a later offer of £1m for 3,000 vehicles. He also spoke of the valuation of £725 per lorry; with 666 of them sold at £400 each, some at £425, others at £387. A Minister confirmed that 666 were sold at £400 each, and that the average price of lorries sold at Cologne was £387. [Hansard, vol. 128, col. 420].

Because of Government control of railways, they continued to be used, free of charge to move vehicles and spares to facilitate this - the original - "car boot sale".

20,000 vehicles were sold at knock down prices. Small operators were willing to work a 100 hour week, maintain vehicles in spare time and overload. [Burton, Page 161].

Many ex-servicemen and others set up in road transport due to the ease with which secondhand vehicles could be obtained. [RCT 3rd Report, Cmd 3751, Para 300].

Having got vehicles on the cheap, they found no laws to prevent them operating as and when they wished, were able to disregard speed limits and to overload vehicles. They also discovered laws which enabled them to undercut rail charges with impunity. (see page 72).

Without such anti rail legislation enabling them to poach rail traffic without risk of retaliation, the road haulage industry would have been stillborn.

One explanation for political cosseting and total freedom for road transport may have been a belated pricking of conscience at the butchery of millions of our own men in the 1914-18 War by military leaders acting under political direction. Where consciences could be eased at the expense of the mighty railways rather than at Government cost would be a continuation of wartime policy. MP's were vociferous in calls to help ex-servicemen, with few skills other than driving. (see page 53).

Those who reduced public expenditure by investing in turnpikes, canals or railways were told how little to charge. Those who used public roads, increasing repair and maintenance costs could charge users as much as they wished and for many years did not pay a penny to use roads, enabling them to build reserves to fund expansion and buy new vehicles. Roads were funded by ratepayers, of whom railways loomed large, and hauliers not at all. As volume grew, so did the wear and tear of bridges, most owned by railway and canal companies who had to bear increasing maintenance costs. (see Chapter 6).

Roads Legislation

Development & Road Improvements Act 1909 - Sec. 8: Gave powers to make advances to County Councils to construct and maintain new or improve existing roads. Sec. 11 [1]: A new Roads Board may acquire land for the purpose of building roads and in addition acquire land either side within 220 yards from the middle of a road. [5] Where the Board cannot acquire by agreement on reasonable terms, any land which they consider necessary, they may apply to Development Commissioners [set up under the Act] for an Order empowering them to purchase compulsorily. They could buy a strip of land a quarter of a mile wide for possible future road building - funded by the State, not the users!

By this Act, Local Authorities were encouraged to improve surfaces. At the start, this assisted 23,500 miles of roads in England & Wales, maintained by County Councils, rather than 95,000 under Rural District Councils. Minor country roads had numerous deep ruts and potholes. Application of tar onto road surfaces was well under way by 1910. This made roads waterproof, more durable, reduced damage and dust. [Hindle, Page 139].

Roads Act 1920, Sec. 3 set up the Road Fund to pay for roads. (Unlike railways, taxes paid by road transport competitors were to be devoted to improving their infrastructure).

The Road Transport Act 1930 was based on the 2nd Report of the RCT. Sec. 19: Drivers' hours for PSV or lorry to be limited to 11 hours in 24 commencing from 02.00 hours, with a maximum of 5.5 hours without a break, and 10 hours rest before commencement of driving. Other sections dealt with the classification of PSV's;

appointment and powers of Traffic Commissioners; issue of licences for PSV's and drivers; appeals against refusal of licences; and authorised local authorities which operated tramway or trolley bus services to run buses.

Governments did nothing to facilitate railway construction. In contrast, they passed the Restriction of Ribbon Development Act, 1935, to keep down the cost of road building and widening by blocking the erection of buildings for up to 220 yards from the middle of classified roads. Highway Authorities were given compulsory purchasing powers.

When roads are built, landowners are paid what District Valuers decide land and property is worth - and it may be much less than the owner believes it is worth, and possibly less than was paid for it.

The MoT told Parliament that Highway Authorities propose bringing 5,000 miles of road under the Act's restrictions in addition to 43,000 miles brought under by the 1935 Act itself. [Hansard vol. 309, col. 2122].

Improvement and development of traffic on roads was aided by the Restriction of Ribbon Development Act 1935 & Trunk Roads Act 1936. [Savage, Page 20].

Claims for compensation for land and for feared loss of amenity if a railway even passed close by, progressively increased during the years of railway development. Railways had to pay the price demanded by owners for land, hence the cost of building railways was inflated. Moreover, many land purchases by railways were subject to a requirement to resell the land back to the original owner at the original price, if no longer used for rail operations, which constrained ancillary uses.

At the start of the century, the surface and condition of roads was poor. Motor vehicles led to a need for roads to have a surface dressing of tar to abate dust and to waterproof them. [RCT 3rd Report, Cmd 3751, Para 162].

Roads Expenditure

The Highways & Locomotives [Amendment] Act 1878, Sec. 13: dealt with disturnpiked roads - half of the rate [for maintaining roads] to be paid by County Councils.

The 33rd AGM of the Roads Improvement Association said that any money raised from motor taxes should be devoted to roads. [Times 4th April 1920, 13d].

They did not call for corresponding, vastly heavier taxes paid by railways, to be used to improve railways. That would not have enhanced road competitiveness. To cater for the growth in the number of motor vehicles, public expenditure on roads was put in hand.

Churchill, Chancellor of the Exchequer said "We are spending more on roads than any country in Europe". [Times 18th May 1919. 8d].

October 1919 - Grants of £8m will be made in 1919-20 for roads and bridges. The total Grant for 1919-20 is £8.61m. An estimate of £7m to strengthen road bridges was made in 1917 by the Roads Board. (Bridge grants were usually to replace level crossings).
[Hansard vol. 117, col. 924; vol. 118, col. 207 & vol. 120. col. 924).

In addition to the Road Fund, (which was inadequate to meet the needs), Civil Service Estimates for the current year provide £8.25m as a Grant in Aid to provide useful employment [Hansard vol. 121, col. 1941, November 1919].

In 1920, Government began contributing towards the cost of road maintenance. Many bypasses were built between the wars. Until March 1937, the basis of paying for roads was the Road Fund which automatically received the bulk of proceeds of motor vehicle licence duties and paid out annual sums in grants for road works as sanctioned by the MoT as well as regular sums of some £6.5m towards Exchequer block grants to Local Authorities to subsidise their road works. [Perkin, Page 330].

£40m will be spent on roads this year in addition to £8m from motor taxes. Lord Montagu of Beaulieu: "Our main roads are the best in the world".
[Times 9th July 1921, 341; and 23rd April 1926, 19c respectively].

In April 1926, the Chancellor of the Exchequer said: Motorists should pay for the wear & tear which they cause of roads. Light and medium vehicles do so, but heavy lorries do not. The railways pay for their permanent way and signalling and pay high rates for the benefit of their competitors. Heavy road transport should not make its way by receiving a subsidy at the expense of the community including its rivals. It is an act of justice to increase taxation on heavy vehicles to a closer correspondence with wear and tear on roads. Of tax proceeds of £21.6m - the Exchequer will take one third on private cars, this proportion being attributed to luxury or pleasure aspects of motoring = £3.5m. The other two thirds ***plus all the yield from commercial vehicles will go to the Roads.***
[Hansard vol. 194, cols. 1711 & 1715].

A 1964 BRF publication "Basic Road Statistics" states that Churchill in his 1926 Budget speech "wanted to protect railways". He did not use the word "protect". Nor did he give money to the railways from the Road Fund as was claimed on BBC Radio in April 1996. The Budget did not allocate a penny to railways, as audited accounts will prove conclusively. His concern at the effect on railways arose because heavy industry was subsidised by railway rates, which would end if "unfair road haulage competition" poached all high rated and profitable traffic. [Hansard Vol. 194, col 1710].

In 1927, £51m was spent on roads. Commercial vehicles paid £4.2m. Railways paid £8m in local rates, that is 19% of net railways revenue. [Pole, Page 228].

The most recent statistics showed £50.97m spent on construction & maintenance of roads and it was still increasing. [Times 7th January, 1927, 7g].

Churchill said Lloyd George's proposal to borrow £200m to spend on roads was a wasteful State subsidised scheme of road development, and more energetic development of railroads would be better. Railways had far more to offer to industry than the development of roads, which were the best in the world and we were spending more than any country in Europe. Railways are capable of modernisation and that could reasonably be undertaken in the next Parliament. [Times 29th April, 1929, 9b]. (No action followed).

When Churchill had an opportunity, after exploiting railways in the next war, he turned his back on them, but used them to subsidise inefficient industry, rural communities and other users and favoured road transport. (see "Blueprints for Bankruptcy", Page 88).

In 1929, a programme of trunk road reconstruction was announced to cost £9.5m spread over 4-5 years. A further five year programme for classified roads would cost £28m. [Hansard vol. 231, col. 666].

In 1930, Parliament was told of the Government programme of £37m on roads and then of a further £20m additional on roads over five years. [Hansard vol. 239, cols. 1358 & 2146].

Also in 1930, Parliament was informed of unemployment relief works of £4m on unclassified, and £33m on classified roads. [Hansard vol. 240, col. 29-30]

The Government announced in June 1930, that £20m pa was the estimated cost of road works over the next five years, and that, over the past nine years, £136m had been spent. [Hansard, vol. 239, cols. 2146 & 2179].

In 1931, Parliament was told that £500m had been spent on roads in the last ten years and that expenditure was proceeding at £60m pa. [Hansard vol. 255, col. 1754].

Sir Josiah Stamp [LMS] told the Glasgow Association of the Institute of Civil Engineers that railways were never subsidised. They were taxed for the maintenance of roads, together with an obligation to maintain, at their own cost, 750 miles of public roads. [Times 5th February 1932, 18f].

The 1933 AGM of the LMS was told that on the railways application for road powers in 1921, the official view was that the question of for how long road users would get the road system free was for Parliament to decide at its proper time.
[Times 25th February 1933, 18a].

In December 1935, 3,500 road schemes were approved for commencement during this year alone. An MP asked if Government will insist on stone from British quarries for the proposed £100m on roads [Hansard vol. 307, cols. 312-3 & 1140].

Statutorily limited sub standard rail rates for mineral traffic were evidently not enough to protect them from foreign competition.

The Minister of Transport was asked for information on the £100m five year road plan recently announced. He said £100m represents the estimated cost of works embraced in a five year programme of road development and improvement put forward by Highway Authorities at Government request. The Road Fund contribution to the programme is in addition to the Grants usually made from the Fund towards the cost of maintaining classified roads. Payments out of the Road Fund in Grants to Highway Authorities include amounts distributed under the Local Government Act 1929 as follows:-

1925/26	£16.2m	1926/27	£17.0m	1927/28	£18.7m	1928/29	£17.0m
1929/30	£19.8m	1930/31	£27.0m	1931/32	£28.7m	1932/33	£23.0m
1933/34	£19.6m	1934/35	£18.5m	1935/36	£20.0m		
Hansard vol. 307, cols. 1567-68							

In 1936, the MoT announced that schemes costing £130m had been submitted by Highway Authorities under the five year programme. The Road Fund will bear 70%. A few months later, the House was told that submissions had reached £139.7m, the Grant for the first year [1935-6] will be £26.65m - £1.65m of it from the Road Fund. [Hansard vol. 310, col. 425-6 & vol. 312, col. 2003].

Railways had to pay compensation when a new railway diverted traffic from road to rail and affected the dues of a local authority. This never happens in reverse. The community owes railways equality with roads in legislation [LMS AGM Times 29th February 1936, 18]

In 1937, the source of road expenditure was £14.9m from the Road Fund, £6.5m, from the Exchequer [under the Local Government Derating Act 1939], £0.5m Grants from other Government Departments, £34.5m from Local Rates [Total £56.4m]. Expenditure was £68.0m, the balance came from £5.6m in Loans and £6.4m was recoverable from Public Utilities. [Modern transport, 31st August 1946].

Reasonable Facilities

Road transport was not obliged to serve all areas, or continue services once an area had become used to them. A DoT Memo, 30th March 1929, to the Permanent Secretary said Jurisdiction [on closures] rests with the Railway & Canal Commissioners. If a railway withdraws reasonable facilities, the R&CC can require reinstatement. [PRO : MT6/3465].

Railways denied road powers

The Balfour-Browne Committee was appointed by Government in January 1921, and reported in March, [Cmd 1228]. Their remit was:-

"To inquire whether it is desirable that railways be given general or limited powers to carry goods by road". (i.e. on roads for which they paid, whilst their competitors did not).

They produced three Reports. Each said that Railways could drive out carriers and create a monopoly. (Why that concerned them, when the 1921 Act was based on the assumption that railways was a monopoly, and was subject to statutorily controlled charges and profits, is not clear). The First Report, by the Chairman & the two railway representatives said railways have lost a considerable bulk of traffic to roads. They ought to be allowed to carry by road on conditions which would prevent a monopoly - the MoT to authorise their road transport and control rates. (Hauliers' rates were not controlled).

The Second Report, by two road transport and two trade & industry members said that railways should be prohibited from operating motor transport. They said that if motor transport was diverting rail traffic, they were suffering, in their turn, what happened to stage coaches. (This was a gross misrepresentation. It was not motor transport, per se, which attracted traffic, but the ability of hauliers to poach traffic due to unfair legislation - notably the iniquitous rates system. That never applied in the pre-motor era. There had been no anti-road or canal legislation for railways to exploit to poach traffic). Road operators objected that railway road transport may undercut hauliers! That might benefit traders in the short term, but in the end may close independent carriers. (see * on page 102).

The Third Report, signed by one member [a Trade Union official] favoured nationalisation of railways and opposed railways having road powers. [Nearly half of the Unions affiliated to the group which he represented were involved in road transport].

"Road transport operators have exhibited unreasonableness in opposing the application of railway companies for powers to use road motor vehicles". [Times, 16th July, 1921, 361].

Without success, railway companies attended a House of Commons meeting to obtain support for road powers. They pointed out they were the largest ratepayers in the country and paid immense sums for the upkeep of roads, but were alone among ratepayers who would be debarred from using the roads without restriction if the Railways Bill was passed into law in its present form. [Times 20th July 1921, 12a].

In 1922, the Railways [North Western & Midland] Bill, seeking powers to operate road transport in the area of the future LMS Railway, was considered by Parliament. Despite the strength of the railways' case, backed by the fact that nine companies had such powers before 1914, and evidence of the total railway funding of roads, the Bill was rejected.

Delaying Tactics

Following many years of complaint by railways about the inequity of rail and road transport legislation, the Government set up a Royal Commission - a time honoured tactic for delaying the need for a decision. It made no recommendation on its prime objective to resolve the railways' complaint. (see page 78).

In February 1932, the railways again asked the MoT to revise legislation, which they said was inequitable - railways being totally regulated and controlled by numerous Acts, whilst road freight transport was totally free. The Government appointed the Salter Conference on 11th April 1932. (see page 83).

Road & Rail Traffic Act 1933

The Salter Conference led to the passing of the Road & Rail Traffic Act 1933.
Sec. 2: Road Goods vehicles will be licensed - "A", "B" or "C" ["A" was for public hauliers, "C" was for a vehicle owned and used by Traders to carry their own goods, whilst "B" was a hybrid]. Sec. 11: Provided for objections to the grant of "A" or "B" licences by existing transport operators. (An impression was later created by the road lobby that opposition to expansion in road haulage was solely from railways. The BTC 1951 Report reveals otherwise - Para 66: "A" & "B" licence holders are not exposed to free competition. They compete with each other and with BR, but applications for licences are firmly opposed by existing carriers"). Sec. 22: Costs of Licensing Authorities to be paid by the MoT.* Sec. 46: Set up the Transport Advisory Council.

* The Railway Rates Tribunal was funded by railways. (see page 47).

Road Traffic Act 1934

Sec. 1: Specified a 30 mph speed limit in built up areas. Sec. 6: An applicant for a driving licence must pass a driving test, unless he has held a licence before 1st April 1934 or a licence under the Motor Car Act 1903. Sec. 31: Required drivers of heavy goods vehicles and PSV's to have a licence for the purpose.

Evidence of the Inequity

DoT Memo, 15th October 1940 to A.T.V. Robinson: Para 3: Few dreamed of the keen competition after the First War, at first by means of cheap surplus Army lorries. The continuing bitterness led to the Salter Conference and the requirement that heavy vehicles should pay a fairer share of road costs. The Road & Rail Traffic Act 1933 extended the role of Traffic Commissioners [from passenger, which was introduced in 1930] to freight. Goods was a bigger problem. There were 5,000 operators & 50,000 vehicles in passenger transport, compared to 60,000 Goods operators with 150,000 vehicles plus 180,000 traders with 360,000 vehicles. [PRO : MT47/275].

When the 1921 Act was passed, the internal combustion engine was still regarded merely as a threat. By the time the Rates system came into operation in 1928, the threat was a reality, and a menace to the financial stability of railway companies. In the absence of fresh legislation, that is largely going to be the position after the cessation of hostilities. [C.E.Jordan, Modern Transport, 29th July 1944].

The MoWT stated that whatever the merits of competition in stimulating enterprise and efficiency, it is evident that if it is carried so far as to undermine the stability of services essential to the community and to commercial interests its effect will eventually prove damaging to the national interests. He pointed out that if railways, on which coal and many other basic industries depend, are deprived of their high grade traffics by the competition of road transport, they must in the long run, either obtain compensating revenue by increasing their rates on traffic they can retain [largely traffic in classes 1-6, coal, iron ore, pig iron, limestone etc], or sink into financial impotence. He said that until this persistent road-rail problem is solved, neither the railway companies nor professional road hauliers can plan their future with confidence. Railway rates have in the main been based on "what the traffic will bear" though there have been other factors such as canal, coastwise and road competition. ["Coming of Age", 1944]. [HoL Hansard vol. 129, col. 383].

He overlooked an alternative - that legislation would finally make railways insolvent. (see "Blueprints for Bankruptcy").

Lower Safety Standards

The lack of legislation on hours of driving, maintenance, safety and design standards of vehicles was in marked contrast to railways.

• Disparity in Drivers' Hours

MoT Paper "Public Transport and Traffic" 1967, [Cmnd 3481]

Para. 1: Many bus and coach drivers are working hours substantially in excess of these limits". (In 1919, Government had arbitrarily, against the wishes of railway companies introduced an eight hour day for *all staff,* not merely those at the sharp end of safety. Monitoring rail staff hours was easy and open, but difficult in respect of road. Indeed for many years it was impossible because no records were kept, nor required to be kept).

Para. 108: "Legal limits on hours of professional [PSV] drivers have remained unaltered since the 1930's".

Para. 110: Maximum length of the working day - 14 hours; the rest period before work will be 10 hours, but on one day per week, it may be reduced to 8 hours.

"There was much evidence of flouting the law". [Barker & Gerhold Pages 62-63].

• Vehicle Design.

In June 1914, MP's pointed out that there is a failure to provide lifeguards [sideguards between the front and rear wheels] for this form of transport [London buses]. Repeated experiments to fit suitable guards have been condemned by Scotland Yard. They also condemned the provision of an audible warning. It transpired in questioning that their Technical expert was "in the habit of getting expert advice from the builders of motor vehicles"! [Hansard vol. 63, col. 609].

On 27th March 1919, The President of the Local Government Board was asked whether his attention had been drawn to deaths caused by lorries which are not fitted with proper side guards and that coroners' juries had recommended that lorries should be so protected. He was asked to consider issuing an Order that all Army and commercial lorries must be provided with similar guards to those on motor omnibuses. He replied that the question was considered last October by a Departmental Committee on Road Locomotives and Heavy Motor Cars which were unable to come to any definite conclusion and recommended further investigation. (This contrasts sharply with railways, where Ministers wasted no time telling railways to improve safety). [Hansard vol. 114, col. 582].

In 1919, A London coroner suggested all heavy vehicles should be fitted with side guards similar to those on buses, as if they were fitted many fatalities would be avoided. [Times 22nd July, 9f].

A Select Committee of the House of Lords considered the 1928 Road Vehicles Regulation Bill which had safety as its objective, but decided not to recommend it and the Bill was abandoned. The object of the Bill had been to diminish the large number of road accidents. It envisaged examination of drivers before the issue of licences, a mechanical check on the speed of vehicles, improved construction of vehicles, prevention of dazzle, third party insurance and alterations in the level of roads to prevent excessive speeds. [HoL Select Committee, vol. 397].

Implementation of many of these essential safety measures did not come into operation for many years, the latter item, only in recent years!

In 1946, the MoWT was asked whether the regulations proposed in 1931 and promised by successor Ministers, enforcing the provision of guard rails between front and rear wheels of motor lorries are likely to be introduced shortly. He replied that the matter was fully reviewed in 1938 when the Minister accepted the advice of the TAC that it would not be likely to effect a contribution to public safety which would justify its imposition. [Hansard vol. 218, col. 181]. (Side-guards did not become mandatory on articulated vehicles until 1983; even later, on rigid vehicles!)

An even more surprising development, was the issuing of Regulations permitting the withdrawal of red rear lights from motor vehicles in 1919. The change was condemned by the London Safety First Council, which said that before the war, the absence of such lights cost many lives. [Times, 22nd August, 7d].

- Speed

In the 1000 mile trial in 1900, vehicles were speeding at 30 mph. [Sutton, Page 33] - (***the limit was 12-14 mph, raised to 20 mph in 1903***).

Not one in a thousand obeys speed limits. [RCT 1929, Cmd 3365, Para 4].

County Councils Association stated that lorries are travelling at 40 mph. [RCT 1931, Cmd 3751, Page 72, Para 259]

"The nominal speed limit of 20 mph for heavier vehicles was often exceeded". [Barker & Gerhold, Page 62].

Acts specified mandatory, not "nominal" limits. Definition of "Nominal" is "not real".

Licensing Authorities gave approval to buses exceeding limits. (see page 79).

- Overloading

Weights carried are much in excess of the legal maximum. 5 ton vehicles are carrying 9/10 tons. There was much overloading. [RCT 1931, Cmd 3751, Pages 72 & 76]

The "normal procedure is to buy a 2.5 tonner, double its capacity by calling it a 5 tonner and loading it up to 7.5 tons". [Barker & Gerhold Pages 62-63].

(Government had been dictating safety standards in railway operations since 1840. Their policy towards comparable unsafe practices on roads was one of laissez-faire).

Taxation

The road lobby frequently demands that all taxation raised on road transport should be spent on road improvements. They dismiss the cost of consequential items such as accident and emergency costs, and the effect on national health of air pollution created solely by motor vehicles. Accident costs are not ignored when justification is sought for new or improved roads - then all accident costs and every conceivable fringe element is taken into account.

Even if the claim of the Road Lobby to have all taxes raised from road transport spent on roads had any validity, they conveniently overlook the cost of collecting the taxes. This fundamental error was not made by their predecessors in 1909. "Motorists accepted that the proceeds of the tax less the cost of collecting it should be spent on roads". [Plowden, Page 88].

When Government originally conceded the idea of spending road taxes on roads, in contrast to the deployment of taxes in any other field of activity, they clearly did not bargain for the huge disparity in vehicle speeds which are experienced today, and which is the main cause of poor road utilisation. Neither could they have foreseen, juggernauts using roads to unload goods to the detriment of other users. (see "Blueprints for Bankruptcy").

Taxes raised on railway profits from 1830 to 1947 inclusive were not spent on rail improvements. In addition, railways also had to pay a tax on gross passenger revenue from 1832 to 1929. (see page 18).

Worse still, Government sequestrated railways in two world wars and skimmed billions of pounds from them. Finally, they enforced a rates system on railways, from 1921 to 1957 which was specifically devised to subsidise agriculture and industry. When road transport has made an equal contribution to the Exchequer will be time enough to consider spending all road taxes on roads. (See "Blueprints for Bankruptcy").

Limited Railways' Road Powers Granted

In 1928, the four main line companies obtained powers to operate road transport on the public roads, towards the cost of which, which they had contributed handsomely, their competitors hardly at all. To achieve this, each of them had to have a Bill passed through Parliament. The four Acts were nearly identical. The LNER [Road Transport] Act, 1928 can be taken as typical. Sec. 3 : May only operate in a district served by the LNER. Sec. 4 Cannot operate buses if the MoT decrees there is an adequate service. Sec. 6 : Must give notice to the MoT before commencing operations. Once approved, a service cannot be withdrawn if anyone objects without the consent of the MoT. Sec 7 : Cannot manufacture parts for their own vehicles. Sec. 8 : Must publish rates for inspection. Sec. 10 : Must convey mails if requested by the Postmaster General. Sec. 13 : The MoT can set up a public inquiry if he believes the public interest has been prejudiced. Sec. 14 : Must maintain separate accounts for road transport and submit details to the MoT. Schedule : Must submit statistics of the number of vehicles by type every six months, and monthly of vehicle miles, passenger journeys, tons and receipts.

Not a single one of these restrictions to free enterprise was imposed on their competitors. It would be hard to conceive that their competitors, anxious to keep railway companies off the roads, could have themselves devised a more obstructionist Act.

Railway investment in goods and parcel road vehicles, by 1937 totalled £4.2m, which included vehicles purchased to replace horse drawn vehicles on town and city collection and delivery work. Including all investment in passenger road vehicles, horses, stables and garages brought the total to £7.3m, or £730,000 pa. [MoT Returns Table A1].

Chapter 6 BRIDGES & CROSSINGS

The expansion of mechanical road transport, and the increase in axle weights created a new and costly problem for railways. Bridges were designed for horse drawn traffic, not badly sprung, heavily overloaded motor vehicles travelling at higher speeds.

In Swain v. SR., [Kings Bench, 1939, vol. 2, Page 560]: It was held "that the duty on the defendant [SR.] in respect of the bridge was to maintain the road over the bridge and its approaches in a condition suited to traffic as existed when the road was made in 1856".

A Royal Commission on Transport, [RCT], was set up to consider problems arising from the growth of road transport. (see below and also page 78).

RCT 3rd Report, [Cmd 3751], December 1930

Para. 198: There are 7,000 bridges including those owned by railways & canals. The legal requirement to strengthen them was based on needs when they were built.

Para. 199: Recommended a strengthening programme of 1,000 pa.

Para. 202: All private bridges should be vested in a Highway Authority.

Para. 204: No compensation to be paid to bridge owners but they should pay the amount saved which would have been spent on maintenance. (No mention was made of repaying capital invested in bridges. They were not biased in the railways' favour!).

Legislation

Government passed laws to protect bridges from collapse from loads they had never been designed to take. It was not implemented, as it would reduce the freedom of hauliers to carry on their business whilst bridge owners - their competitors - picked up the tab.

Road Transport Act 1930, Sec 25 (which was never implemented) :

[1]: A Bridge Authority may exhibit a notice prohibiting the use of a bridge by vehicles exceeding a specified weight provided it is not less than 5 tons.

[5]: Anyone aggrieved by any restriction may appeal to the MoT who may order removal or variation of a restriction.

[7]: An MoT order shall not prevent re-imposition if the Bridge Authority considers it is necessary due to changed circumstances, but a new appeal may be made.

The Salter Conference called for bridges to be the responsibility of road authorities and to be paid for by new road licences. (See page 84).

Road & Rail Traffic Act 1933 repealed Sec. 25 of the 1930 Act, replacing it with Sec. 30 of the 1933 Act, which had two significant variations - bridge owners must give the MoT 28 days notice before exhibiting a notice; and were precluded from placing another [if circumstances changed]; whereas they could under the 1930 Act.

Legislation undermined

Road users will learn with satisfaction that Sec. 30 is deferred. Recently, the MoT decided all bridge authorities should forward to him a list of all such bridges on class 1 & 2 roads together with maps. He is anxious, on bringing this Sec. 30 into operation, to cause the minimum of impediment to road transport generally, hence the decision for its postponement. [Modern Transport, 30th December 1933].

The MoT has decided to defer the introduction of Sec. 30. All bridge owning Authorities must report on which bridges they consider it necessary to restrict vehicles over twelve tons laden or with axle weights of eight tons. Sec. 30 required 28 days notice to restrict five ton vehicles. The list of weak bridges supplied by the railways totals 1,324. [Modern Transport, 13th January 1934].

7th February 1934, the MoT told Parliament he had asked Highway Authorities for lists of weak bridges in connection with Sec. 30 of the 1933 Act, and was ready to fund 75% towards the costs of strengthening or reconstructing weak bridges owned by railway and canal companies. Sir Gifford Fox referred to further restrictions which may be imposed under the Act. Will the MoT give an assurance that before provisions are put into force a sufficient number of adequate bridges for use of road rollers, threshing machines, steam ploughs and other heavy agricultural equipment will be provided.
[Hansard vol. 285 cols. 1124 &1126].

28th February, Captain Strickland referred to over 2,000 bridges on class 1 & 2 roads where notices may be placed. The MoT replied they were 1,180 on class 1 & 2 roads, the rest were on unclassified roads. [Hansard vol. 286, col. 1111].

On 5th March the MoT was asked what steps he would take to mitigate hardship and avoid serious dislocation of [road] traffic [if prohibition notices were placed on weak bridges]. He replied that in deciding on what date Sec. 30 should be brought into operation, he would not overlook the considerations [potential dislocation and hardship] brought to his attention. When this section is brought into operation, a bridge authority must give 28 days notice of their intention. There is a right of appeal by any aggrieved person or body. [Hansard vol. 286, col. 1527].

The Act was passed and effective 17th November 1933. They expected railways to forecast 28 days before traffic volume and weight caused a bridge to collapse.

On 14th March, the MoT was asked, whether, in view of the impossibility of repairing essential bridges scheduled as weak, within a reasonable immediate period of time he will consider postponing the operation of Sec. 30 of the 1933 Act. MP's were reminded that 28 days notice is required. [Hansard vol. 287, col. 357].

On 21st March, the MoT was asked in Parliament what steps he would take in the case of a main road bridge scheduled as now unsafe for heavy traffic and which neither Bridge or Highway Authority is prepared to repair. He was asked whether he would give assurances that road traffic would not be prevented from use of that route for an indefinite periods. He said he would await a definite case of this kind before he made a reply. [Hansard vol. 287, col 1200].

"If, and, when Sec. 30 [of the 1933 Act] is implemented, road transport interests will call for a 100% Grant for reconstruction of bridges". [Modern Transport 8th February 1936]. Improved facilities for private enterprise road transport to be funded by the State.

The MoT is unable to relieve the BTC of bridge costs, but proposed a fact finding meeting between BTC & Highway authorities! [BTC 1952 Report, Para 15].

Was a meeting necessary? Traffic had increased since 1932. DoT files must have bulged with data. Three years earlier DoT files record the MoT view that the costs should be transferred to the highway budget. [PRO : MT39/671].

In October 1994, the DoT could not find a Report on any Fact Finding Meeting. On 24th April 1995, they wrote: "As far as we are aware, Sec. 30 was never commenced. It was repealed, re-enacted as Sec. 41 of the Road Traffic Act 1961, but never commenced with the rest of the Act [see Schedule 20]. It was repealed and re-enacted as Sec. 17 of the Road Traffic Regulation Act 1967, but not commenced with the rest of the Act. Finally, Sec. 17 was repealed by Schedule 7 to the Local Government, Planning & Land Act 1980. We recently checked the 1980 Bill papers, but they did not explain why the provision was repealed then".

This is baffling. Unquestionably there were, and still are, bridges which need to be subject to weight restrictions. The non enactment of the provision certainly did the road transport industry and Treasury no harm.. What effect it had on maintenance and renewal costs of railway bridges is another story, and a hidden factor in their losses.

The scale of the bridge problem

28th November 1933, Mr. Peat told Parliament that there were 7,000 dangerous bridges - many in private hands, e.g. railway owned - which could impede "transport along our great trunk roads!" He urged Government to pressure the railways and local authorities to put bridges right as "it means steel". [Hansard vol. 283, col. 803]. (Industry was in a period of deep recession. Any large scale programme would help industry - at railways' expense).

On 12th December 1933, the MoT was asked how many bridges were rebuilt in England & Wales in 1931, 1932, 1933 and at what cost. How many were scheduled for reconstruction? Lt. Col.. Headlam PS to MoT: During the years ended March 1931, 1932, 1933, the number of bridge strengthening schemes approved were 830, 522, 194 respectively. He could not give the cost!. [Hansard vol. 284, col. 198].
It speaks volumes on cost consciousness where road transport was concerned.

28th March 1934. The MoT told Parliament that in 1932-3 there would be no funds for strengthening bridges owned by railways or canals, but he had made a Grant to Highway Authorities of £0.29m for bridging level crossings, and that in 1933-4, there would be another £0.5m. [Hansard vol. 287, col. 1971-2].

December 1934: the MoT said that £500,000 was being made available for reconstruction of weak bridges from the Road Fund. This was in addition to 80 schemes for reconstruction of weak bridges and replacing level crossings at a total cost of £0.67m. [Modern Transport, 29th December 1934].

There are 1,200 weak bridges in a priority list. A 5 year programme has been submitted for reconstruction. 357 are to commence this year. [Modern Transport, 10th August 1935].

Level Crossings

Level crossings should be speedily eliminated. Highway Authorities should have compulsory powers, to buy land to replace them by bridges. [RCT 3rd Report, Cmd 3751, December 1930, Para. 208]

Road & Rail Traffic Act, 1933 Sec. 42: The MoT could direct level crossing gates to be normally closed across a railway instead of across the road as had applied from earliest times.

This reduced road delays. Government could reverse practices introduced for "Good and sound reasons" - if road interests would benefit, whereas they did not if railways would benefit. Government used the phrase "Good and sound reasons" to justify forcing BR to retain ultra sub standard fares in 1952, after the ostensibly independent Transport Tribunal authorised them being raised to standard levels, still leaving fares below the RPI. (see "Blueprints for Bankruptcy", page 102).

Increased road traffic on level crossings, hitherto manned by resident keepers, giving 24 hour cover, required more staff as a result of Government enforcing the eight hour day. When the early railways were built, there was very little night time road traffic. (see page 30).

In February 1934, the MoT told Parliament well considered schemes for the elimination of level crossings are eligible for Grants. [Hansard vol. 413, col. 1124].

A new problem

The bridge problem was exacerbated by increases, over the years, in the size of road vehicles. Bridges were built to cater for horse drawn vehicles, and hence, not only was weight not then a problem with bridges over railways, height was not a problem with bridges under railways. It would seem that the road transport industry has not been able to train its drivers to relate the height of their vehicles to the height signs approaching bridges. Hence, some collide with bridges and disrupt rail traffic. Whilst railways may sue for damage, and for the cost of delay - if the offender has not disappeared, some traffic diverted from rail to road due to ensuing delays may not be recovered. Pending a bridge engineer's examination, trains must be diverted, stopped or delayed. Recently, the road lobby has suggested that to end the problem of lorries crashing into bridges built, to cater for the horse & cart, bridge authorities, including railways, should pay for a device to stop drivers from being careless! It is typical of the road lobby to try to get others to pick up the tab for their malpractices and incompetence.

Post-war reviews

Government failed to respond to pleas to relieve BR of rapidly increasing costs for resurfacing and strengthening bridges and level crossings, and for increased staffing costs of level crossings to cope with heavier road traffic, which arose from the inequitable rail/road rates policy. Here, as elsewhere, Government ignored its' own advisors and, time and time again, shied away from implementing recommendations which were potentially beneficial to railways, and prejudicial to road transport.

On 2nd December 1949, the BTC wrote to the MoT:-

"Maintenance of bridge surfaces"

The BTC believe the cost should be transferred to Highway Authorities. The BTC should be relieved of a heavy and inequitable burden. The MoT should take over the obligation from the BTC and make arrangements with Highway Authorities. The total cost of re-surfacing BTC overbridges is £190,000 pa. [PRO: MT39/671].

Internal DoT Memo, December 1949: It is the DoT view that responsibility for bridges should be transferred to the Highway Authority. The Treasury opposed a change. [PRO: MT39/671]

The BTC urged a review of Bridge costs which Government's 1932 Salter Conference on Road and Rail Transport had agreed should be the responsibility of road authorities. [BTC 1950 Report, Para 17].

If Occupation* & Accommodation* crossings user increased, Highway Authorities should take them over, or if the use has been changed by development, users should pay to make them safe or provide alternative access. [BTC 1951 Report, Para 18].

*These were not public crossings, but had restricted user rights.

"BR should be relieved of the cost of overbridges and burdens which dated from when they had a monopoly". [Cabinet Minutes, 12th March 1951].

DoT papers show that the BTC sought to have bridge costs dealt with in the MoT 1956 White Paper, "Proposals for Railways", but were blocked by bureaucrats: "I wish to have the BTC paragraph on liability for maintenance on road bridges deleted. It is unrealistic of the BTC to suggest Government can help obtain relief from liability to Highway Authorities, as they would not agree unless Government paid". [PRO: MT132/32].

Government preferred to leave the burden on BR, thereby inflating their losses instead of taxing road users realistically to cover these costs.

In 1956, BR reported that level crossing staff costs had increased £0.2m pa to £1m pa, due to increased road traffic. BR could not try modern methods for level crossing design and operation to reduce rising costs without a change in the law. [Cmd 9880, Paras. 78 & 79].

The 1957 Railways Bill sought to end some provisions of the Highways [Railway Crossings] Act 1839 and the 1854 Act and to introduce new methods of control. These specified that crossings must be provided with gates and manned at all times. Parliament was told: Crossing costs were over £1m pa. (see "Blueprints for Bankruptcy"].

The Prime Minister is ***considering*** affording relief on bridges & crossings. [BTC Minutes, August 1958]. (26 years after the Salter Conference recommendation).

In 1958 the MoT contributed £2m pa towards bridge and level crossing costs, but after 1960, it was withdrawn. Deducting level crossing staff costs left £1m to cover maintenance costs at 33,000 overbridges and 2,800 crossings, equating to £28 pa per location. (see "Blueprints for Bankruptcy", Page 84].

BRB continue to bear the costs of bridges and level crossings estimated at £2.5m. With increasing road traffic, the burden of manning and maintaining level crossings has grown greatly in recent decades. [BRB 1964 Report, Page 79].

An MoT Paper in November 1967 stated: For two years up to 1960 MoT agreed to pay BR £2m towards the cost of bridges and crossings; it was stopped because "it was thought administratively more convenient [for Government], to deal with this through the revenue deficit". [Thereby inflating BR "losses"]. Recommended that costs of bridges and crossings "be taken into account in re-capitalisation". BR costs in 1965 of Road Bridges were £1.5m. If bridges were transferred to Local Authorities, compensation [to local authorities] would be £100 to £500 per bridge pa", (between £3m and £16m - i.e. between twice and ten times as much as that accepted as BR costs). "BR pay £40,000 pa to the MoT for trunk road bridges, and have to find £327,000 pa for road surfaces of bridges". The Paper recommended BR's £40,000 to MoT [which began in 1946], for trunk road bridges be ended and responsibility for surfaces of overbridges be borne by Local Authorities. The present statutory framework for bridges is complicated and unsatisfactory. The main disadvantages are a lack of clearly defined obligations and [external] administrative difficulties which often prevent removal of bridges which are no longer necessary". BR costs in 1965 of Level Crossings were £1m. £1.5m is mentioned as the cost of crossings elsewhere in this White Paper. [Cmnd 3439, Pages 19 & 51]. This policy would obscure the scale of the problem and future cost increases.

Under the 1968 Transport Act, Sec. 116: Bridge surfaces became a highway authority responsibility, but the more costly sub structure of bridges remained as a heavy burden.

BR are entitled under EEC regulations to half the cost of providing and maintaining level crossings. This contribution amounted in 1975 to £9m. [1977, Report of Select Committee, Para 19].

This indicates total costs of £18m in 1975, when prices were 2-3 times as high as in 1965, when the total cost had been put at only £1m by the MoT. A significant under estimate.

The cost of level crossing modernisation, which would lead to reduced delays for road traffic, had to be borne by BR and justified by staff economies which would arise from replacing old style crossings. No contribution was made by Government or local authorities.

In 1995, it was reported that Railtrack is likely to spend £400m to strengthen road bridges as the Government "has refused to meet this bill". Government did not dispute the amount.

Chapter 7 THE DEADLY RATES SYSTEM

From the opening of a railway line, rates and charges were specified in the enabling Act. (see page 14).

The original principle of rates based on mileage was replaced by one based on "tapering" when maximum charges were introduced in 1892 as a result of the Railway & Canal Traffic Act 1888. With tapering, charges per mile decrease over longer distances. For example, for one class, the rate per ton per mile was - first 20 miles: 3.1d [about 1.3p], the next 30 miles: 2.6d, next 50 miles: 2.0d, over 50 miles: 1.8d. To these were added a fixed element to cover terminal and handling charges, as appropriate.

[Jordan, "Modern Transport", 29th July 1944].

Until January 1928, except for the period 1914-20 when Government controlled railways and their charges, the classification of goods and their rates were governed by the Railway [Rates & Charges] Order Confirmation Acts 1891/2 applicable to individual railway companies. The classifications were identical and divided goods into eight classes, and a maximum rate per ton mile was prescribed for all articles in a class. Within these maxima, companies were free to vary rates subject to certain statutory safeguards for traders. As a result, a very large proportion was carried at rates below the maxima, and these were referred to as Exceptional Rates.

Classification of Merchandise

The allocation of goods into Rate charges bands was decided by the Rates Advisory Committee set up by the 1919 Act. Their General Classification of Merchandise [GCM], was completed in June 1923 - 8 classes were expanded to 21, exclusive of coal, coke and patent fuel. It listed every item known to man, and was described as "a Nonsense Novel, because it prescribed, for example, that in sending fish products, you had to separate oysters from periwinkles and from crabs because all go at different rates. Goods - say shoes, packed in different containers - hampers, sacks, casks or cases go at different rates". Nominally, there were 21 classes, but, sub divisions increased this to 66. The RCA said that classification was appropriate only if there was a monopoly. ["Clear the Lines", Page 10].

A new Railway Rates Tribunal [RRT] had to undertake the duty of fixing standard charges for each of the classes for each Group company - a task which occupied some years. Ultimately they were fixed at a level broadly about 60% above 1913. It was hoped that the new standard charges would result in the cancellation of the bulk of the Exceptional Rates, but this was nullified by the unforeseen and extremely rapid growth of road motor competition. [Sanderson, Page 141].

The GCM and outdated law created the "Killing Fields" of rail freight traffic by retaining archaic monopoly-inspired rates systems from 1928 on the assumption that railways still had a monopoly, although that had been steadily vanishing since 1919. Any proposed change in the Classification had to be submitted to the Tribunal by traders or railways. Only the Tribunal had power to reclassify existing commodities or classify new commodities. (see page 77 for an extract from the GCM as used in "Clear the Lines").

In contrast, Government had helped Canal companies to compete with railways by permitting them to vary charges under the Canal Tolls Act 1845. Canal Carriers had complete freedom on rates charged, as did road hauliers who had unique freedoms denied to railways. Despite glaring evidence of a loss of traffic from rail to road, directly attributable to the inequity of their respective rates systems, Government did not try to redress the balance, as they had done for canals. Instead they enforced the continuation of their "pack-horse" rates system, which enabled road haulage to "cream-off" higher value traffics which was intended to subsidise low value traffic. (see page 72)

Under the 1845 and 1854 Acts, Railways had to offer equal facilities to all at the same price. Road could, and did, discriminate. As if this poison chalice were not enough, an 1873 Act compelled railways to open rate books to everyone. Thus hauliers knew by how much to undercut rail, usually 10% was enough - no question of blind tendering for them.

"The present [1928] classification was arranged on the basis of traffic available when road transport was not regarded as a serious competitor, but since then, there has been a considerable and permanent diversion of highly rated traffic from rail to road. The Railway companies are left with a classification based on a pool which no longer exists. [Jordan, "Modern Transport", 29th July 1944].

Railways Act, 1921

The Act specified a basis for determination of rates to be charged which was unique in industrial, even in railway, legislation. They were to be decided by the Government appointed Railway Rates Tribunal [RRT] - a Court of Law, which took until 1928 to implement a monopoly based strait jacket, by which time, Railways had ceased to be a monopoly! Railways had to submit a schedule of Standard charges [based on the Classification], to the Tribunal which would consider objections and fix the Appointed Day for implementation. Railways' proposed schedule was submitted in 1923 - there were 1,812 objections by Trade and Industry. Hearings dragged on for four years. The Act included the following provisions:-

Sec. 32: On and from the Appointed Day, Standard charges would be the only permitted charges, with no variation up or down, except for Exceptional Charges, (the latter were only downwards - no variation was allowed above Standard). Agricultural products were given concessions. Within six months of the Act, Railways had to submit Terms & Conditions of Carriage for consideration.

Sec. 58: Charges fixed in the first instance "will be sufficient with efficient & economical working and management [in the opinion of the RRT] to yield equivalent to the Net Revenue in 1913 of constituent companies", [amalgamated by the Act], together with a sum equal to 5% on Capital Expenditure. In determining Standard Charges, and to encourage economies from amalgamation, the Tribunal shall make a fair allowance in respect of economies achieved not exceeding one third of such economies". (Efficiency improvements arising from amalgamation, which improved net revenue would result in a claw-back so railways would be denied a major part of their economies. No other industry was ever denied economies and profits arising from amalgamation nor had its profits legally pegged in perpetuity).

Sec. 59: The RRT was required to review charges each year [the MoT could order no review after the first two years]. "If on any review, the Tribunal find that the Net Revenue obtained, or which could with efficient and economic management have been obtained by a company, is substantially in excess of the Standard Revenue of the company, they shall modify charges so as to effect a reduction of the Net

Revenue of that company in subsequent years to an extent equivalent to 80% of such excess, unless the Tribunal is of the opinion the excess is not likely to continue". [This would return the excess to users in the form of lower charges].

Inputs were made on the proposed scheme by agriculture, industry, traders and railways to the Tribunal, which was empowered to modify all or any Standard or Exceptional Charges to enable Companies to earn the Standard Net Revenue. (How they would assess whether the four largest companies in the UK were inefficient, was not prescribed. In 1938, Capitalisation of railways amounted to £1,127m, whilst ten top publicly owned companies had a combined capital of £68m. Sir Josiah Stamp, said the LMS was the largest privately owned organisation and largest employer of labour in the whole of Europe. In April 1953, the President of the Transport Tribunal - post 1948 successor to the RRT - said: "This is not a proper body to examine the efficiency of London Transport" - much smaller than any of the four pre-war main line companies).

The Special Advisory Group, a secret Government appointed committee said in 1960: "The RRT was inflexible and railways were placed at a disadvantage in meeting competition from a growing road haulage industry". [PRO : MT132/82].

Coal Traffic

The 1925 Coal Commission [Cmd 2600] was groping after means to avert trouble in the coalfields by reducing costs of production. As in all periods of slack trade, there was a cry for lower rail rates from coal mining and other heavy industries, which the Commission rejected. They recommended establishing a Standing Joint Committee to improve methods of conducting mineral transport. They were of the opinion that 20 ton wagons should be gradually introduced over a term of years and District Pools should be formed by their owners. Not until 1927 was the Standing Committee set up and it failed to persuade the coal trade to show any enthusiasm either for larger wagons or District Pools, in spite of the tactful and persistent efforts of its first Chairman, Sir Arthur Duckham to secure agreement on a forward policy. ["Coming of Age", Page 13]. (See Felix Pole's comment - on the coal industry - page 37, and two views on the profitability of bigger wagons - page 156).

It has been claimed that the cost of carrying lower value traffics was significantly lower than that of higher value traffics, because wagon loads of the former were higher. Whilst there was a difference, the disparity was diminished as coal and mineral wagons were usually returned empty, whilst goods wagons mostly had return loads, and by the slow train speeds of the former. The turnround time of goods wagons tended to be better than other types. The cost of poorer mineral wagon utilisation was underrated.

1928 Freight Rates

The basis of the 1928 Charges scheme was that the Standard Revenue [that achieved in 1913] would be earned given the prevailing volume of traffic in the prevailing ratio in each of the 21 Classes of freight in the GCM - and also taking account of passenger revenue. It was based upon an analysis of a week's traffic in March 1920 - so by the time the Rates system was implemented in 1928, its' basis was well out of date. Traffic in lower classes was subsidised by profits from higher classes, in accordance with the theory: "What the traffic will bear". As railways could not increase charges to test what the traffic would bear, the validity of this concept to the prevailing rates was unproven. No industry or trader would ever admit a willingness to pay more, and lacking the opportunity to test the market by price variations - ***up and down*** - the concept was a wholly discredited theory. Some traffic could have been priced higher. (see page 113).

A DoT Report in August 1943, admitted that heavy industry was being subsidised through uneconomic rail rates. (see page 105).

If higher class traffic was "creamed off", the balance was destroyed. The privileged status of hauliers allowed them to charge a discriminatory rate for every job, after exercising a legal right to check the rail rate, and thus cream off 16.9% of merchandise tonnage by 1937, and 26.9% by 1938, compared to 1927.

[1927 data from BoT returns, 1937/8 data from Parliamentary Papers].

The 1928 Rates Book, was unaltered until a 5% increase in 1937. Apart from four increases during the eight years of Government Control [1939-47], and those permitted by the MoT between 1949 and 1956, the basis of the Rate Book remained unchanged until 1957. Except for additions and minor alterations, the GCM was also unaltered until 1957. Hence, the vulnerability to "creaming off" was not diminished throughout that time. A general rate increase brought more traffic within the poaching zone.

Creaming-off

The margin for undercutting rail rates is illustrated by an example from the 1928 Rate Book: For 100 miles, the rate for the lowest class was 9s 11d per ton [50p] and for the highest class, 90s 7d per ton [£4.53p] both including wagon provision. Thus the highest rate was nine times the lowest, whereas the cost of carrying, ton for ton would be broadly the same. Before the onset of road competition, goods were, in aggregate, carried at a profit, the carriage cost per ton being at a point below the midway level of rates. All below is subsidised by all above that level. (see Graph on page 73).

When road began to "cream off" top layers offering 10% below the rail rate, rail lost profitable traffic which was, by law, subsidising the loss makers. In 1928 railways earned - Coal: £33.5m; Minerals [Classes 1-6]: £15.3m; Merchandise [7-21]: £49.4m; Livestock £1.9m. Road attacked only the vulnerable Merchandise classes.

Legislation encouraged creaming-off. The 1854 Act designed to ensure that Railways treated all potential users equally, facilitated unfair road competition. The 1873 Act which required all rates to be open for inspection, enabled hauliers to examine rate books and undercut rail rates with impunity. Legislation prevented railways from retaliating or even from preventing traffic losses. A flat rate or percentage reduction below a rail rate was sufficient to secure the business to road.

Hauliers were not bound by Common Carrier law which meant that they could pick and choose the more profitable flows, and reject any traffic for any reason, indeed, without reason - whether due to a temporary shortage of resources or because the flow would be unprofitable at the price a customer was prepared to pay.

Between 1924 and 1935 road transport increased its share from 13% to 50% of the total market of the vulnerable merchandise traffic. ["Railway Crisis", Page 14].

The complex Standard rates were imposed on railways, who, by law, may offer "Exceptional Rates" [to all, without preference] of not less than 5% nor more than 40% below Standard. Upon application to the RRT, approval may be given for less than 5% or more than 40% below, by which time the traffic had moved by road. All new Exceptional

Rates or changes had to be reported to the MoT, who could refer them to the RRT to review. Variations were subject to notice, some of prior approval of the RRT, who decided on any objections. Any trader could apply for a new Exceptional Rate. Sections 36-40 of the 1921 Act laid down the complex conditions governing Exceptional Rates. In the period 1928-37, 1.45m new Exceptional Rates were granted. [PRO: MT6/2876].

The expansion in Exceptional Rates took place to try to retain some of the profitable traffics, but it was done at the expense of reduced profits. [Sanderson, Pages 141-142].

To offer Exceptional Rates more than 40% below Standard was constrained by law, so road could always win on price with the higher valued goods.

No one realised that the traditional method of railway charging was going to play right into the hands of a rapidly developing rival. High value goods were particularly susceptible to road competition. A book was produced of all exceptional rates as a useful guide to hauliers. [Dunbar, Pages 9, 46 & 89]. (Dunbar was in the road haulage business).

It was the policy of "a group of hauliers to ascertain a railway rate and quote 10% below". [Bonavia[2], Page 63]

"At present traffic is diverted from railways by competitors who have full knowledge of railway rates whilst their own rates are veiled in secrecy". (see page 85).

As light industry progressively transferred traffic to their own vehicles or public road haulage, the burden of subsidising heavy industry increased and thereby reduced railway profits. The guarantee of profits fixed at the 1913 level, in exchange for statutory control of rail charges was worth less than the paper it was written on.

The graph below shows the Standard rates and the mean average of the Exceptional Rates railways were allowed to offer and haulage rates at 10% below them. The rail cost of carriage is for purposes of illustration only, as no separate costs could be calculated.

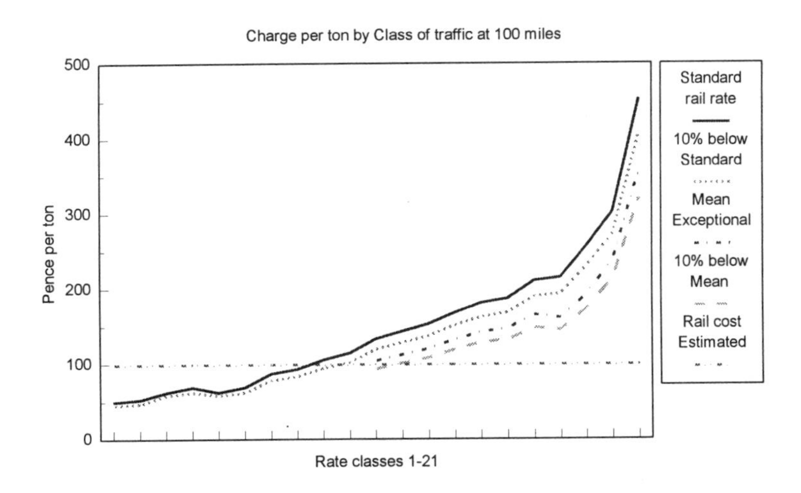

In October 1943, the House of Lords was reminded "how after the last war, ex army lorries were purchased for next to nothing and operated at cut rates to skim the cream of long distance railway traffic". [Hansard vol. 129, col. 360]

Railway Rates Tribunal

The RRT had a legal obligation to adjust charges from year to year, to ensure the earning of Net Revenue, but never did so, despite the fact that in no year was it achieved. There was no valid, legal reason to prevent them from increasing low and decreasing high rates to achieve the statutory objective, thus limiting the unfair competitive position of road haulage. DoT files show that some bulk traffic could bear more cost, and that there were undisclosed political factors - to protect inefficient industries. Under the 1921 Act, the MoT could direct no review [Sec. 58]. (see pages 105 &113).

In the 11 years preceding the Second War, the annual shortfall was between 10% and 44%, amounting to £172m, or 3.5 years total Net Revenue. [Railway Crisis, Page 12]. Railways were promised Standard Revenue in exchange for Statutory Rates control. Government got its part of the deal - subsidisation of rural transport and of UK heavy industry, both at railway expense.

Railway Rates Tribunal Hearings [PRO : MT67/35, except where shown].

1923. Railways submitted proposals affecting charges in 1922. Objections were to be made by 9th January. On 20th February Railways submitted proposals on charges for coal class traffic. Thirteen objections were made. The RRT sat on 2nd May and gave their decision at the end of May. The Schedule of proposed standard charges for freight traffic [under the 1921 Act] was published on 31st July. There were 1,812 objections. They sat in public to hear proposals on five days between 27th February and 5th March. Judgement was given on 22nd March that provision should be made for Standard Charges for Workmen's and Season tickets. Railway submissions were made, 26th April. Five passenger associations, a local authority and a trade association objected. They sat again on 29th to 31st May inclusive.

1924. Consideration proceeded on Standard Terms & Conditions. A Hearing took place on Standard Revenue on 11 days between 26th May and 25th June. The MoT expressed disappointment with progress.

1925. Against railway company advice, they reduced demurrage rates for wagons, an action detrimental to wagon utilisation and hence on costs, efficiency and competition. The consequences were disastrous for freight profitability over the next 40 years, and was counter productive in the 1939-45 War when traffic increased by 50%, (see page 141).

Had the companies taken this irresponsible action, the RRT could have said that it was detrimental to achieving Standard Net Revenue and penalised them accordingly.

1926. A further 55 days of hearings on the new Rates Structure and Classification.

1927. A Schedule setting out standard charges had been lodged with the RRT on 31st July 1923. Notice of objection was given by 612 trade association, public authorities, passenger associations and individual trades. The RRT had still to deal with owners risk rates, low charges fixed under agreement or by statute, terms of carriage and schedules for circuitous routes. [Times 8th July, 11d].

The RRT decided that the "Appointed Day" for introduction of the new system should be 1st January 1928. [Times 29th September 1927, 9b]. The pace had been uninspiring.

1929. They dealt with the new Railway Freight Rebates scheme, designed to give a further subsidy to heavy industry and agriculture. (see page 91).

1932. They heard the case of J.Robinson & Co. of Avonmouth who despatched cattle food to 208 stations on the GWR at a flat rate of 7/2d per ton. (Based on an average of cost by rail and the customer's vehicles). They heard it on 18th - 24th October, and decided against the GWR on the grounds that railways had no power to apply average rates. The GWR took the case to the Court of Appeal who dismissed it on 31st May 1933. The concept was authorised by the Road & Rail Traffic Act 1933. Road hauliers could and did offer flat rates (without let or hindrance). [Dunbar, Page 133]. (see also page 76).

1933. The Tribunal meets for a review on May 16th. If the deficit is not due to lack of efficiency or economy of management, it is their duty to modify charges to enable railways to earn Standard Net Revenue. Efficiency results are favourable. They will have little difficulty satisfying themselves as to efficient management. [Economist 22nd April, Page 857].

1936 The Tribunal hearing noted that railways had overpaid £9.76m to the Railway Freight Rebates Fund [Times 4th December, 4d]. (see also page 91).

On 25th May, the MoT told Parliament: Railways are precluded from charging in excess of standard mileage rates [for fares] as laid down by the RRT. [Hansard vol. 312, col. 1645].

1937 [PRO : MT67/182 & MT67/193]. The RCA wrote to the RRT on 23rd April:

> "As none of the Companies has attained Standard Revenue, the provisions of the 1921 Act appear to impose on you the duty to make such modifications in Charges as you may think necessary to enable the Net Standard Revenue to be attained".

The RRT asked railways for their suggestions and they proposed a general increase of 5% or thereabouts. The Tribunal wrote to the RCA on 11th May, seeking amplification as to the spread or make up of the suggested 5%. The RCA replied 18th May, proposing Merchandise 5%, Passenger 5%, [with some exceptions in regard to cheap fares]. The RCA pointed out that the Companies had noted that the cost of manufacturing had increased in nearly all directions and prices of raw materials were rising. Coal had gone up. Total UK production was rising, unaffected by these price increases. The price of potatoes had risen 77% between 1932 and 1936. (Agriculture was given special treatment under the Act and the Rebates system, see below). The Tribunal sat on 16 days between 14th June and 1st July. On 27th July, the Judgement of the Court of the Railway Rates Tribunal read:

> Following the application by the Railway Companies, the Tribunal announced that as from 1st October, fares throughout Great Britain will be increased by 5%. Excursion fares, Season tickets, workmen's tickets, coal, livestock and General Merchandise will, with certain exceptions, be included in increases. Suburban passenger fares inside the London Passenger Transport area will not be affected.

The RRT was asking for proposals when it was their statutory duty to determine the charges! This farce delayed increases for which railways called six months earlier. They were acting on railway recommendations, which could have been implemented in April.

1938. On 21st May, Railways told the RRT, that they gained from an increase in rates in 1937, there was no loss of traffic. (Contrary to popular belief that only railways' increases reduce business. If true, we would be buying new cars at £100).

1939. Sir Wm.Wood [Vice President, LMS], said that "Railways were told that packed confectionery and packed explosives are carried at the same rates by road and that the same must apply to rail, although the rail rate for explosives is, at 50 miles, double the rail rate for confectionery. No suggestions were received that the converse should apply and the rates for traffic in lower classes increased to the level of road rates". He told the Tribunal that 235 miles had been closed to all traffic, and 951 miles to passenger traffic.

On 10th January, an application was made by the LPTB and four main line Railways to the Tribunal for a fares increase in the London Passenger Transport Area. The Hearing took place over ***16 days*** between 20th March and 4th May. Judgement was given on 24th May and implemented 11th June. (Such delays were unjustified).

Railway Freight Rebates

Government policy on pre-war Municipal Rate relief was another example of its disparate attitude to railways. The Local Government Act, 1929 relieved railways, industry and agriculture of Municipal Rates. Railway relief including that for their factories, was used to subsidise industry and agriculture. (see page 91).

Road & Rail Traffic Act, 1933

Sec. 37: Authorised railways to make "Agreed Charges" with any trader. Each case required the approval of the Railway Rates Tribunal, and hence, became public knowledge, including road hauliers (enabling them to undercut). Other traders could object to any such Charge, and could apply to have an Agreed Charge fixed for his traffic. Other traders could then object to that Charge.

Sec. 39: Made special provision for the protection of coastwise shipping.

Agreed Charges could not be offered for traffic which could be accepted under Exceptional Rates. That cut out all the one-load consignment type of traffic which was the thing on which road won all along the line. [Bonavia[1], Page 62].

Other railway subsidies to industry

In August 1922, there was a general reduction in all merchandise and coal rates, and again in May and August 1923, following representations by traders that trade would be stimulated by reduced rates. This experiment proved unjustified, having failed to earn sufficient revenue to carry on business on an economic basis. MoT statistics show that average per ton mile rates fell 31% from 2.076d in 1921 to 1.439d in 1925.
[Times 10th January 1927, 10a].

Had 1920 rates still applied [they had been reduced], 1925 revenue would have been £56m greater. Optimism which brought the reduction in August 1923 was not justified. Purchase of foreign coal in the 1926 coal strike cost the GWR £1m. Unlike Gas, Electricity & municipalities, railways did not raise charges to compensate. [Pole, Page 227].

Coal owners were not satisfied with having total pricing freedom, whilst able to object to any proposed rail increase in a Court of Law. They submitted a proposal to the 1926 Royal Commission on Coal, 1925/6 for a reduction in railway wages rates to finance reduced freight charges. [Cmd 2600].

Pole pointed out that unlike railways which worked round the clock, seven days a week, coal was only cut on less than six hours per weekday! [Times, 15th January 1926, 10d].

The Coal Industry did not modernise to reduce prices and increase sales, nor did the Commission urge them to do so, as railways were urged to do by the RCT. (see page 80).

BAS
44

GENERAL CLASSIFICATION OF MERCHANDISE

	Class
Basins and stands, lavatory, earthenware:-	
4 tons	13c
2 tons	15c
Less than 2 tons	17c
[Exceptional rates for baths apply]	
Note - if not packed, as damageable goods not properly protected by packing	
Basket, trunks, nested	19
Basket work, e.o.h.p., minimum 10 cwts per truck	20
Baskets, Bass or rush, in bundles	18
" Coal [colliers']. rough	13
" Dress - [as trunks]	
" Fruit, cardboard, with tinned iron handles, nested, in bundles, minimum 10 cwts per truck	18
" Iron	16
" Japanese, minimum 10 cwts per truck - [as Baskets, e.o.h.p.]	
" Japanese, nested - [as Basket trunks, nested]	
" On wheels or castors	19
Note if not packed, as damageable goods, not properly protected by packing	
" Osier or twig - [as hampers, empty, e.o.h.p.]	
" Spale, or spale swills, or chip in crates or in bundles, not packed nor wrappered minimum 10 cwts per truck	18
" Wooden, nested, for plants, fruit or vegetables	18

	Class
Baskets, workmen's', tool [as bags, workmen's', tool]	
" E.o.h.p., minimum 10 cwts per truck	20
Bass baskets, in bundles	18
Bass or whisk, not prepared for making brooms or brushes:-	
2 tons per truck	12
30 cwts per truck	15
less than 30 cwts per truck	18
Bass or whisk, prepared for making brooms or brushes - [as fibres, vegetable]	
Basswood - see timber classification	
Bates or pures, dog, hen & other, in barrels, drums, sacks or tins	9
Bath brick powder:-	
In sacks	8
E.o.h.p	11
Bath bricks	7
Bath chair & trailer bodies, basket work or wickerwork wrapped in paper & canvas, minimum 10 cwts per truck	20
Bath chairs	20
Bath cubes - see bath salts	
Bathing salt [common salt], not perfumed - as salt common	
Bath salts [soda crystals] perfumed	
In casks, drums or sacks	13
In tins or cartons in cases	13
E.o.h.p.	18
Bath seats, wood or iron, with cork tops & wire hangers	18

Every conceivable item is listed. There were more than 400 pages like this.

Chapter 8 THE VAIN SEARCH FOR EQUALITY

Inequitable road/rail legislation, which began in 1921, continued through the 1920's and 1930's, as timid attempts were made to consider the problem.

A railways' deputation met the MoT and said that they did not desire to be protected from fair competition, but the diversion of traffic was made possible by the fact that motor carriers were provided with roads, to the cost of construction and maintenance of which, they only contributed a relatively small sum, whereas railways had to provide their own permanent way and were compelled by statute to provide services which were often unprofitable and accept all classes of traffic. Road hauliers were free to run when and where they liked and to select only the most profitable business. This diversion of profitable traffic to subsidised hauliers would place a burden on the heavier traffic and could not be in the national interest. They asked that hauliers be called upon to pay the whole of the expense of road maintenance and construction which was due to the use of roads by them. The MoT replied that the Government were aware of the diversion which was taking place. He assured railways the matters raised would have full consideration by the Government. [Times 1926, 11th March, 16c]. (12 years later, nothing had changed).

Royal Commission on Transport

The Commission chaired by Sir Arthur Griffith-Boscawen, was set up in August 1928 after years of railway protests regarding the disparity of legislation between rail and road, and of the consequential unfair competition. It was to look into the issue of rapidly increasing, totally unregulated road transport and its effect on an over regulated rail industry. Its' Remit:

> "To take into consideration the problems arising out of the growth of road traffic, with a view to securing the employment of the available means of transport in Great Britain, [including transport by sea - coastwise and ferries], to the greatest public advantage; to consider and report what measures, if any, should be adopted for their better regulation and control and so far as is desirable in the public interest, to promote their co-ordinated working and development".

The Commission decided that there were three questions involved in the Remit:-

1. Free and easy movement of road traffic and its control from the point of view of safety.
2. Licensing of PSV's.
3. General co-ordination and development of all means of transport.

They made three Reports between 1929 and 1931, dealing respectively with these three questions.

1st Report: The Control of Traffic on Roads, [Cmd 3365], published July 1929. They were asked to consider a Road Vehicles Regulation Bill, to be put before them, but referred instead to a Select Committee which rejected it - was "not proceeded with" in the House of Lords - i.e. abandoned. (see page 61).

Thirty days were occupied in Public Inquiries. 54 witnesses were heard. The Commission said that the present "road transport law was obsolete and often disregarded".

Para 4: "There was a need to revise legislation. Not one in 1,000 motorists observed speed limits. Bus companies have had timetables approved by Local Authorities which were based on speeds in excess of legal limits". "Accidents have been increasing, but official statistics are not sufficiently comprehensive". (This contrasts with railways for which the Government had, under an Act of 1842, been supplied with such data). They recorded in Paras 5 & 6 that 6,127 were killed in 1928 by mechanical transport, and an increase in accidents - 1909: 27,000; 1928: 148,000. Recommendations included:-

[iv] no general speed limit for vehicles with pneumatic tyres,

[xi] driving licences issued on ***self declaration*** as to fitness to drive, and

[xxv] the need for Third Party insurance.

(It always appears that whenever road transport ignores laws aimed at safety, then Governments bow to the road lobby and relax the law. When railways' actions infringed safety, new, more severe, laws were passed and regulations imposed).

2nd Report: The Regulation of PSV's, [Cmd 3416], October 1929, recommended the establishment of 14 Licensing Authorities - Traffic Commissioners - who would issue PSV licences, be empowered to grant or refuse licences, approve timetables and fix maximum and minimum fares. They would approve timetables and fares - the aim would be "a controlled monopoly" within each Area. PSV's would require a certificate of fitness, and Insurance cover. Trams and Trolley Buses were excluded and proposals would not apply in the London Area. (Licences for PSV's, were enacted in the 1930 Road Traffic Act).

Final [3rd] Report. The Co-ordination & Development of Transport [Cmd 3751], December 1930. There were 44 days of Public Inquiries with oral evidence from 47 bodies and five individuals, and 54 written submissions. The Board of Trade expressed themselves in no uncertain terms of the value of coastwise shipping. (Government seemed determined to protect any transport other than railways from competition. Policies gave protection for railways' competitors at both ends of the spectrum - coastwise for large consignments and road at the lower end). It said:

"Parliament fixed a maximum profit for railways, (unlike hauliers), if this was exceeded, four-fifths of the surplus must be given back to the public as reduced charges".

Para 165: The total highway mileage in 1929 was 179,095*, of which 68,000 were receiving grants for maintenance and improvement. Para 168 The Finance Act, 1920 repealed Duty on imported motor spirit. Para 178: £20m came from the Roads Fund for expenditure on roads against £60m spent by Local Authorities. It noted the development of road transport had caused serious loss to railways, "which will continue to lose traffic to road". They suggested merging "Joint lines" [those owned by two or more of the "Big Four"] into one of those companies, (but identified no economies). They said there was much to commend closing little used, unremunerative branch lines. To ensure public have other facilities in place of those discontinued by railways, companies should be required to inform the Area Traffic Commissioner of their intention to close any station or branch and when closing thereof actually takes place. (* In 1909, it was 118,500 - see page 54. New roads were funded by rates, to which hauliers contributed little, but railways paid heavily).

This would prolong losses arising from reduced use by customers who had transferred much of their business to road. There was no recommendation that road hauliers should give notice of an intention to withdraw from any area or cease to serve any trader. None of the rail proposals would affect the creaming-off of freight traffic. Clearly the Commission was unaware of the statutory role of the R&CC. (see DoT Memo on page 100).

Page 16: British railways suffered as pioneers - due to heavy capital expenditure.

Page 22, Para 65: Locos, rolling stock and sleepers were sent overseas, especially to the Western Front. Workshops had to produce special wagons to carry war materials (howitzers, tanks, etc). Para 66: Lack of adequate materials in the war resulted in minimum attention to maintenance and repairs. By 1919, railways needed a complete overhaul. Para. 67 Permanent way sadly in need of attention, a great shortage of locos and rolling stock - most in use was overdue for repairs at the end of the war.

Page 29: Railway "Disabilities" include Control of charges; Obligation to carry; Undue preference; Facilities for HM Forces and workmen at cheap fares; Control of wages and conditions of service by the National Wages Board set up by Government; Accounts & returns; Passenger Duty [tax]; Safety; Maintenance of roads over rail bridges; Standardisation of equipment [by Government decree]. (A lack of similar control of road wages, conditions, hours or vehicles made road transport cheaper). Para. 99: Railway companies asked for removal of these disabilities and said that most problems would be resolved by equal regulation of road transport.

Para. 101: Railways called for an end to liability for maintenance on bridges.

Para 103: Sir Josiah Stamp said economies are very large and progressive - a fall in prices of purchases was worth £20m pa.

Para 112: Referred to the 1929 Standing Committee on Mineral Transport [1st Report - Cmd 3420] which noted that only 3% of wagons are over 20 tons capacity. Drastic reconstruction is needed at terminals and sidings, estimated to cost £8.75m and is essential for extending the use of 20 ton wagons. The RCT recommended no wagons below 20 tons be constructed after 1st January 1932 without authority. (see page 155).

Para 120: The POW system is defective and costly.

Para 125: ABCC criticised slowness of obtaining a rate, (through the Tribunal).

Page 37: They criticised passenger train speeds, when Railways were complaining about loss of freight to unregulated road transport! (See LMS response - page 81).

Page 41: They criticised railways for buying into road haulage [having said a loss of freight to road was inevitable], and said railways should use capital to electrify suburban lines. (There was no data on cost or revenue). They said that companies do not require express authority to close a line or station. (But see page 100).

Para 160: They concluded that the country cannot afford to lose the railways. The aim should be to harmonise and co-ordinate the newer and older forms of transport.

Para 536: Lower rail fares were suggested to recover traffic. All suburban lines to be electrified. (Fares had not kept pace with inflation, reductions would throw the burden onto freight. It would not recover a ton of freight and would decrease profits. They had no data on costs or benefits of electrification, and made the common assumption that improved quality on railways, unlike elsewhere should be at lower prices!).

They made recommendations on bridges and level crossings. (see page 63 & 65).

They recommended an Advisory Council on Transport to advise Government on co-ordination and proposed another Inquiry into rail and road freight competition. They said that "without unification, (a euphemism for nationalisation), co-ordination would not be successful. Transport should not be for profit - a policy adopted by German, and other, railways before the War".

There was no prospect that road haulage would accept that, but events proved Government inertia, policies and legislation would ensure that the recommendation was applied to railways.

Railway Reaction

The RCT Final Report reads like a long drawn out attempt to reach agreement by compromise and shirked the main issues". ["Coming of Age", Page 25].

At the 1931 AGM, the Chairman of the LMS Railway referred to RCT criticism on road transport expenditure vis a vis suburban electrification. "They omitted to say that it would have gone hardly any way to fund suburban electrification and would have left the bulk of the country where it was before road powers. Road transport charges are based on illegal and undesirable practices and labour conditions which we could not employ. The RCT criticised the speed of trains, seeing no improvement. A Royal Commission sixty years ago considered the question and took the fastest and average speeds from London to principal towns. The present RCT did not follow this lead, indeed it is difficult to know how they arrived at their conclusion. In each of the instances shown in 1867, the present speed on the LMS is markedly greater. The RCT also ignore the implications on speed of heavier trains". A table presented at the AGM showed that the fastest trains were 50% faster, and the average, between 27% and 47%. [Times, 28th February, 17a]

Rail expenditure on road transport, including those required for C&D in the 10 years from 1928 to 1937 inclusive was £7.3m. At £0.73m pa, electrification would have taken 357 years! (see page 62). Weir said the return would come after completion. (see page 93).

In "Fair Play for Railways", the RCA criticised conditions enjoyed by "unduly favoured" hauliers, who "should be subject to the same statutory regulations as railways. They urged Government to pass legislation to give them fair treatment as compared with road competition. Railways have to buy their land, build their permanent way and maintain it at their own cost. They pay for policing and signalling it. Rail charges were regulated. Anyone with a vehicle could operate on roads and choose the cream leaving the rest for railways. Every road user should pay his full share of road costs - construction, improvement, maintenance, signalling, policing. Railways are bound by Parliamentary regulations. Road haulage should also be regulated. The existing situation is a serious and unfair handicap to railways. Its correction is essential to their efficiency and vital to the sound economic development of the transport of the country. The Railway Rates Tribunal stated: "We do not fail to recognise the great services railways have rendered and are rendering to the country. We are profoundly conscious of the importance of maintaining an efficient and prosperous railway system".

For 1930 as compared to 1924, after allowance for bad trade, the loss from road competition was £16m in net revenue - one third of the profit the law stipulated they should be allowed to earn. As road competition had reached a considerable stage of development in 1924, £16m is an under statement of the loss. But for loss of traffic, railways would have earned, in most years since amalgamation, more than the profit fixed by Parliament and 80% of the surplus would have been used to reduce fares and rates. In fact, railways had to increase rates on freight traffic by 7% in 1927. This would have been unnecessary but for road competition. Reduced expenditure in 1930 compared with 1924 was £18.8m and further economies were being made. The RRT annual review found that railways are being managed efficiently and economically. All railways ask is equality of treatment with road competitors. Road costs are a burden on ratepayers. Expenditure on roads is £60m pa, split between £20m Road Fund [from licence duties on vehicles], and £40m Local Rates. The local ratepayers [and railways are large ratepayers] are today funding two thirds of road expenditure. 25 years ago it was proper that the cost of roads should be met from local rates. Roads were then used almost entirely for local traffic. The MoT told the Royal Commission that apart from the use of the roads by mechanical transport, other users are negligible from the point of view of highway expenditure. Diversion of rail traffic to road is a burden on ratepayers. Road transport has the free use of 177,000 miles of road, which they use as "business premises". Railways claim that all road users should pay their share of road costs. Railways paid Local Rates throughout the UK, hauliers did not. £40m rates [spent on roads] is a subsidy to the road industry at railways' expense. Heavy motor vehicle owners pay too little in relation to other road users.

The Royal Commission recognised the consequences of the problem, and recommended the imposition of substantially higher licence duties on the heavier classes of motor lorry. Expert evidence to the Commission said £1,600-2,000m had been spent on road construction. In the nine years to 1929, £490m was spent on roads and vehicle owners paid £180m in licence & petrol duties. Railways have invested £1100m, including £800m on permanent way. Road users pay no interest on capital [spent on roads].

Parliamentary Regulation differs :-

Railway: Charges for passenger and freight are regulated. No preferential treatment is allowed to customers. Must convey all traffic offered [but for a few exceptions of dangerous goods], and are bound by strict safety regulations.

Road Haulier: Charges what he likes. Accepts or refuses traffic as he likes. Operates over any road he likes. Operates at any time he likes without regard to regularity of services. Under no obligation to State or industry. He chooses the cream and leaves the rest to the railways.

Railways claim that road transport for freight traffic should be regulated on lines corresponding to that applicable to rail e.g., such vehicles should require a licence granted subject to:- Fitness of vehicles; Fair wages & conditions of staff employed; Necessity for service on grounds of public interest; Publication & control of rates charged. Rail and road transport must be placed on an equal footing. Railways seek to place no burden or restriction on road transport which is not fair and reasonable and for which railways has not a corresponding burden and restriction.

The Railway Stockholders Union said : Parliament needed to be convinced that a line was needed and then only granted permission subject to a number of exacting conditions. Railway costs were enormous. Motor vehicle cost is negligible and any man might purchase a lorry and put it on the road without any Authority asking him what he hoped to contribute in the direction of new and improved services. The revenue of railways has fallen from £45.6m in 1923 to £26.4m in 1932. It is impossible to see how railways can compete with motor transport under existing conditions and at the same time fulfil the intention of Parliament by assisting the basic industries. ["Your Concern"]

Had this applied today, Railways would have tested archaic laws, as some tested illogical Sunday trading law, by pulping the GCM and Rate books and charging on an unfettered commercial basis on exactly the same lines as road haulage.

Support for Railways

In April 1932, the Association of British Chambers of Commerce called "for the removal of disabilities and restrictions on railways which made it difficult for them to compete efficiently with road transport". [Keesing, 281A].

In October 1932, the National Organisation of Trade & Industry stated: "The [Royal Commission] Report entirely failed to deal with the most important subject included in the terms of reference - division of function [between rail and road]. It failed to set out the agreed facts in relation to the competition of road and rail transport and in relation to measures to be taken to deal with such unfair competition as may be found. It must eventually deprive Trade and Industry of any effective alternative means of transport, destroying the reasonable competition which is their safeguard". [Keesing, 528K].

All pleas fell on deaf ears.

The Salter Conference

Sir Arthur Salter, a journalist, and one time civil servant, was appointed by Government on 11th April 1932 to head a Conference between rail and road interests. Their remit was:

> To establish a fair basis of competition and division of function between rail and road transport; to give advice and information to the MoT; to consider the nature and extent of regulation which should be applied to goods transport by road; to make recommendations which will enable the two sides of the industry to carry out their functions under equitable conditions which adequately safeguard the interests of trade and industry. (The remit acknowledges that existing conditions were not equitable).

The Conference said there were 364,000 road goods vehicles - it was not concerned with passenger. The Conference reported on 29th July 1932. It also recommended a new Central Advisory Committee to advise the MoT on road licensing and the division of goods between different modes and that road haulage should pay towards the cost of building and maintaining roads. Report highlights:-

> Para. 30: Rail tariffs are based on charging less than cost for certain traffics and more to others. This is possible as they were carrying both groups. Even when we have corrected the incidence of highway costs, the question remains as to whether it is possible to retain in permanent equilibrium two systems whose charging principles differ. Industries, and communities dependent on them, will be seriously affected if all bear full costs of services.
>
> Para. 31: Drew attention to the limitations of solving the road/rail problem merely by allocating fair road costs.

Para. 90 : As part of the recommendation for new road licence duties, we recommend that road authorities should assume responsibility for the anomalous and inequitable cost to railways of bridge surface maintenance. (Government acted on this in 1968!).
Para 96: Railways cannot be placed on a footing of equality in competition by releasing them from obligations as common carriers, or from the control of charges.
Para. 119: Railways would have preferred that the question of publication of rates be dealt with forthwith. They accepted a recommendation that the MoT be asked to examine the question. (Six years later, the MoT had done nothing).
Para. 124: Agreed with the Royal Commission that it is not in the national interest to encourage further diversion of heavy traffic from rail to road.

Sir Josiah Stamp urged Lancaster Chamber of Commerce to read criticisms of the Salter Report and see how they confuse current maintenance costs with total road costs or refer to pre-war conditions as though they were still maintained. They say that as road costs before the motor era were £10m [now equivalent to £20m] this sum ought not to fall on motor users. Motor vehicles had taken the place of almost all pre-war non motor traffic. Much of costs paid by private cars were in excess of costs they entailed, whilst freight vehicles paid less. Transferring costs from ratepayers and taxpayers to users was a reduction in tax not an increase. [Times 31st January 1933, 7c].

"The Salter Report was in Government hands for seven months, with no sign of action". [LMS AGM, 1934].

It is essential that the Government lose no time in placing competition between road and railway on an equitable basis. [Times, 22nd February, 1933].

Road & Rail Traffic Act 1933

The Act created the Transport Advisory Council, which was formed in 1934. Sec. 41: Railways needed MoT approval before opening a new line [including lines on land already owned], and needed approval before converting any line to electric traction! The Act authorised the concept of Agreed Charges. (see page 76).

The Act gave no power to Licensing Authorities to attach conditions to road licences as to charges. It empowered railways to make "Agreed Charges", and gave a trader the right to apply to the RRT to fix such a charge if his business was detrimentally affected by the another trader's Agreed Charge. Such charges have not proved a rich source of revenue. ["Coming of Age", Page 26].

The MoT said on the 3rd Reading of the Act: "It is far better that this kind of co-ordination, which has got to come, should come through the voluntary agreement of the interests concerned". ["Coming of Age", Page 31].

Transport Advisory Council [TAC]

An Advisory Committee was recommended by the Royal Commission and the Salter Conference. The Chairman of the Council had been Chairman of the Royal Commission. The TAC was asked in 1935 to consider the railway complaint, and produced a Report: "Service & Rates" in July 1937:-

Page 3, Sec. 7: Internal reorganisation of road transport must be regarded as an essential preliminary to further progress. Appendix 1: Railways did not ask to be exempted from controls, as Traders prefer the present system, but consider road transport should accept the position of a public service with appropriate regulations. *At present traffic is diverted from railways by competitors who have full knowledge of railway rates whilst their own rates are veiled in secrecy.* If such legislative restrictions of one transport agency are beneficial to the public, they are likely to be beneficial in the case of their competitors.

The Report stated that its' Programme Committee recommended, in November 1935, that a Committee be set up to investigate Service & Rates in relation to goods by rail, road, canal and coastwise, and that the first part should be on road transport. Eleven meetings were held, and a sub committee held four meetings. Evidence was given by Railways, the Canal Association, the Grand Union Canal, the Chamber of Shipping and the BRF.

The Committee concluded:-

Services. Any attempt to direct traffic by different modes would not be tolerated by the public. All transport should be rate controlled with publication of rates and non discrimination to ensure a fair basis of competition. It referred to the view of the MoT during the 3rd Reading of the 1933 Act: "Co-ordination has got to come through voluntary effort and the voluntary agreement of transport interests concerned".

Rates Railways: have an elaborate rate structure. Coastwise interests claim that economic control of coastwise rates is more effective than the rail system, (a good reason to abandon railways' statutory control). Canals are subject to maxima to a limited extent, excluding bye traders. Coastwise shipping is not controlled. Road transport is not controlled. Opportunity should be afforded for road hauliers to build up a rates structure. They also recommended setting up Area Rates Committees.

They recommended :-

1. Traders should have an unfettered right to select any form of transport.
2. It is impracticable to dictate goods by certain forms of transport.
3. All transport should, where practicable, be rate controlled.
4. The co-ordination of rates between different forms of transport can best be achieved by voluntary agreement. (A pious hope for which they advanced no evidence).
5. An internal reorganisation of road transport is essential to further progress towards co-ordination. The steps to stability are regulation of wages and charges [both already existed on railways]. Area Road Rates Officers should be appointed and there should be a Road Rates Tribunal dealing also with publication of rates and enforcement.

Reaction to the TAC Report

At the LMS AGM in 1937, Sir Josiah Stamp produced data to demonstrate that performance on the LMS was better than in Germany or the USA.

The Government accepted the Report, but did nothing, apart from minuting it, very briefly, at Cabinet Meetings in January and February 1938 :-

"Whilst the licensing system has done much to remedy evils against which it was directed, the position is still far from satisfactory - in faulty maintenance of vehicles, long hours, exploitation of workers, with reaction on safety prevalent". The MoT told the Cabinet: " I should have looked to the TAC to propose a more complete and a more scientific scheme". [Cabinet Minutes, 28th January 1938, Paper CP 17 (38), Para 2]. (But he still remitted the Square Deal claim to them - see pages 103 & 106)

MoT Paper on the Stabilisation of Rates & Charges in the road haulage industry. The MoT explained recommendations in the TAC "Service & Rates" Report as steps necessary to secure stability in the road haulage industry which included regulation of wages and charges. He sought approval for an early announcement that Government accepted the Report and proposed in due course to introduce legislation accordingly. He would then be able to consult interested organisations and determine a number of points in detail not covered in the TAC Report, which must be settled before a Bill could be prepared. Legislation was not contemplated this Session. The Cabinet approved the proposals and authorised the MoT to consult those concerned.

[Cabinet Minutes, February 1938].

Twelve months later, no legislation had been initiated.

"The generalities of the TAC Report 'Service & Rates' and the vague scheme amounting to little more than a pious hope, were far removed from the solution to the freight problem, railways have demanded. If they had formulated a practical scheme for co-ordination and Government had taken steps to implement it, railways would not have made the present [Square Deal] claim. Undue preference mitigates against local discretion - lest a trader elsewhere claims similar rights. It enforces centralisation. Railways attach more importance to this [restraint] than any other. [Bonavia, "Modern Transport", 10th December 1938].

Publication was strongly resented by railways. In the absence of Undue Preference, publication would be of no value.

On 7th December 1938, the MoT told Parliament: The whole question of transport co-ordination was receiving my earnest attention in the light of the Report of the TAC on Service & Rates. [Hansard vol. 342, col.1159].

The Report had been ***published 17 months earlier***. Doubtless, his sudden announcement was precipitated by the demand for equality by freeing railways from inequitable legislation as an alternative to equality through like legislation on road transport, on which the Government had been so completely inactive.

Internal DoT Memo, 15th October 1940 to A.T.V. Robinson: Para 10: The TAC involvement led to little, if any, constructive control of rates before the War.

[PRO : MT47/275].

The BRF tried to claim that, railways could find out hauliers' rates from Licensing Authority hearings, but railway spokesmen responded that that was untrue. They had no jurisdiction over rates and could not quote them. [Railway Gazette, vol 66, Page 454].

The road haulage industry was unenthusiastic about the proposals. If Railways were able to prevent traffic being poached, let alone recover any lost traffic, hauliers would be the losers. They claimed that road haulage would be vital in war, in case railway bridges were bombed. Railways, of course, were dependent on home produced fuel, which was unlikely to be unavailable due to enemy action. Hauliers did not explain how they proposed to ensure that tankers carrying imported fuel - prime targets in war - would not be sunk. Oil at the bottom of the sea was irretrievable, bombed bridges and track were soon restored, as letters of gratitude from the military reveal. (see page 171).

Chapter 9 MORE INIQUITOUS POLICIES

When Government began, in 1929, to tackle unemployment and assist industry, its attitude to railways was in stark contrast. Public money was used to finance road improvements, reducing road transport costs, which, Public Inquiries had shown were already subsidised by not paying for existing roads. (see Chapter 8).

Industry and Agriculture were aided by subsidies - from railways! (see pages 90 & 91).

An Inequitable & Iniquitous Passenger Tax

"Over a period of 60 years, railways had pressed Government to abolish Railway Passenger Duty on fares in excess of 1d a mile". ["Coming of Age" Page 15]. (see pages 18-20).

In March 1929, Government seeing that railway investment may reduce unemployment, offered to withdraw a discriminatory and inequitable tax - the Railway Passenger Duty, provided that railways used the money [i.e. their own income] to finance expenditure, which would not normally have been approved by the Railway Rates Tribunal, as its return was inadequate. Investment with an adequate return was being pursued anyway.

The Chancellor, [to stimulate employment], said that he could not abolish the Duty unless Railways bought up 600,000 outdated and low capacity POW's and replaced them with 20-40 ton wagons.

Railways said it should be abolished without strings, as the road passenger industry had no comparable tax, (and did not then pay taxes to use roads). Railways said that larger wagons would be useless unless colliery owners rebuilt facilities to accept larger wagons. They pointed out Government's powers in the 1919 Act to buy them. The Chancellor changed direction, but insisted that repeal must be used to create employment by being invested in projects which may otherwise be uneconomic. [PRO: MT47/128].

Parliament was told: If railways turned to using 20 ton wagon, there are 51% locations where they could not be used. [Hansard vol. 231, col. 664].

On 1st April, the Chancellor stated : Railway passenger duty receipts for 1928/9 were £366,967 - the last full year of the Duty. The Capital equivalent was estimated by my predecessor in Budget last year at £6.5m. [Hansard vol. 237, col. 1110]

The RCA wrote to the Chancellor on 5th April:
The Duty is difficult to justify. It was introduced in 1832 in substitution for duties on stage carriages and horses let for hire. No similar duty is imposed on other transport. In 1883, it was reduced in urban areas, on account of competition by omnibuses. The intense competition to which railways are now subjected justifies abolition. Duty declined from £484,000 in 1923 to £368,000 in 1928. Not more than 75% should be available for capital at 5% which amounts to £5.5m. They urged the MoT to prohibit construction of POW's under the 1919 Act. This would give collieries funds, [otherwise used for wagon repair & replacement] to modernise screens & sidings and thus cut unemployment. [PRO:MT47/128].

Government did not pick up the challenge, to buy up or prohibit the construction of coal wagons - they had no similar iniquitous tax on coal which could be repealed as a lever.

A DoT Memo dated 9th April, said: Repeal will, on the basis of the amount paid in 1928, mean a saving of £370,842 pa to railways. As Duty has been falling, a deduction of

10% will be made of duty paid in 1928 to calculate the capital value. It will enable them to finance £6.675m projects creating employment & improving services. There will be a knock on effect in the steel industry. [PRO: MT47/128].

A week later, the Chancellor told Parliament : I am glad to be able to make this modest contribution to a policy to modernise railways. Railway companies have repeatedly sought relief from this tax [Passenger Duty] which they regard as an invidious survival. [Hansard vol. 227, col. 58].

The Traders Co-ordinating Committee on Transport objected to railways raising charges to remunerate this new capital. The DoT pointed out that this would preclude any benefit to railways. [PRO: MT47/128].

The RCA wrote on 1st May to the DoT: We accept the proposal by the Chancellor of the Exchequer that:-

1. A Sum representing 90% of the amount of charges in Accounts for Passenger Duty, for 1928, will be capitalised on a 5% basis and spent on improvements.
2. Government will promote a Bill to raise the Capital.

The tax was repealed in the Finance Act 1929, which required 90% of the capitalised sum amounting to £370,000 per year, to be spent by Railway companies on schemes of development and capital projects worth £6.7m.

The FBI wrote on 18th May to the MoT saying that railways should be told to place orders with industry not railway workshops! [PRO: MT47/128].

Passenger Duty works of £7.34m were authorised involving LMS, LNER, GWR, SR & Metropolitan Railway. [Hansard vol. 231, col. 866].

By March 1930, works had begun costing £6.6m. The SR extended electric working to Brighton & Worthing, other railways were building locos, yards & relief lines and modernising rolling stock, stations and coal-shipping appliances.

Development [Loans, Guarantees & Grants] Act 1929

After these works started, the Government asked railways to assist Government in carrying out further schemes to find work for the unemployed. The railways agreed to undertake, with modest Government assistance, viz. refund of interest, about £8m further projects, which would not otherwise be constructed. [Railway Gazette, Vol 52, Page 319]

This was arranged under the above Act which would make Grants or refund interest on loans of capital spent on approved schemes spread over not more than 15 years. Railways qualified only under Sec. 2 of the Act for refund of interest. These works would otherwise be commercially uneconomic. Grants were made to local authorities to finance public works, among which roads figured prominently. Meanwhile, Parliament was continually being informed of more road schemes. (see Chapter 5).

The Act specified that the Treasury would guarantee loans for public works.

Sec 1: Relates to development, construction & re-equipment in public utilities. The Treasury to have regard, in considering a grant, of the effect on employment.

Sec. 2: The Treasury may make grants to public utilities, to defray, in whole or part, interest payments on any Loan under the Act mentioned in Sub Sec. [1] of Sec. 1, with a 15 year limit. [for projects to relieve unemployment, which would not have been undertaken without financial help]. (This could apply to railways).

Sec. 3: Public Utility Undertakings means an undertaking carried on under statutory powers but not one which is referred to in Part II [Local Authorities].

Sec .4: Local Authorities may receive [capital] grants to create employment.

Government made Grants of £103m for public works. [Hansard vol. 239, col. 1435], and would incur about £200,000 pa refunded interest on approved railway schemes, which pales into insignificance alongside roads expenditure. (see Chapter 5).

The Railway Agreement Act 1935

In 1935, to further reduce unemployment and improve the economy, Government decided to spend nearly £100m on roads, later increased to £130m, (see page 57), but offered an *interest bearing* ***loan*** to railways to be spent with UK industries!

This Act authorised the Treasury to guarantee securities issued in accordance with an Agreement made with the railway companies on 30th November 1935. It provided for a Treasury guaranteed loan of £27m at 2.5% repayable within 16 years. Railways had to pay the same interest rate paid by the Treasury. Naturally, and for legal reasons, railways limited the use of such loans to self financing works.

Sec. 1: Provided for Agreement between the Treasury, GWR, LMSR, LNER & SR. Schedule: The Government is desirous of increasing facilities for transport of passengers and merchandise by railway by electrification and by provision of new equipment and improvement of railway works. The total cost was estimated at £29.5m, Treasury to guarantee £26.5m. Railway companies shall borrow from a fund of £26.5m, and pay interest to the Railway Finance Corporation formed for the purpose.

The Government had never shown any desire to improve railway facilities at its own expense, and it was not making this offer for altruistic reasons, but because it was in a very big hole arising from vast unemployment. Its advisors had warned of the prospect of war in 1939, and Government knew that railways were vital in war. (see page 96).

The issue of £27m, 2.5% Guaranteed Debenture Stock of Railway Finance Corporation at 97% was announced on July 29th 1935, in accordance with the Railway (Agreement) Act with the objective of financing an equipment programme of the four main line Companies. [Keesing 1968C].

On 25th November 1935, Sir Josiah Stamp [President, LMS], responding to Government proposals, told stockholders it was not the railways' job to act as a political agent. The LMS will only borrow money from Government if its expenditure is economic and will produce a return, not for relieving unemployment. There would be an interest gain of 1% [compared to the rate railways would have had to pay on the open market. [Times 26th November 1935, 8a].

Sir Wm. Wood [LMS] wrote to the MoWT, 20th April 1943, on the Railways [Agreement] Act 1935. "Railways raising of capital is normally to improve or maintain net revenue. The RRT would oppose [investment] if it drained away revenue. Government developed the 1935 Scheme and asked Railways to undertake Works, which otherwise would not have been undertaken, to relieve unemployment. To make this possible an interest rate of 1% lower than the Railway companies' credit could have afforded was obtained by Government guarantee. Government were in turn guaranteed by Railway Debenture Stock as security. None of the Works would have normally been undertaken at that time. It was done through low interest to stimulate unemployment". A DoT Memo says: "Sir Wm. Wood states fully and completely the circumstances underlying the Railways Agreement Act 1935 so far as the main line companies are concerned". [PRO : MT47/275].

This would not cost the Treasury a penny, since railways paid the interest at the precisely the same rate as it cost the Treasury to raise the loan. The loan was repaid by the nationalised BTC in 1951. [BTC 1951 Report, Para 183].

Government policies to protect industry & others

On the same day on which the Railway Agreement Act was passed, Government also enacted the Public Works Act to grant money for the purpose of certain local loans [to businesses] to be made through Public Works Commissioners.

Agriculture and industry received a hidden subsidy as a result of impoverished railways in Scotland, Wales and other rural areas being subsidised by profits from the major English main line railways. Without the amalgamations of 1923, many such lines would have closed. Government took no steps to enable railways to earn their 1913 net revenue as they had led them to expect would be assured as a quid pro quo for enforced amalgamations under the 1921 Act between profitable and struggling companies.

Internal DoT Memo 29th June 1929, states that Unemployment Grants - are not likely to benefit railways. [PRO : MT47/128],

A 1930 Channel Tunnel Committee Report [Cmd 3513] opposed the development of a Tunnel [at railway expense] because potential losses to shipping, agriculture and other industries would be greater than the estimated advantages.

A tunnel would have substantially increased rail traffic. Sea and road transport would have lost traffic to rail. It is another example of Government's discriminatory policy towards railways and its protectionist policy to shipping, agriculture and industry at the expense of railway viability. It was also opposed by the military who could not guarantee a land frontier, the width of a tunnel. Today, denationalised railways are set to reap the benefit of increased business as a direct result of the long delayed Tunnel, which BR had promoted long before present companies even existed.

Agriculture, industry and transport were subsidised directly by Government:-

Agriculture & Industry was given a total subsidy of £55.4m between 1932 and 1939 Further subsidies of £6.4m were promised to Agriculture. [Hansard vol. 348, col. 55].

Airlines - Imperial Airways and British Airways were subsidised between 1924 and 1939 by a total of £6.54m. [Hansard vol. 348, col. 54].

Shipping - Government said in January, 1937 that it intended to subsidise tramp shipping in 1937 at the same level as 1935 and 1936 - £2m pa. On 28th March 1939, they raised it to £2.75m pa for 5 years. [Hansard vol. 348 col. 55].

In July 1938, the Chancellor said that Government subsidies to industry since October 1931 amounted to a total of £55.08m. They covered agriculture [including £5.8m for milk, which also benefited from Rail Freight Rebates], shipping, aviation, and road transport. On 13th July 1939, legislation was being progressed to give shipping and shipbuilding further grants. [Keesing 3148A & 3503D].

These subsidies were in addition to those arising from low freight charges implicit in the Government enforced railway rates system. They also benefited from another subsidy from an anti-rail policy arising from the concept of Railway Freight Rebates.

Railway Freight Rebates [RFR]

Government policy on pre-war Rate relief was another example of its disparate attitude to railways. The Local Government Act, 1929 gave relief from municipal rates, to industry and agriculture, to effect a reduction in production costs. They were then given a further subsidy through railway freight rebates, which were funded by the same rate relief to railways, including their factories. The Act relieved railways of 75% of local rates payable on hereditaments used wholly for transport purposes, the relief to be passed to railway users by rebates on charges of prescribed traffics in the 11th Schedule. A Rebates Fund was created to subsidise coal, iron, steel, and agriculture. The Railway Clearing House administered the Fund and took out a small proportion for administration expenses.

MP's urged bringing forward railway derating to help subsidise the coal industry. The ABCC suggested bringing it forward to help industry. [Times 1st May 1928, 6e & 16th May, 17c].

Rebates planned for October 1929 were brought forward to December 1928 to help coal and Iron & Steel. [Supple, Page 263].

The Chancellor told Parliament three quarters of rates on production industry and the whole rate on agriculture will be abolished. [Times 16th April 1929, 10c].

(Freight Rebates were an extra bonus to industries already subsidised by railways rates).

The Railway Rates Tribunal announced that the new rebates for 1930 were - Agriculture: 10%, Coal: 30%, other traffic: 10%. On Gross charges of £21.2m for traffics concerned, the total rebate was £3.99m. [PRO : MT67/35].

The Chancellor told railways they would get nothing out of this relief [Industrial Derating]. Railways' relief is to be passed onto industry [through Freight Rebates]. Those industries benefited twice, railways, not at all". [LMS 1936 AGM].

On 6th April 1943, the MoWT said that the Rebates were to assist agriculture, coal iron & steel, then in a depressed state and by increasing volume now carried by rail to indirectly assist the railways*. Annual net revenue of the Rebate Fund was to be distributed 20% to agriculture, 70% to coal, coke & patent fuel selected traffic and 10% to other selected traffic, mostly Iron & Steel. [Hansard vol. 127, cols. 1 & 2].

* This theory was flawed, because traffic from these industries was carried at sub standard rates. Companies do not become profitable by increasing output of loss making goods - the same principle applied to railways. They needed to hold onto and recover the profitable merchandise traffic, which was unaffected by the Rebates. Moreover, it will be noted that the Chancellor had said *at the time* that "railways will get nothing out of this relief".

The SR and LNER appealed against the rating valuations to the R&CC who reduced the assessment of the SR from £1.8m to £1.07m, and the LNER from £2.6m to Nil! Local Authorities took their case to the House of Lords, who confirmed the R&CC decision.

"The 1929 Act treated railways more disadvantageously than other ratepayers". [Economist, 3rd October 1936, Page 244].

The Big Four became entitled to a refund of £10m overpaid over five years, but there was only £1m in the Fund. No repayment was sought from industries which had received

Rebates. The Government created a Loan Fund to repay the debt over 15 years! Railways which had lost the use of this money for five years were to wait 15 years for settlement. (Shades of the 1914-18 War skulduggery). This led to the Railway Freight Rebates Act 1936 which curtailed the traffic on which rebates were allowed - to milk, livestock and export coal. The proportion devoted to each class was fixed by the Acts and only alterable by Parliament. The net revenue of the Fund was £1.6m, the sum payable in rebates was £1.5m. Proposed rebates are Agriculture: $16^{2}/_{3}$%; coal exports: 1.5d per ton + 26.5% of the remainder of the carriage charges. [Modern Transport, 31st December 1938].

Railway Returns to the MoT show £31.5m was paid in rebates on selected traffics up to 30th September 1938.

The Railway Rebates Act, 1943 transferred coal rebates to the Ministry of Fuel & Power, as he was paying subsidies to the coal industry. An Internal DoT Memo, 30th September 1943, to Page and Keenlyside stated "Railway Freight Rebates were designed deliberately to be a subsidy to heavy industry". (They were already subsidised by low rail charges). [PRO : MT47/275].

In 1943, the MoWT said: Assessments of railways were made in 1936 on the basis of which rate relief had been paid into the Fund during the previous five years Railways became entitled to reclaim £9m from the Fund. The result would have been that no rebates could be paid for years until the debt was paid off. To avoid this and enable the debt to be met, Parliament passed the 1936 Act which authorised the issue of redeemable stock secured on the Fund and a sinking Fund for repayment of annual instalments. The reduction in assessments reduced the revenue available for rebates. The Act made a drastic reduction in the lists of selected traffics so that 20% went to agriculture, 80% to coal. The reduction would not continue after 1943 unless continued by an Order made by me and ceases in any event at the end of 1952. During the War, the carriage charges on milk and livestock have not varied substantially. A fall in coal exports has created an extraordinary situation. At 30th September 1942 there was £0.9m in the Fund. The Bill suspends coal rebates until such date as I may appoint. The purpose of coal export rebate has ceased to exist. The Fuel Minister is paying abnormal transport charges incurred by reason of wartime conditions to reduce the cost to home consumers of coal brought coastwise at relatively high rates. Money paid to the Minister will be used as the Treasury directs. [Hansard HoL vol. 127, col. 1-5].

In 1949, 20% of the fund was used for rebates on milk and livestock, the rest went to the MoT to subsidise coastwise shipping. (Which could object to low rail rates). Between 1948-50 total rebates credited to the Fund averaged £3.8m pa. The Scheme was wound up on 1st January 1951 and the balance paid back to the BTC. [BTC 1950 Report, Para 32]. The Regulations implemented to wind up the Scheme provided for the outstanding principal and interest on the loan to be borne by the BTC, not the Treasury. Railways wait for refund of overpaid rates was in vain. [Hansard, vol 482, col. 210].

The facts clearly show that the reduction in railways' municipal rate burden was passed on in full to other industries to help them. The facts show that road haulage did not begin to pay licence fees to make a modest contribution towards road costs until 1933. They paid nothing, of course, to cover usage over the preceding 30 years. The road lobby confused taxes which they paid to the general Exchequer, as the railways did, albeit railways paid far more, with the funds needed to pay for the highway.

Weir Report on Electrification

Except where shown, the source is PRO : MT6/3335 - another non security jeopardising file locked away for 50 years.

Among inter-war issues which excite criticism, is the refusal of railway management to electrify in the thirties. Government set up a committee under Lord Weir in 1929, which reported in March 1931. There can be no doubt that Government saw this as a means to relieve unemployment, without using Government money, in contrast to its willingness to spend public money on roads. The Committee's Remit :

> "In view of the progress being made towards widespread availability of HT electrical energy, to examine economic and other aspects of electrification of railway systems with particular reference to main line working and to report their conclusions".

Conclusions All main lines could be electrified for £261m net, giving a gross return of 6.7% and 2% after interest. This represents the position in year 21, when electrification is complete. The study is based on two lines, which on detailed examination may be incorrect. Risks cannot be predicted accurately. They lie in the fallibility of estimates, possibility of traffic loss due to competition or reduced national activity. Such a return would not appear from a business angle to warrant adoption of a scheme of such magnitude. The margin would be too narrow for the risks and contingencies. The expense and scale should not prevent serious consideration by railways, Government and the country. Suburban electrification brought increased traffic, but the economics of main lines rest on those deriving from existing traffic. Electrification of small sections is unlikely to be justified. The main reasons which led to electric haulage in foreign countries do not apply here. The scheme would involve expenditure of £80m by the Central Electricity Board, on which they would earn normal revenue. They estimated employment at 60,000 men pa over 20 years.

Reaction to the Weir Report.

The RCA wrote to the MoT on 26th March pointing out the fall in traffic since 1929. The companies could not finance the work out of their resources. The return is speculative, and raising money from the public, impossible. They asked what assistance there may be from Government. At a meeting on 31st July the MoT asked the railway companies what financial assistance was needed; and the Railways replied: Capital at a non commercial rate.

The assumption that traffic of 1929 will still be on rail in 20 years may not be justified. The scheme would give manufacturing industry fuller employment. £520m has been spent on roads in the past 10 years, and spending was still at £60m pa - compared to £13m on railways. [Economist, 2nd May 1931, Page 931].

Railways could not carry out the work without borrowing. [Aldcroft[1] Page 248].

The Central Electricity Board said that the increased load on the national system which electrification of railways would contribute would react favourably on the cost of energy produced for all purposes. The additional transmission network required would do much to accelerate rural electrification in the country. [Times 25th April, 7b].

From personal involvement in electrification schemes, I know that BR found energy costs did not fall. The Electricity Board imposed elements in the charges to cover provision of extra generating capacity and a further premium for peak demand, in addition to a basic charge for each unit consumed.

Lord Weir wrote to disabuse those who believed his committee recommended the Scheme: "We expressed no opinion. We were not asked to do so". [Times, 31st July, 8d]

It is surprising so much has been heard in favour of electrification, and so little against. The publicity campaign conducted by interests likely to benefit has aroused some likely to be adversely affected. The Gas Council point out the return leaves little for reducing transport costs. Railways will be fortified in their view that they cannot recommend expenditure of so large a sum on a speculative undertaking. A loss in sales of 7m tons of coal pa is forecast. [Times, 1st August, Page 444].

Electrification on the wholesale scale envisaged in the Weir Report is out of the question on financial grounds. Suburban extension must be a matter for serious consideration. [Times, 12th August, 16c] However, Para 46 of the Weir Report refers to suburban electrification as being superimposed on main line electrification, not independent of it.

The MoT told the Cabinet that the RCA had written to say that the scheme would bring development to the country, and might enable railways to make economies, but they criticised the Committee's estimates. [Cabinet Minutes, 15th July 1931].

The Prime Minister said it was important to avoid any impression that Government was seriously considering electrification of railways. The RCA letter should not be published. [Cabinet Minutes, 30th July 1931].

One MP cast doubt on the reliability of the Weir Committee estimates, pointing out that a Weir Committee on the Electrical Grid had estimated costs at £33.5m and they had now reached £50m. Another pointed out that electrification was forecast to cost £30m pa. In maintenance of roads in last 10 years, we have spent £500m, and now proceeding at £60m pa. [Hansard, July 1931, vol. 255, col. 1717 & col. 1754].

The ABCC wrote to the MoT on 24th May 1933, urging a programme based on Weir to reduce unemployment and reduce the cost of electricity to all users. (They did not undertake to transfer all traffic back onto rail to help to remunerate the cost of electrification). Beneficiaries from electrification would, it seemed, be anyone but railways - Industry, Unemployed, Rural communities, and consequently, Government.

The Cabinet was anxious to progress suburban electrification to relieve unemployment. The MoT explained that since the passing of the LPTB Act 1933, the main line railways had no power to proceed with work in the LPTB area until it had been examined by a Standing Joint Committee, which had only just been appointed. The Act provided for the pooling of receipts for suburban services. No reference was made to Government cash. [Cabinet Minutes, 27th June 1933]

PART III

THE SOLUTION

"The railways are not asking favours. They are only asking to be placed on the same footing as their competitors".

["Clear the Lines", page 18].

Chapter 10 THE 1938 "SQUARE DEAL" CAMPAIGN

Public Record Office file MT6/2876 [last item dated 1939, was closed until 1990] and contained DoT files SRC/32, 32A, 32/6, 32/12, 32/13. Customary practice would have numbered sub files consecutively. However there was no trace of sub files numbered 32/1 to 32/5 and 32/7 to 32/11 inclusive. Except where shown in the text, information is drawn from this file. PRO staff could not trace any other sub files.

In 1938, having failed to persuade Government to enact equal Statutory controls on Hauliers, to those to which railways were subjected, the "Big Four" companies called for statutory control of rail rates and conditions to be abolished to give them an alternative form of equality. In this approach, rail rates would be confidential and at "cost plus" instead of what it was assumed "the traffic would bear" which was so vulnerable to "creaming off". They asked for a meeting with the Minister.

Hauliers were well aware what railways had in mind. Even before the launching of the Square Deal campaign in November 1938 there had been a steadily increasing press campaign conducted by road haulage for the purpose of representing [or as the Railway Gazette said, misrepresenting], that the railways were trying to interfere with the rights of traders to select the form of transport which best suited them. [Nock, Page 89].

The road lobby did not suggest that hauliers take the acid test of exchanging railways' restrictive legislation and statutory rates control for road transport's total freedom, nor even to be subject to equal legislation.

Internal Memo [unsigned] dated 21st November 1938 to the MoT: "In view of the dependence of heavy industries on cheap rail transport [secured by the application of 'what the traffic will bear'], the maintenance of an efficient railway system is essential in peacetime, while in war the need for economising on petrol or other imported fuel is likely to ***necessitate the use of railways to an even greater extent than in peace*** as the main transport machinery of the country. It is suicidal to encourage road transport at the expense of crippling the railways".

A clear acknowledgement that railways were in danger of being destroyed. The scenario of increased use in wartime was later dismissed by Civil Servants as too fantastic. (see page 120).

There are three directions to ameliorate railways' position:-

1. Increase receipts - more traffic or higher rates.

2. Reduce expenses - wages, facilities, branches, amalgamation.

3. Capital reconstruction.

These were evaluated as follows:

1a. Due to road competition, higher rates are only feasible for coal, iron & steel and agriculture which may not be able to stand increases and might be contrary to Public Interest. One cause of the difficulty is that road, charging on a basis of cost rather than what the traffic will bear, has been able to undercut railways in respect of a large percentage of the more highly graded traffics on which railway charges are comparatively high. It is doubtful if relief can be found in this direction, unless road competition for higher graded traffic is limited.

1b. Freedom of Charges. A proposal which finds support and is being adopted by railway companies is that they should be relieved of all statutory restriction on charges and left free to fight out the issue with road transport on equal terms. No doubt, ***the Companies suffer from disabilities*** compared with road transport, e.g., the ***necessity for publishing charges,*** the need for approval of the Tribunal to reductions over 40% below Standard, liability to law against undue preference, etc. Their competitive position might be improved if they were relieved from these restrictions, but such a course, involving as it would, the complete abandonment of the rates structure, which in one form or another, has existed from the earliest times, would be a leap in the dark, the outcome of which would be uncertain and might conceivably prove disastrous to traders or railways or both. To make such a departure at a time when it is actually proposed that a rates structure be evolved for road transport would, inevitably, kill any prospect of early advance in that respect. Nor can one look forward to a sort of all in wrestling match between road and rail transport with anything but alarm.
(The road rates structure solution was proposed six years earlier, but no progress had been made at all. Despite, the DoT recognition of the significance of publishing rail rates, the Ministry subsequently blocked the railway call for an end to publication - see page 109. The historical angle was irrelevant, as it related to the pre-motor transport era).
1c. Increase of traffic. Apart from a trade revival, any important increase must depend upon restraint of competing road transport. There is much to be said for the view that the road haulier and ancillary user ["C" licences] has been allowed too great an inroad into rail traffic which on a broad national view is most economically carried by rail. Some active step will have to be taken to reverse the process of the past few years. An immediate step might be the reversal of recent policy of Government Departments, particularly Service Departments and those concerned with ARP, of obtaining competitive tenders from rail and road and using each to undercut the other. Such a policy of which numerous examples have been furnished by railways involving carriage by road of heavy loads over very long distances at cut rates is opposed to the Ministry's policy of preventing cut-throat competition and promoting co-ordination. This would touch only the fringe of the subject, but in view of the dependence of Departments on railways in war, the Minister would be in a strong position in urging on the Treasury reconsideration of the present policy. I suggest that the time has come to seriously consider severe restriction, amounting in normal circumstances to prohibition on long distance goods traffic by road hauls of over 40 miles, save in exceptional circumstances, to be reserved for railways. The TAC [1937] Report "Service & Rates" insisted on Traders' unfettered right to select the form of transport. No great deference is due to the implication that Traders' convenience should take precedence over national interests.
(They did not attempt to restrict road transport until wartime problems with oil imports enforced fuel rationing).

2. Reduction in expenses.
[a] The possibility of a cut in wages has already been threatened. There may be justification for such a cut, but this would encounter the strongest opposition from the unions [precipitating a strike], and would be counter to the policy of ensuring adequate wages on road transport.

This was no groundless fear - railway wages had been cut in the past. Government had done nothing about road transport wages. (See Keesing 567D, 1326D, 1490C, 2053F).
[b] To seek a solution by a general closing down of branch lines would be defeatist. Small sections may be closed if running at a loss, but they are few in number. The moral effect may well be bad and the loss of efficiency in wartime might be serious.
[c] More amalgamations are of doubtful expediency. 60% of rail traffic is already subject to pooling [of receipts], which means that economies from mergers are already secured. Companies are already unified in large measure.
3. Capital Reconstruction.
Replacement cost of railways exceeds substantially either the capital expenditure or capital issue. Writing down capital would be a serious blow to financial confidence. [An enclosure sets out the railways' capital situations. It shows that some 37% of their combined capital was without remuneration - the LNER was worst with 52%]. In short, without some change the railways will be back in the position they were in 1932, during the worst period of the depression.

DoT Brief, 23rd November, for the Meeting with Railway Chairmen:
Every study since the First War had been in favour of co-ordination not competition, but nothing had been done to advance co-ordination or retard competition. The DoT is concerned that Railways could undercut Coastwise shipping. The liquid reserves of Railway Companies are practically non existent. (They were unconcerned that Road was undercutting rail, and rail was legally debarred from retaliating).

In December 1938, shipping asked for £5m pa subsidy and protection from railways and foreign ships! [Savage, Page 25].

Submission from the RCA

The RCA handed their submission for abolition of restrictive legislation to the DoT at a meeting on 23rd November: They pointed out that Railways had made representations to Government for 15 years on legal disabilities, most recently on 24th May regarding damage caused by one sided control, and that conditions of competition over the last 15 years were inequitable. They pointed out that the TAC set up in 1935 to investigate Service and Rates, had recommended in July 1937 the creation of a rates system for Road. There has been no action by Parliament. Since that date, the situation has become seriously worse and meanwhile extensive propaganda has completely misrepresented the railway position. They warned of consequences if Railways were required to respond to a National Emergency, adding: "The extreme urgency is apparent". They called for:-

[a] Repeal of existing statutory regulation of charges for Merchandise, including classification, publication of rates and undue preference.
[b] Railways to decide their own charges and conditions. When equality was achieved, new regulation could be imposed equally on all forms of transport. Railways are not asking for preferential treatment or artificial protection.

MoT Press Release : Under Railway Accounts, wastage of assets is not dealt with by depreciation, but by renewal funds provided out of revenue. Referring to the 1913 Net

Revenue: "No adjustment was made to reflect the post war decrease in the purchasing power of money".

A further meeting took place on 1st December between DoT Civil Servants, [Browett, Hill, Page, Clark, Clarke] and Railway Chairmen. Railway Chairmen said it "took six months to obtain an increase in charges from the Railway Rates Tribunal by which time the boom was over, losing the Railways £3m. They said that a simple Act on one piece of paper was needed to repeal specified Parts and Sections of seven Acts. The DoT called for a list of the worst restraints and proposed that the Railway Companies should meet the Minister on 8th December 1938 with a revised (less demanding) submission. (The 1937 Application led to a 16 day Public Inquiry and a six month delay, despite proof of unhindered price increases by trade and industry. The £3m was another subsidy to industry and agriculture at railways' expense).

Memo, 1st December, from Hill to the Permanent Secretary [for the Minister]. I support restriction in road transport, even if rail proposals are adopted. Freedom of choice is a luxury which cannot be sustained. We are already convinced that restriction will be necessary in war, it may be sound policy in peace. Suggest limit the radius of "A" & "B" licences. He referred to a recent letter to the Times from Mr. F. Smith [Unilever] which "welcomed the railway proposals, and said:-

1. It would readjust traffic so each form of transport carried that most suitable to it.
2. Once freed from statutory restrictions, railways will deal on a purely commercial basis and are unlikely to antagonise customers by granting preferences which are not commercially justified".

Hill's Memo continued: There is a danger that railways may act to obtain wide control over industry. Any relaxation of rate restrictions will need to be examined with great care with safeguards against possible abuse.

Internal DoT Memo, unsigned, December: Railway companies were Statutory Carriers under the 1854 Act rather than Common Carriers. I advocate modifying the Classification (he meant "tinkering with it" - see page 101) rather than sweeping it all away and leaving traders with rights to apply to a Tribunal for a reduction in rates. We could consider ending the Statutory obligation to carry. It would deal with traders who use rail for low class and road for high class traffic, which was not justified. Immediate Action could be taken by a short Bill on the following lines:-

1. Repeal equality and undue preference provisions and give dock authorities a right to complain to the Tribunal of charges prejudicing their docks.
2. Subject to the provisions of Sec. 28 [1], [a] of the 1921 Act, give Railways power to vary the Classification. [This retained the role of the RRT to rule on changes].
3. Relieve Railways from obligations under Secs 37 & 38 of the 1921 Act of reporting Exceptional Rates to the MoT and obtaining sanctions of the RRT to rates which were more than 40% below Standard Rates.
4. Repeal Sec 40 of 1921 Act. (A minor issue dealing with the disintegration of exceptional rates).
5. Repeal the first proviso of Sec. 35; repeal Sec. 59 of the 1921 Act. Add to Sec. 35 that if a Company earned more than Standard Net Revenue in a previous year, charges to be reduced so as to produce not more than Standard Net Revenue in future years.

[The Sections provided for variations to Standard Charges and periodical reviews by the RRT of charges]. (No limit was to be enacted on road profits).

6. Rail & Road Traffic Act 1933, Sec. 37 - repeal proviso dealing with approval of the Tribunal to Agreed Charges and substitute right for a trader detrimentally affected by an Agreed Charge to apply to the RRT to fix a charge. Such a Bill would give Railways a considerable measure of freedom at once and their use of this freedom would be a guide to the formulation of permanent provisions.

(The author appears to have been S.J.Page. It did not approach the Railways' reasonable demand for equality).

Hill wrote to Browett, reviewing the lines open to the Minister:-

1. Reject Railways' demands.
2. Reply not satisfied a case has been made, but prepared to recommend a Bill on amendments as per S.J. Page's Memo. (see above).
3. Not indicating how far he would go - will consider, consult and recommend legislation to Cabinet which appears to him justifiable.

Adoption of options 2 & 3 would mean Railways would not be able to say the claim has been rejected. Companies may force the issue and embarrass Government by :-

[a] Reducing wages.

[b] Asking the RRT to increase charges on coal and heavy industry.

[c] Refusing to co-operate on ARP.

[d] Announcing that Government, by not taking action, will bankrupt the Railways. [e] Sitting back, letting events take their course and leave the onus on Government.

(Note that the DoT foresaw the prospect of bankruptcy this early).

December 2nd, Internal DoT Meeting [Browett, Hill, Birtchnell, Page, Clarke]. Purpose: to advise Minister for meeting on Thursday next:-

1. The proposal is counter to Government policy - we have pursued for years to bring all transport under control in proper relation to each other. (They had taken six years to do nothing - see DoT Memo of 7th December, below).
2. Some relaxation may be possible.
3. Restrictions on mode of transport are difficult.

Advice:- Minister to say he is not prepared to recommend the Railway claim to Cabinet, but will prepare a remit to the TAC to investigate and recommend.

December 7th, Internal DoT Memo, unsigned: Railways cannot abandon lines without the approval of the Railway & Canal Commission. (Their original role was to safeguard the interests of investors and creditors, not users). If the present classification represents what the traffic will bear, railways could not raise low rates without killing traffic which is the last thing they wish to do. The Railway proposals are a reversal of views expressed to Salter Committee [1932], and the TAC [1936] and ***are justified by the absence of prospect of settlement in time to avoid serious deterioration of their finances.*** If the new proposals are accepted, Railways fate will be in their own hands. The Memo postulated a sequence of events - rates increase, cut throat competition, industry demanding subsidy, line closures, eventual merger of road transport companies, co-ordination between rail and road. Judging by the progress on co-ordination as regards rates in the last six years, it seems probable that the process will be interrupted by the advent of a Labour Government which will nationalise all forms of transport. By this time rates may have fallen below cost and transport will need a subsidy. He urged control of road transport instead, but not their rates. Railways to have powers to modify rates freely, within the present Standard. This would not bring about equality, but will give time for a permanent policy to be worked out. (Preventing lower rates being increased, but decreasing higher rates would still bring ruin. They had forgotten that Government had enforced a system whereby the higher rates would offset losses on lower grade traffics. If higher rates were reduced - how could they do that?).

Second Submission from the RCA

The RCA's Second Memo to the MoT, was handed to him at a Conference on 8th December 1938. He had asked railways to amplify their claim.

It stated that they had in mind legislation which was short and comprehensive. It entailed repeal of Part I of the 1921 Act and of other Acts and sections of Acts. The proposals did not extend to passenger fares, and therefore the Rates Tribunal would remain. They pointed out that hauliers have complete liberty to vary charges up or down, if he abused his freedom, he would lose his business. The same would apply to railways - competition, even for heavy industry, would see to that. The Minister had invited Railways to specify particular features in the present system which are exceptionally galling. They regretted they cannot follow him into this field. They are not seeking a little relief, which may help keep up an unequal battle through another round. They are seeking equality with other forms of transport and they believe the sense of justice in this country will support this elementary demand. The MoT had asked what use will be made of the powers. They had no scheme for embarking on a general increase or to make wholesale reductions. Charges will be known to customers just like a price list of any large manufacturer or retailer, which will be varied as circumstances demand. The elaborate rates system applied to railways could not be applied to road. Co-ordination of transport, which the MoT sought, will not advance without equality of conditions. Railways pointed out that when they acquired road powers in 1928, there were similar fears of abuse. Nothing of the sort occurred. Competition would control the risk of abuse. Hauliers have a virtual monopoly in some areas, without abuse occurring. There was, therefore, no need for safeguards for heavy industry. Railways had no monopoly over iron & steel - some traffic already moved by road. Rates increases could lead to transfer to road. (The Railways claim could be implemented on one piece of paper, - a short list of repeals to specified parts of seven Acts dating from 1845 to 1933).

The MoT said that he did not want to ***tinker*** with the problem, but it was easier to consider relaxation of certain definite regulations. Stamp [LMS] said railways wanted complete freedom, subject to safeguards the MoT may suggest. Wedgwood [LNER] said Railways want freedom to quote freight rates as they saw fit, and not to publish. The MoT *admitted that "road transport had creamed -off traffic* (which subsidised lower rated rail traffic), but **did not think Parliament would agree to complete freedom**. Under Statute, he was bound to refer it to the TAC which he would do at once". (He had taken it upon himself to decide how Parliament would vote! When in doubt - set up a fourth Public Inquiry. He said he did not want to "tinker" - but that *was* their policy - see page 99).

The Railways' Case

"British railways are the only railways in Europe which have not received a taxpayers' subsidy. Restrictions were put on when they were a monopoly, which is no longer the case. Competition has doubled since 1930. Railways are not allowed to run on commercial lines. They have to transport anything offered to them, but road competitors concentrate on heavy flows between main centres. Road carriers often take loads of full cases, and the empty cases are sent back by rail. A statutorily imposed General Classification of Merchandise [GCM], ran to over 400 densely printed pages, in which every item known to man was listed and allocated to a rate class - of which there were 66. Railways have never been able to earn the return which Parliament had prescribed, and hence, were unable to attract new capital [to improve facilities] on reasonable terms. Nothing has been accomplished on the TAC's 1937 Report, nor is there any prospect for years to come. Meanwhile, the position of railways has become more serious. The removal of restrictions would not put the railways in a privileged position. They ask only for the same freedom as other transport. They dismissed the talk of co-ordination - which may take five years, ten years - and the railways' problem is here today. ["Clear the Lines!", Page 12].

In January 1939, Lord Stamp, President, LMS told the Manchester Chamber of Commerce that the patience of railways in waiting for Government to introduce a comprehensive system of control in rates for all transport had been ill rewarded. It was obvious that many [hauliers] had much to gain and nothing to lose by delay. The trader gets a short run advantage, but snap bargains are no good for commerce in the end*. Railways pleaded only for equality, and then traffic will find its level according to public convenience and the economic character of goods and services. He pointed out that no trader has any redress if he finds the road competition somewhere else is keener than in his own neighbourhood. Except on the few occasions where there is no possibility of road competition, the whole concept of undue preference has broken down. He said that it has been suggested that this "leap in the dark" for the trader and the terrible experiment of giving the railways the same freedom as other people would be less risky if it were not permanent. Railways have agreed to a five year clause and offered regular conferences to the coal and steel industries - at which not only railway rates, but prices for coal and steel, and the price paid for railway scrap would be discussed. He compared 1937 with 1929 - the index of national production rose 13%, but motor vehicle tonnage rose by 42%, LMS traffic fell 4%. Answering criticisms that railways object to road haulage licences, he said railways objected to less than 10%. He said that Standard Revenue was never based on a return on capital, but on the actual return being made in 1913. (*see page 58).

(Objections to road licences were based on the adequacy of existing transport capacity, which, in view of statistics on production and transport growth, was unarguable).

Compared to 1929, freight receipts susceptible to road competition fell 14% in 1937 and 22% in 1938, against falls of only 6% in coal in 1937 and 10% in 1938, and in passenger of 6% in both years. On the basis of these figures, the fundamental feature in declining railway revenues is the activity of road competition. The Economist Index of Business Activity in 1937 was up by 13%, and in 1938, by 6% on 1929. The Rates Tribunal was not merely enabled to adjust charges to ensure Standard Revenue was earned, they had a legal obligation to do so. Classification is applicable only where there is a monopoly of all traffic, as its efficacy depends on preserving a balance between goods carried at a low rate and those at a high rate. When the balance is disturbed, it becomes bottom heavy. The 1921 Act perpetuated the restrictions based on monopoly at precisely the moment when the monopoly began to disappear. ["Railway Crisis", January 1939].

The statistics confirm losses were attributable to unfair road competition and not trade depression as some critics tried to claim. (See also pages 81, 82, 104, 106 & 110 for other statistics).

On 15th February 1939, Lord Stamp told the Glasgow Chamber of Commerce: "There is no restriction implicit in the Square Deal for competitors or customers, it seeks to give railways the same freedom as competitors. In Europe & the USA, State restraint by outdated "anti-monopoly" legislation forced railways into bankruptcy or to be subsidised by the State. In the USA one third of railways were in receivers hands, which a [US] Government Commission said stemmed from policies favouring rail competitors. It was the clearest warning that Britain's railways would be forced into bankruptcy if legislation was not changed. The historic monopoly has now vanished. Industries who have no control by outsiders over their own prices and conditions think railways should have hardly any power to raise charges without first having to do what no other trade in the country is required to do - get the permission of the Tribunal. The need for a Square Deal was now or never - if out of date laws were not changed railways would succumb. The Square Deal they sought was the same treatment as road haulage - both free of control".

Of the options "now" or "never", Government chose the latter. Had war been deferred railways would probably have become too run down to meet war demands. Partial freedom, but not full equality came, alas, too late, in 1962!. [see "Blueprints for Bankruptcy"].

"The Square Deal was aimed at Road Transport and Coastwise Shipping". [LMS AGM 1940]. Coastwise shipping retained protection against railways until 1980. (see page 186)

The Railways mounted the "Fighting for Freedom" exhibition at Waterloo in February 1939 to put over their message. An exhibit likened the Railway Rates Tribunal to the Old Bailey. "Railways are 'tried' for wanting to reduce a particular rate to avoid losing £100 worth of business. All the majesty of the law is invoked. The cost is enormous".

Independent views

In December 1938, the Council of Chambers of Commerce stated that railways are seriously handicapped by the unequal treatment of different forms of transport and called for legislation to free railways at an early date. [Times, 15th December, 8d]. (See also page 83).

"The railway monopoly ceased to exist long ago". ["Modern Transport" 26th November 1938].

Government inaction

A week after his statement that he was giving his "earnest attention" to the 15 month old TAC Report - of which he had secretly told the Cabinet he was critical, (see pages 85 & 86), the MoT asked the TAC to consider the problem, saying that there was a prime facie case for relaxing statutory regulations. (see Chapter 11).

Having set them an entirely opposed remit, his inaction with the earlier remit did not bode well for any alacrity in dealing with the "Railway Crisis".

December 14th, MoT Paper to the Cabinet: "Railways have never been within sight of Standard Revenue. Last year, it was £38m, this year, it is £28m. In 1937, £78m of capital received no dividend, this year it will be £416m. They constituted the iron backbone of the State and were essential to the community alike in peace and war. They wanted freedom to quote rates, free of statutory conditions, which would be contrary to 100 years experience. No solution could be found which did not include control, and provide for appeals by consumers. Given complete discretion, they could refuse to carry a colliery's coal if a single ton of coal is carried by road. He was satisfied that ***railways were handicapped by antiquated controls***. He had remitted their request to the TAC, and had given a hint that the railway's request should not be met by a complete refusal. If they were given a blank refusal, they were capable of reducing wages. This would involve a real risk of a railway strike. He was not without hope that it would be possible to afford railways a considerable measure of relaxation from restriction. It must provide for a right of appeal and include some modernisation of the concept of equality of treatment for all. He referred to the absurdity of the present system, of machinery brought by road from the North, and empty crates returned by rail at exceptionally low rates based on the assumption that profitable traffic had passed by rail".

This malpractice was only possible if a company falsely declared that the crates had been used to convey goods by rail. How the MoT could fear a refusal of railways to carry coal when the "Square Deal" was about merchandise, which they were losing, not low rated coal, is incomprehensible. The blinkered focus on 100 years of statutorily controlled railway rates - a period without competition, explains how the UK fell behind. It is incredible that Government could not see that Controls on railways alone were driving them out of business. Any "solution" which retained controls on railways only and not equally on road transport was not a solution, but a preservation of the status quo.

December 21st, The Cabinet had before it Memo CP 278 [38]. Other Ministers to submit views. They may appoint a sub committee.

CP 278 [38]: "The Finances of Railways".

Para. 3: Finances have been declining for years. This year the decline in gross receipts is £6m and the increase in costs of wages and materials £4m. It is estimated that the Net Revenue for this year is £28m against £51.5m under the 1921 Act. The LNER is in the worst position.

Para 5: Railway companies say "this is due to unfair competition and nothing less than complete freedom will do; and something must be done at once".

Para 10: Freedom would include an end to Railway Freight Rebates (which subsidised industry). Railways propose the Rates Tribunal would remain for passenger fares only.

Para 12: A rates war is forecast where road is competing and increases where road competition is not fierce. (A rates war would benefit industry).

Para 13: Initially, Railways wanted their whole proposal or nothing, but on December 8th said they would consider safeguards for traders. (Under pressure).

Para 14: It is feared that a Government refusal to act would cause Railways to lay the blame on Government and reduce wages resulting in a strike. They could refuse to co-operate on defence measures unless all costs are borne by Government. (This explains Government's cuts in ARP and War Damage Compensation after the War had started).

Para 15: There is a case, in the MoT view, for material relaxation:

[a] Remove the obligation of the Rates Tribunal to adjust charges, but retain Net Revenue as an overriding limit.

[b] Remove the obligation to notify Exceptional Charges including obtaining approval for over 40% [below Standard Rates].

[c] Repeal equality of charges and undue preference, but replace it with the right of a trader to claim equal treatment with other traders. (i.e. No change).

Para 16: I have referred the matter to the TAC set up under the 1933 Act.

Para 17: The final objective of the Government is co-ordination. The LNER is in serious trouble. All have insufficient revenue to service capital.

Secret admissions in Whitehall of the justice of railways' case

Internal DoT Memo, 15th October 1940 to A.T.V. Robinson : Para 20: We must have either like publication of rates or like freedom to quote rates. Hauliers must give up the freedom of road quotations or the ***railway fetters must go.*** [PRO : MT47/275].

(This is very revealing. Senior Civil Servants admitting that legislation relating to railway rates were "fetters").

DoT Memo, 3rd August 1943, Keenlyside to Hurcomb, Page and Hind: The source of the railway problem is being left with unremunerative traffic. That being so, it seems to me that an unwieldy monopoly is not a solution, but it is to rationalise the railway rates system. Under this, heavy industry would have to pay rates consonant with the cost of the service they receive. It is to these industries the railways are essential and it is these who should pay for their existence. The policy of light industry subsidising heavy industry (via rail rates) is easy but wrong. It is short sighted and imposes obstacles on industrial development and maintenance of export markets in the face of international competition. Low freight rates on heavy industry have undesirable effects in the location of heavy industry. It should be close to raw materials and sea communications. Government need railways in wartime and should contribute to their upkeep. [PRO : MT47/275].

Memo, 30th September 1943, to Keenlyside & Page stated Railway Freight Rebates were designed deliberately to be a subsidy to heavy industry. [PRO : MT47/275].

The continued obsession of Ministers and Civil Servants with Standard and Exceptional Rates shows an unwillingness to contemplate railway rates being on a purely commercial and economic basis. It demonstrates an inability to project their thinking forward from 19th century practice to relate to 20th century developments.

THE RAILWAYS ASK FOR A SQUARE DEAL NOW!

Chapter 11 THE "SQUARE DEAL" INQUIRY

On 12th December, 1938, the MoT asked the TAC to consider the problem, as there was a prime facie case for relaxing statutory regulations. DoT files show that the remit required control to be retained over maximum rates, and that Standard & Exceptional Rates should be preserved. He saw "no reason to suggest modification of Classification, and Publication is necessary".

They would still be tied by the main restraints which caused traffic loss. This was no open remit to an independent body. He marked their cards before they started. Clearly, referring it to the TAC was a charade, a delaying tactic. On 22nd December, the TAC informed the MoT that 19 people had been appointed to form the Committee to consider the remit. Except where shown in the text, information is drawn from PRO : MT6/2876.

At the initial meeting, railways were criticised for demanding the freedom enjoyed by others. Road Transport representatives said: "It was discourteous of Railways to go behind the back of the TAC to the MoT. It was a reversal of a policy to which railways subscribed". Railway managers said that when railways decided the only way out was freedom in charges, the only course open was to the Minister. Lord Stamp [LMS], said freedom would promote co-ordination. Sir Arthur Griffith-Boscawen, TAC Chairman said "It is no wonder the Railways took the action they did. It was the Minister's fault for doing nothing tangible for so long on the [1937] Rates Report". [This was endorsed on the papers in the DoT file as "This is rather hot!"]. Sir Arthur's background was military and political, rather than business or financial.

Railways Submission

Railways had lost by 1937, £32m in Merchandise receipts after adjustment for reduced traffic caused by changes in the structure of industry. Between 1926 [the earliest census of road goods vehicles] and 1937 - the number rose by 86%, and the unladen weight by 73% - much greater than justified to meet a rise in production of 46% between 1924 and 1937. The use of trailers further increased carrying capacity. On Publication of rates, Railways were prepared to accept publication of rates if the principle applied also to all forms of transport, instead of only to rail [and to those canal companies which were statutory carriers]. They said that undue preference had been broken down by road transport except where railways are the only available mode. Railways pointed out that hauliers could see proceedings of the Rates Tribunal on Exceptional Rates and Agreed Charges (both identified customers), and obtain information which places railways at a disadvantage in competition.

The TAC Chairman suggested that changes should include a five year review clause, which Railways accepted.

Views of Trade & Industry

Agriculture: The existing statutory regulation of charges for merchandise, classification and undue preference should be repealed. They did not object to non publication of railway rates.

Birmingham Chamber of Commerce : Maintenance of bridges including approaches should be vested in the Highway Authority. No objections to non publication of rates.

Coal & Rail Sub Committee: Co-ordination cannot be effected between transport systems whose charges are based on widely differing principles and we agree it would not be practicable to apply the present railway rates structure with its elaborate classification, restrictions and obligations, to other transport. No objections to non publication of rates.

Industry - Mr. F.Smith, Unilever: "Undue preference was unnecessary, it should be wiped from the statute book, and railways allowed complete freedom. Nothing in the railway proposals or in the method of applying freedom will change the situation [on relative rates paid] one iota from the point of view of the small man. Even parts of Unilever pay different rates for similar transactions". (He had made the same points to the Institute of Transport Congress in May 1938). No objection to non publication of rates.

Iron & Steel Industries had no objection to the non publication of railway rates.

Mining interests had no objection to non publication of rates. Railways should give the Mining Association 14 days notice of submission of price increases to the Tribunal. If they [Mining companies] refuse to agree to increases, the Tribunal will give a decision in one month and decide an implementation date. The Tribunal to have regard to what the traffic will bear, its effect on volume and not to have power to approve any charges for coal traffic to make good losses incurred in competing with other transport, or Ancillary businesses. Export coal to be treated as a special class entitled to Exceptional Rates. (& Railway Freight Rebates!). They called for :-

[1] No reduction in charges in favour of a particular trade or sector of trade until approved at a Conference.

[2] No increase should be operative until the Tribunal has made an award, and then only from a date considered to be appropriate.

[3] A new Statutory Tribunal, having seven members including four Trading and one railway, to decide matters which cannot be agreed at District or National Conference.

(Needless to say, mining was not subject to arbitration on its prices. Railways were to continue to subsidise a grossly inefficient industry from foreign competition and be a minority in deciding their own charges! Railways' responses are shown on page 109).

National Chamber of Trade : Railways should be free to reduce rates, but not to increase them! (No Trader would accept that).

Scottish Commercial Motor Users Association favoured a gradual acceptance of reasonable regulation by road & rail. (Rail was unreasonably regulated already).

Views of other Transport Bodies

British Road Federation [BRF] Their Memo on the Railways claim for freedom in rate fixing said that there can be no equality of competition between four railway companies operating 10,000 motor vehicles of their own and 61,000 independent hauliers with "A" & "B" licences operating 138,000 vehicles including 9,400 "Contract A". The BRF ***agrees*** railways have just grounds for complaint in the difficulty experienced in closing down small stations and branch lines, which would never have been constructed had the internal combustion engine been invented 50 years earlier. (Their history was weak - railways had been around for 100 years). They claimed that the recent fall in rail traffic is not due to competition of road hauliers, but to decline in industrial activity. They said that there was no justice in killing the independent haulage industry and called for amendments in law affecting road haulage industry if railways obtain a relaxation of control. These include reduced taxation but not reduced drivers hours. The BRF does not wish to stand in the way of removal of any reasonable grievances railways may have, but call for a removal of restrictions on road at the same time. They had no objection to non publication of rail rates.

(They expressed no outrage at the prospect of killing the independent railway industry. Their Memo concentrated on trade levels over the past 12 months, railway traffic losses to road had been occurring over the past 20 years).

Canals sought equal statutory relief and raised no objection to the non publication of railway rates.

Coasting Liner companies attach importance to statutory protection as regards rail competition, but it has been lessened by development, under inadequate regulation, of road companies against which they had no similar protection. They raised no objection to non publication of railway rates.

Coastwise Tramp shipping representatives supported the railway proposals as now before the TAC. [These included non publication of rates].

Docks & Harbours raised no objection to the non publication of railway rates.

Mansion House Association: As a member of the Traders Co-ordinating Committee, its presence was an unnecessary duplication. All the other organisations present were representative of thousands of companies. It is no surprise that they opposed non-publication, which would curtail their ability to cream-off.

Traders Co-ordinating Committee on Transport : Agree that railways are operating under certain limitations and restrictions in connection with charging powers and conditions which place them at a disadvantage in competing with other forms of transport which are not restricted. They saw difficulties in applying a different system of rates. They agreed to certain relaxations :-

A. Simplification and modification of classification and rates and conditions.

B. Abolish Railway Rates Tribunal jurisdiction of certain matters now under review.

C. Railways to have the right to quote an Exceptional Rate without reference to the Tribunal or reporting to the MoT. (i.e. free to quote lower but not higher rates, unlike themselves. A case of "Do as I say, not as I do").

D. End undue preference to enable a rate to be reduced to meet competition [of which proof would be needed].

E. Repeal Standard Revenue.

They said Railways should go to a Tribunal to increase rates, and opposed non publication. (Traders owning vehicles would continue creaming-off, others would help hauliers to cream-off, whilst submitting to no Prices Tribunal themselves).

TGWU drew attention to the MoT's statement in Parliament on Proceedings before the Licensing Authorities: He said "In 1937 there were 8,000 convictions for driving over hours; 10,000 for hours not recorded; 4,500 for unserviceable vehicles; 2,750 for vehicles without licence; 200 in use whilst under prohibition order; 550 for heavy vehicles driven by unlicensed men and 7,300 for speeding. A total of 26,000 excluding speeding, all involving road haulage". (All of which kept costs down).

Railway responses

to BRF:

Objections to road licences are made by all forms of transport [including other hauliers] not merely railways as the BRF infer.

to Mining:

[1] Unacceptable to railways, as it is worse than now.

[2] Unacceptable - makes an increase inoperative however much it has been fully discussed.

[3] Railways said it would be unfairly weighted and slow. Basically most proposals are unacceptable.

to Trading Interests:

On 13th January 1939, railways submitted proposals designed to meet fears expressed by trading interests, and were prepared to accept a five year period.

An internal DoT Memo from Dickson to Stedman, referring to the BRF claim to end licensing restrictions, stated: "Railways could also show an equally imposing list of legislative restriction on their physical operations".

On 14th January 1939, the Chairman of the TAC wrote to the Railways that he "felt maximum rates must stay". He noted that Railways had said they would be better off with no concession, but he felt that "maximum rates were the crux". A 'Square Deal' can be made with good will, including the retention of maximum charges. He could not be a party to advising the MoT to abolish maximum charges. "The other difficulties were Publication and coastwise shipping, but these should not prove insuperable. I understand that satisfactory arrangements are in the course of being reached by representatives of coastwise and docks". He said that the "letter is private and confidential and will not be communicated to any interested party", but a copy was on the DoT file, and Government was a very interested party! (How could he advise the MoT to abolish the principle of maximum charges, when the remit to him had effectively proscribed it?).

The DoT quickly picked up his thinking on non Publication. On 26th January Dickson [DoT] wrote secretly to the TAC Chairman: "We must insist on publication of Standard Charges & Exceptional Rates as provided by Sec 54 of the 1921 Act. You were anxious to give [railway] companies some relaxation on classification. I agree this is desirable and am of the opinion they should be given power on giving ***due notice*** to modify the classification [GCM], provided that if that increases existing charges, and a trader objects, the modification should not have effect unless and until determined by the Railway Rates Tribunal, and the onus of proof lies with the [railway] companies". This letter was endorsed "Sent by hand at the request of the Chairman of the TAC".

The Chairman must have phoned for guidance. The remit proscribed non-publication. Dickson was replacing chains by ropes, this gave the railways nothing. It was obvious that traders would object to every change of classification which would increase charges.

On 6th February, an agreement was reached at the TAC Inquiry when Road Haulage withdrew objections. (It is incredible that railways needed competitors, who were using the law to poach traffic, to agree that railways should have, not the same legal freedom as themselves, but a watered down substitute!).

Road representatives claimed that they were constrained by law, because any application to set up in haulage was subject to opposition from other transport. They demanded that all forms of transport, except road haulage should have no right to object - but they wished to retain the right of existing hauliers to object to new hauliers setting up in business! (Railways needed an Act of Parliament to set up, and anyone could object).

The LMS AGM in 1937 was told that there are far fewer objections to licences where traffic is already on rail than MP's alleged, but with little effect. In 1939, Lord Stamp said railways only objected to 10%. (see page 102).

A Joint Memorandum [Rail/Road] was submitted to the TAC, for a consultative committee of the two industries to establish agreements on rates to be charged by road and rail, requiring approval of the Rates Tribunal supplemented by a member experienced in road transport, which would hear objections by traders or road carriers. They proposed safeguards to protect industry and trade and there would be no interference with the right to use "C" licence vehicles. Views of coastal shipping, canals or traders would be considered before the TAC reported to the MoT

On 26th February, the DoT [Stedman] wrote to the TAC Chairman: "You suggest the Railway companies might be given power to exceed proposed maxima by 10% in the case of particular articles. I dislike giving railways an opportunity of altering rates of their own volition". (This was claimed to be an independent Inquiry, whose advice, the MoT had told railways he was required by Statute to obtain! DoT files reveal that the TAC Chairman was keeping the DoT informed of his thinking, tacitly seeking approval, even, before he prepared a Draft Report).

Draft Report, 27th February 1939

DoT files show that paragraphs supporting the case for freedom, **were *deleted at the DoT***, from the Draft Report of the ***independent*** TAC as were statistics which proved that transport capacity had increased well above production indices, although the 1933 Act was designed to prevent excess capacity being created. These statistics were the clearest confirmation that road transport had "creamed off" top rated traffic. Four paragraphs of the Draft were not carried into the Final Report:-

> Para 3B: Railways estimated that they had lost by 1930 [from 1920], £7.7m pa due to road competition.
>
> Para 3C: For 1930-37, Railways estimate a gross loss of receipts from Merchandise of £25m in 1937 after making adjustment for reduced traffic caused by changes in the structure of industry. Therefore, Railways total loss of gross revenue due to road competition for 1937, compared to 1924 is £32m.
>
> Para 3D: Between 1926 [the earliest census of road goods vehicles] and 1937 - the number rose by 86%, and the unladen weight by 73%. Railways state this is much greater than justified to meet a rise in production which between 1924 and 1930 rose from 100 to 106, and from 1930 to 1937 by 100 to 138 (an overall increase of 46%

between 1924 and 1937). The use of trailers further increased carrying capacity of road haulage. (The 1933 Act had been passed to prevent excess transport capacity). Para 15 [ii]: "The principle of fixing charges to produce Standard Revenue, entails a corollary that if undue reduction is given to one trader, a corresponding burden must be placed on other users of the railway".

In addition to the above deletions, paragraph 16 [i] on private sidings was amended:

"Railway companies said that there were throughout the country, large numbers of instances where rates, tolls and charges are regulated by special agreements". The underlined words were replaced by the less emphatic words "there are".

Final Report

On 24th March, the TAC reported its unanimous recommendations based on agreements reached between railways and other interests, except coal mining.

The Report recommended:-

1. The present system of control of railway rates to be abandoned: Repeal GCM, Standard Charges, Exceptional Rates, Agreed Charges, and the concept of a Standard Net Revenue.

2. Railways to be entitled to make such reasonable charges as they think fit, subject to safeguards. Repeal Equality of Charges and Undue Preference provisions, but replace by a trader's right to appeal to the Tribunal [RRT].

3. Safeguards for trade & industry should take the following form :-

[a] A periodic conference on a voluntary basis.

[b] Current charges only increased by agreement, [by the appropriate conference in the case of a general increase or by traders concerned in the case of an individual increase], or by authority of the RRT.

[c] Right of appeal to the RRT on the reasonableness of any charge; (despite users having options of road haulage - not subject to "Reasonable Charges", or "C" Licence, and not being themselves subject to "Reasonable Prices". This, in effect, would retain trader rights to equality and nullify the repeal of Undue Preference).

4. Safeguards for other forms of transport should be :-

[a] A periodic conference on a voluntary basis.

[b] Agreement as to rates with road haulage interests [subject to 3b above].

[c] Certain specific provisions to prevent unfair competition.

The TAC said that a material relaxation of statutory control of rail goods charges was necessary, but because of the ultimate [Government] objective to co-ordinate all forms of transport, recommendations were to be regarded as a temporary measure and should be for not more than five years or such shorter period as might be necessary to establish adequate co-ordination. They said that assurances given by railway companies, of no major change in respect of private sidings, had been accepted by the Iron & Steel industry. There would be no change in arrangements for conveying mails. The Report set out the facts on Railway Freight Rebates and stated that they would be incompatible with relaxed railway charges.

This would concern Government as they would have to replace these railway subsidies to coal, agriculture and industry with additional Government subsidies.

No recommendation was made on the Publication of Rates. (This was illogical, since given the repeals set out in paragraphs 1 and 2, publication served no purpose. An overwhelming majority at the Inquiry had no objection to ending publication. Railways had said that they were prepared to accept publication of rates if the principle applied to all forms of transport, instead of only to railways, and those canal companies, which were also statutory carriers).

The proposals did not meet the basic demands of the railways and seemed to have been based on a unique definition of Commercial Freedom. Quite clearly, the DoT, which had copies of those views, and even edited the Draft Report of the TAC, had interfered in what was supposed to be an independent Inquiry. (see page 109).

The prospects of Railways gaining commercial benefit get slighter as proposals become encompassed by safeguards and stipulations. Rates will be constantly under review by railway-cum-traders committees and trading associations with a right of appeal to an enlarged Tribunal. ["Modern Transport", 25th February 1939].

Without freedom to adjust the charges of coal and minerals at will, and with all the delays implicit in thousands of traders looking to increase profits at railway expense, by alleging unreasonable charges, railways would still face ruin. They could not reduce charges for merchandise to compete with road, unless they were free to increase under-priced traffics to compensate. Introducing a statutory principle of "Reasonable Charges" would be a lawyer's dream. Moreover, there was never any real prospect that an industry, so disparate as road haulage would ever establish a common rates structure to facilitate co-ordination.

Political response to the Report

Sir Wm. Bruce Thomas, President of the Railway Rates Tribunal, (whose powers would be reduced by railway freedom), secretly urged the MoT that "A Bill should specify that Railways may make such charges as they think fit not exceeding those they were entitled to make at the passing of the proposed Act - [preserving existing Maxima]. The Tribunal would determine the reasonableness of a rate if a trader objected. There would be no presumption that an existing rate was reasonable or unreasonable". (The Tribunal had decided existing rates after considering objections - surely they must be reasonable).

It is clear from the instructions to Parliamentary Counsel for the drafting of a Bill, that discriminatory restraints were to remain, railways would not be free.

Memo dated 28th November 1939, to Parliamentary Counsel on the points to be embraced in a Draft Bill, to amend the law relating to the carriage of merchandise by rail, [coal and minerals were excluded]. The Act was to remain in force for five years. Provisions to be included:-

- Any trader or body of traders may apply to the RRT to fix reasonable charges.
- Appeals against unreasonable charges, even if these had been approved by the RRT.
- To empower Coastwise shipping to object if placed at an undue disadvantage.

•Provision to be made to an entitlement to object if placed at an unfair disadvantage - particularly dock, port and harbour authorities.
•Railways to confer with traders or industry, and failing agreement could give a month's notice - it would then be put to the Tribunal to decide what is reasonable. The Tribunal was to have regard to public interest and all other relevant matters.

It should be noted that the Draft Bill would exclude coal traffic, which confirms the irrelevance of the MoT "fear" that, if railways were free, they might refuse to move coal, an improbable scenario against which they could easily legislate. (see page 104).

Memo of Internal DoT Meeting, April 27th: "The onus would be on railways to justify any rate they wished to implement. They would have to prove it was reasonable". A Memo dated 3rd May recorded that the Permanent Secretary had decreed that "The Rates" would, in effect be the "maximum" rates.

Unsigned DoT Memo, during May, endorsed "SECRET": The TAC reported to the MoT on 4th March 1939, on its remit. "It does not seem possible to accept the claim of railways that they should be put on the same footing as other forms of transport", [with regard to the publication of rates]. "The contention of the Traders Co-ordinating Committee that all rates and charges should be readily accessible appears to be justified. Publication of rates to be applicable only to rail". (These comments clearly confirm the unwillingness of the DoT to move an inch. Railways were pressured to curtail their claim for complete freedom. There was no plan to amend the Railway Freight Rebates Scheme).

May 6th, DoT Memo from LB [L. Browett] to MoT: "Publication of rates is vital to the interests of Traders".

Memo of DoT meeting on 21st June 1939 : Secretary, Deputy, Hill, Stedman, Page, Thompson, Clarke. They discussed public interest in regard to charges and "what the traffic would bear". Stedman pointed out that coal for power stations could bear considerably more than other traffic - the only result would be to increase consumer prices. They agreed not to send Document 'D' [Publication of rates], to the Railway companies. The MoT is of the opinion that publication is desirable. They said Agreed Charges should be listed and open to inspection; present arrangements were subject to direction by the RRT. The meeting noted that the R&CC had power to level down railway rate to ports which complained of unfair discrimination.

Consideration by the Cabinet

The MoT wrote to the Prime Minister on 4th April : I have today received the TAC Report which has the unanimous approval of the Council. The TCCT & Mansion House consider Publication should be retained., whilst Iron & Steel and the NFU accept that the obligation to publish Rates should be repealed.

This gave the false impression of two against two. In fact, nine organisations did not object. The Mansion House Association was a member of the TCCT. This was effectively double counting. As the BRF, shipping interests, mining industry, docks, canals, etc numbered members in tens of thousands, the "vote" was overwhelmingly in favour of non publication!

On April 5th, the MoT reported to the Cabinet that he had received a Report from the Chairman of the TAC, and said it was being carefully reviewed by his [MoT] officers, and he hoped to put a paper before Cabinet shortly after the Easter recess.

May 11th, Memo to Cabinet, CP 109 [39] SECRET, entitled: "Railways Square Deal Campaign". The Paper included the following key points:-

Para 4: The existing rates system was devised when railways had a virtual monopoly of inland transport. The situation has been radically altered by the development of road transport.
Para 5: The TAC recommended the existing structure be abandoned.
Para 6: Publication of rates - Railways will contest a proposal that they should be required to do more than they have volunteered, namely to make their charges known on appropriate commercial lines. It does not seem possible to accept the claim of railways in this respect - that they should be put on the same footing as other transport. The Traders Co-ordinating Committee on Transport is justified in contending that all rates and charges should be published.
Para 8: No agreement was reached with mining, possibly because of conflicting interests within coal mining itself.
Para 12: Legislation must refer to Conferences to give them legal standing.
Para 13: Railway Companies would be required to apply for a Certificate that the Conference or Conferences are appropriate. The Tribunal is not suitable, it would need to be done by a Government Department, presumably Board of Trade, Ministry of Agriculture, or Scottish Departments. (Certificates were a piece of bureaucracy not deemed necessary by the TAC, and would have delayed overdue action further. Other Trade Associations did not need Government certificates to enable them to function).
Para 19: Departure from past practice contains risks which can only be revealed by events.
Para 23: Will need to strengthen Ministry staff engaged on checking abuses [in Road Transport] e.g. excessive hours of driving.
Para 25: An efficient transport system cannot exist side by side with competitive rate cutting. Any increase in rail charges must be agreed with traders or by the Tribunal.
Para 36: The Bill will still be contentious.
Para 37: Railway companies have stressed the urgency - Government will pressed to act. The whole question is so complex - it involves consideration of a century of railway and canal legislation - that even if Parliamentary time was available, I doubt whether it would be possible to prepare a Bill in time for it to receive proper consideration this session. Action should be taken as early as possible and the necessary legislation prepared so as to be ready for introduction at commencement of next session. (It was a gross exaggeration to say that so much legislation had to be considered - railways had prepared a very short list of what needed to be repealed).

I [the MoT] ask :-
[a] Authority and direction be given for the preparation of a Bill to be introduced at the commencement of next session.

[b] Authorisation to announce at once that the Government accepts the Report in broad principle. Whilst specific proposals require careful examination and consideration, it is intended to introduce legislation as soon as possible.

He added that he needed to determine points not covered in the Report which must be settled before a Bill could be prepared. (As his staff had directed the TAC Chairman and edited the Draft Report, there should have been no points to determine. The file contains no record of his "points" nor of any action on them).

Approval was given for a Press announcement:-

"At an early stage, Railways modified their demands. There will be no change in the 'Reasonable Facilities' provisions, or through rates and Standard Conditions. There will be regular meetings with Trade Associations. Railways will make reasonable charges as they thought fit, subject to the right of traders to appeal". (Modifying demands was "Hobson's choice" - Government would not agree to their original demands).

Legislative delay unjustified
Government was expeditious in other matters

A meeting took place on 16th May between the DoT and Railway companies which talked of war compensation as well as the Square Deal, "because of work on [war control], compensation is no longer academic". (Conveniently, the Square Deal began to take a back seat).

There is no reason to believe that the War precluded action. Government moved quickly enough in passing complex Defence Laws but were paralysed by this Crisis. They quickly established, before the war that Railways would play a vital part in evacuation, and could move 100,000 persons per hour from London, on top of the movement of war and industrial traffic, and millions travelling to work by train. Railways moved 1.3m evacuees in the first four days of September 1939.

Four weeks before War was declared, Government found time to pass the 50 page BOAC Act, which did not exercise any control over their charges. (The Railways' just and moral claim required a one page Act). A 1939 Act created the BOAC and enabled it to acquire certain air transport undertakings. Under Sec 2, they were given pricing freedom: "It is the duty of the Corporation to operate services at reasonable charges". (There was no provision for a Tribunal, certificated Associations, appeals or public inquiries!). Sec. 24: Government would make Grants [subsidies] up to 31st March 1941.

They found time long before they knew that the War could be won, to plan post war housing, debate a post-war health and welfare plan and improve Civil Service leave: Cabinet Minutes in July & August 1941: "Civil Servants should be given an extra weeks leave". They also found time to draft and pass the Restoration of Pre-War Trade Practices Act, 1942, to restore restrictive practices in industry to persuade "craft" unions to accept "unskilled" labour on wartime work!

A Railway [Charges] Act could have been passed in 1939 or prepared ready to implement at the end of the war, for this problem was not going to go away and would only get worse. During the War, Government was thinking ahead about the pressing need for post war exports to repay enormous debts and pay for the welfare state. Ensuring that rail did not lose more traffic to road, after the war, would have released road vehicles for export and killed two birds with one stone. Railways only sought legal equality with their competitors. Government could have prepared legislation to implement this overdue moral change.

The demand for equality could have been dealt with more swiftly, had the Government had the inclination to be fair. "Much of the time of the TAC Inquiry was taken up with the co-ordination aspect. In view of the large measure of agreement, the view was widely held that legislation to implement TAC recommendations would be introduced immediately. There was widespread disappointment when the MoT announced it would be next session, which transpired to mean March 1940 at the earliest". [Railway Gazette, vol. 70, Page 965].

Postscript

In 1943, Lord Leathers said that whatever the merits of competition in stimulating enterprise and efficiency, if it was carried so far as to undermine the stability of services essential to the community and commercial interests its effects would prove damaging to the national interest. If railways are deprived of higher grade traffics by road competition, they must increase rates in other traffic or sink into financial oblivion. The rail-road problem remained the main one which must be solved. The war had made it clearer than ever that railways were a national asset which must be retained in full efficiency. It followed that the financial position of railways must be firmly established. We could not allow so vital a service to be starved of proper maintenance and improvements owing to shortage of funds or inability to raise new capital. It could be achieved by rationalisation or by creating conditions in which railways could operate on a reasonable profit margin. Shortly before the war, Captain E. Wallace, speaking on behalf of the Government, promised legislation to implement the TAC recommendations on the railways "Square Deal". Those proposals fell short to reach the root of the problem. Both the TAC and Government regarded them as a stop gap. He did not believe that the "Square Deal" proposals put forward by railways before the War could by themselves solve the trouble. If it should be appropriate post war to proceed with those proposals he was convinced that some more radical solution had to be found. He had no suggestions to make.
[HoL Hansard vol. 129, cols. 383-4].

Within a few years, his Party jettisoned these commitments. He referred to the railways' Square Deal proposals but these had never been entertained. He was really referring to the TAC's pale substitute, which the Government also rejected.

The Fawkner Committee which had been set up arising from the Square Deal: "To investigate and produce, as soon as possible, a classification and national rates structure applicable to the road haulage industry based on standard conditions of service". The Committee rejected the railway classification and proposed to classify by weight. The Interim Report made "No commitment", but said that after two years work, there were many years work ahead. [Modern Transport, 24th November 1945].

Rates freedom should have been embraced in the 1947 Act. Giving post war railways freedom to decide their own prices in line with other industry, especially suppliers, would have been just. Instead, Government compelled BR to devise Charges Schemes which would be subject to Public Inquiry in a Court of Law - the Transport Tribunal - to prevent BR exercising monopolistic powers railways had lost 30 years earlier!.

PART IV

THE RIP - OFF

"Railways were taxed three times - by Government taking 50% of net revenue, by withholding all revenue over the Standard Revenue, and by Excess Profits Tax.
No other industry was so heavily penalised".

[Lord Stamp, LMS 1941 AGM].

Having failed to prevent war or protect the country against attack, Government exploited railways to bail them out. This is no overstatement. Military experts and historians had known since 1830, that railways were indispensable to the conduct of war.

In 1914, with 120 railways to integrate and horse and cart the alternative, there were practical, but no moral grounds for sequestration. In 1939, the UK lacked the finance for war, and again sequestrated railways (to contain War costs). It was not justified on practical or moral grounds, as railways had been given no funds by Government, whose inertia and anti-rail policies had denied them adequate profits to service capital and fund improvements. The £0.8m or so refunded interest on the loan to help unemployment was as nothing compared to rail investment of £1 billion. A liaison organisation to prioritise traffic would have sufficed. Government did not take control of, nor integrate, nor seize profits of 60,000 road hauliers, (see Chapter 13). Railways integrated freight working before the war - hauliers had nothing similar long after the war started. Rail operations remained in railway hands from top to bottom. Government had no grounds to seize the lions share of the silver lining emerging from behind the cloud which had overshadowed railways since 1921, which Governments created and obstinately refused to remove.

Their wartime meanness scaled new peaks. Having advised railways in 1937 of the importance of ARP, calculated to cost £5.25m, Government said Railways should cover part as a good employer, (but political failures led to the war). Government would pay up to £4m, but cut it through 50% to 25%, which it paid from fat sums gained from railway sequestration. Blocking the "Square Deal" kept the cost of sequestration down.

The documents referred to are from PRO : MT6/2604, except where shown in the text.

Preliminary discussions

The Committee for Imperial Defence [CID], approved a recommendation by the Chiefs of Staff in 1934 that committees on transport should proceed on the basis of a possible war with Germany in 1939. [Savage Page 51].

1937

Talks on Wartime Control started in earnest.

2nd April. Internal [unsigned] DoT Memo to Deputy Secretary, (seemed by its tone to be from the Permanent Secretary): In view of the decision by the Committee for Imperial Defence as to control of railways, it is necessary :-

[1] To draft an instrument giving the MoT necessary powers.

[2] To settle in general terms the basis of Compensation which we are *prepared* to offer [for sequestration], and to which we should endeavour to get the railways agreement. Deputy Secretary to form a small committee - comprising himself, Hill, Page, Feirn, with Roke as secretary. [The first meeting took place on April 9th].

Two weeks later, Hill summarised the Kyffin Taylor Report on War Compensation :-

Receipts - Anticipations of 1914 that rail receipts would diminish, during Control, were falsified and receipts were greatly increased. (Had traffic fallen, Railways would have carried Government traffic at bargain rates!). Recommends no payment of arrears of maintenance until the end of the Control Period.

ARP - Railway Companies are prepared to take the risk of damage to railway property which may be very great and will not spend in peacetime. (From a Government which had not invested in adequate defence, this is rich criticism). If Government guarantees net receipts, it will pay all costs. Will also pay for damage pending ARP, which may have been avoided. It is prudent for Government to pay in peacetime for essential precautionary measures. The Committee for Imperial Defence recommended that Government should be prepared to spend up to £5m towards measures estimated to cost £10m. (During the war, they recovered most of these costs - see pages 126 & 139).

Fire - Insurance needed against fire caused by aerial bombardment of which a plane can carry 4-5,000 incendiary bombs which are quite inextinguishable.

Basis for Compensation - Guarantee of net receipts over the preceding three calendar years. In default of Agreement*, it had to be determined by the Railway & Canal Commission under proposed Regulations by a special Tribunal. Government should bear the cost of making good aerial damage. (This was soon changed - see pages 133 & 139).

It may be necessary to send locos and wagons overseas. (They were already deciding to use assets they didn't own in lieu of military assets they had been too mean to fund)

*When there was disagreement, there was no arbitration. (see pages 132 & 142).

On 27th October, the Board of Trade wrote to the DoT: In the last war, railway rates were frozen, shipping rates increased tremendously and railways were overburdened. Queries DoT plans regarding rail rates in any future war. On 10th November. Hill replied: It is useless to forecast.

On 14th December, at a meeting between Browett/Wedgwood/Wood: Railways thought an average of revenue based on the last two years was too low, as earnings were rising. Government thought Standard Revenue was too high. Browett suggested that Railways formulate a case based on being no worse off at the end of the Control Period, only by reason of Government Control, not because of the effects of a War. [PRO : RAIL424/15].

1938

The 4th Meeting of DoT's Departmental Committee on 15th February discussed terms of compensation. Feirn preferred to leave the settlement until the emergency arose, as it would enable Government to secure better terms. The Committee agreed to wait railway proposals, but discussed whether railway bookstall rents should be included!

Whilst Government played pass the parcel from 1937, the Cabinet decided to subsidise the Bacon industry by £5m over three years. [Cabinet Minutes, February]

On 31st March, The RCA Secretary wrote to Wedgwood: Compensation should be based on Standard Revenue. The 1921 Act imposed an obligation on the RRT to ensure Standard Revenue was earned. It was not achieved because of loss to road and also to shipping. If these two were removed, railways will earn Standard Revenue easily. Under an Emergency, both will be crippled. If Railways are taken over they will easily earn Standard Revenue. [PRO : RAIL424/15].

On 18th May, the RCA wrote to the DoT: "Railways propose Standard Revenue should be paid, and objected to Government participation in earnings already limited by Statute, and asked Government to make War damage good". (Whilst Government schemed to exploit railway assets at minimum cost, they bought lorries in profusion for HM Forces).

Hill's Memo of 10th August updated developments: The Railway proposal for Standard Revenue can hardly be taken seriously. Railway contentions that in an emergency, railways would be in a position to earn revenues in excess of Standard seems to be fantastic. There would, no doubt, be increased Government traffic, but on the other hand:-

[a] A falling off of normal traffic. (but see reference to increased coal - page 153).

[b] Increased working costs.

[c] War damage.

We must reject the proposal for Standard Revenue. Arrears of Maintenance to be paid at the end of the Control Period, and be on the basis of the price ruling when it was made and limited to net arrears.

Hills's Memo of April 1937 and the Board of Trade letter in October, both of which forecast increased traffic, were in the same file. On 15th August, Hill's further Memo recorded: The railways are disposed to avoid coming to grips with the compensation issue until the emergency arises. They may say they are being asked to buy a pig in a poke.

In mid September, A Memo to Hill (from Browett?): Have seen Wedgwood. Railways are unable to accept our view that in time of emergency, they would not be working even to the degree they had been working in the last few years. Railways said the emergency would throw considerably increased volume onto railways. At the moment, road transport is carrying a third [of merchandise], but railways said the bulk would have to go back on rail. The DoT view is that any transfer from road would be offset by losses in other directions. Wedgwood could not accept that view, and said there would be considerably greater demand than at present. He said they would wait until the evidence emerged.

The "DoT view" was advanced, despite the fact that they were aware that 1914-18 experience was to the contrary. There were no grounds, nor industrial production data in the file to justify a different conclusion in respect of the next war. Their objective was clearly to seek ways to hold down the cost of sequestration. (see DoT Paper - page 96).

1939

On 7th July, after repeated letters since March 1938, from the RCA regarding the payment for wartime control of railways, the DoT replied: "I am still unable to reply........ I am doing my very best to get it settled". Eleven days later the DoT wrote again: "Am doing my very best to get it [Compensation for Control] settled. [PRO : RAIL424/15].

Two days later, an LMS Memo of a Meeting with the DoT: Browett said only the previous afternoon had he been placed in a position to discuss compensation. (DoT files contained no document to confirm this). He said Government proposed variable compensation - a minimum fixed on pre-war profits plus a share of profits over that. Government could not accept Railways profiteering during an emergency by securing profits greater than in normal times. Railways intervened to point out that a 4.7% return was not profiteering. Browett withdrew "profiteering". Taxation was brought up by the DoT, but Railways said it was irrelevant - tax is raised after profits are declared, and that Standard Revenue had not been achieved owing to the administrative actions of the Government since passing the 1921 Act. No other industry had profits so restricted and further restriction during a period of intensive use was illogical. Railways said Standard Revenue could be earned and adjusted in accordance with Sec. 59 so as to add 20% of the surplus to the Standard Revenue. Browett said he would get back to them as soon as possible, but was on holiday on 4th August. (War was weeks away!). [PRO : RAIL424/15].

At the next meeting on 1st August, the DoT floated a concept which would guarantee Railways a minimum of £34m, rising to £38m, if earned; with 50% of net profits up to £45.5m and 20% over £45.5m. [PRO : RAIL424/15].

The Prices of Goods Act 1939 permitted businesses, but not railways, to increase prices to reflect cost increases. Independent arbitration would hear industrial and trade appeals. Had the Square Deal been conceded, and the 1921 Act provisions on charges repealed, this Act would have been applicable to railways. (see page 159).

On 1st September, the MoT took control of Main Line, LPTB and minor railways under the Emergency Powers [Defence] Act 1939, Defence Regulation 69, to remain in force (enabling Government to move demobilised troops free of charge) for a minimum of a year after the end of the war, (actually extended to $2^1/_2$ years!). This differed from the 1871 Act under which possession was taken of Railways in 1914, but the effects were similar. Railways were to be run on behalf of Government by a Railway Executive Committee [REC] of Railway GM's. Chairman: Sir R. Wedgwood (LNER retired CGM), Sir J. Milne [GWR], G. H. Newton [LNER], F. Pick [LPTB], G. S. Szlumper [SR], Sir Wm. Wood [LMS]. As in the Great War, their salaries and those of staff seconded from railways were paid by the railways! [Wedgwood resigned in 1941 and was replaced by Anderson]. The REC left individual companies to carry on day-to-day affairs in their own way and intervened only in matters arising from the war when it has been essential for all companies to take common action. ["Coming of Age", Page 38].

The next day, Milne [Chairman, GM's Conference] wrote to the DoT: As Government have taken Control, it is necessary to come to an early decision on compensation terms. [PRO : RAIL424/15].

Formal Control Agreement Negotiations

On 4th October, Railways submitted detailed proposals repeating their request for Standard Revenue, saying 4.7% was not an excessive return, a contractor would want 5%.

On 8th November, Browett told railways that Government was unable to accept the basis suggested by them. DoT considered there should be a partnership between Government and railways, whereas under Railway proposals, companies were not concerned with net revenue nor would they incur a risk. [PRO : RAIL424/15].

They did not seek a partnership when revenue was falling due to creaming-off by road hauliers. Their timing was impeccable. This unique partnership required £1 billion of railway assets, reserves and manpower, Government contributed nothing. New assets required for Government purposes, would, if used by railways for revenue earning purposes be subject to a rental! (see page 122).

An LMS Memo dated 8th November: Railways were told Government could not accept the basis suggested, and that there should be a partnership between Government and Railways. Railway Solicitors argued that in a partnership, unlike this one, profits are divided after, not before tax. Government is dividing before tax. They pointed out that Railways are entitled to keep 20% over Standard Revenue. Government decided to include the LPTB in the financial arrangements, despite protests that this would shift the burden of decline in LPTB revenue to be made good by Rail freight receipts. Main Line Railways accepted joint direction of Railways & LPTB, but compensation should be separated. The

LMS harboured doubts about Government sincerity on charges, and observed that reducing passenger facilities to handle Government and other freight traffic would cause revenue loss. Government is silent on destruction of Railways goodwill by loss of net revenue earning services during the control period and upon decontrol when revenue earning would be slow to recover. Solicitors point out that in the Finance Act [2], 1939 Government excluded 1938 as unreal for Excess Profits Tax [EPT], and should do so for Railways. [PRO : RAIL424/15].

On the same day, an Internal DoT Memo set out a Draft Control Agreement:-
Sums for lost ships and assets will be paid into a Trust Fund. Final liability for War Damage not to exceed £10m for a single year. Government are prepared to give a definite undertaking that rates, fares and charges will be raised promptly to meet variations in working costs - wage rates, price levels and operations under war conditions. Also to include staff allowances to men in the Armed Forces*. Maintenance charges will be adjusted for prices in excess of those ruling in the base period, and the Expenditure Account is to be charged with the additional cost. [PRO : MT47/276].

*This principle was to apply in industry and the Civil Service. The word "promptly" was dropped in a later Draft, but restored when Railways objected.

The GM's Conference wrote to the DoT on 16th November: Your proposals are much less favourable than in 1914, although assets are greater and efficiency greatly improved. We object to including the LPTB and minor railways. The Government share in profits was not in accordance with the 1921 Act. They questioned the basis for fare and rate increases in the absence of Standard Net Revenue which is the ceiling. [PRO : MT47/276].

On 21st November, the RCA wrote to the MoT: It would be suicidal to encourage road transport at the expense of crippling the railways [due to the expectation of War]. They asked for a review of Government policy of asking road and rail for the cheapest rate, as road would know by how much to undercut rail. (see page 96).

An LMS Board Minute for 28th November reads: If Government act up to their undertaking to raise charges to meet increased costs, it is unlikely that the minimum will be operative, unless there is a wilful subsidising of industry. [PRO : RAIL424/15]

At the end of November, the MoT replied to Milne's letter of 16th November: [PRO : MT47/276 & RAIL 424/15]:

<u>Financial arrangements for Government Control of main line railways & LPTB</u>

- Charges will be those in operation at the outbreak of war, modified from time to time, so as to be not less than those required to meet variations in working costs and the cost of meeting War Damage on the basis agreed. Government traffic charges will be fixed broadly on the same consideration as apply to large commercial concerns. (They were referring to Agreed Charges - see pages 75, 76 & 125).
- Adjustments of charges shall be made promptly.
- Works ordered by, or for the use of the Government will be paid for. If they have a revenue earning value, Railways may be charged rent.

- Regarding the "Remuneration for loss of revenue for property requisitioned for non railway purposes - hotels, steamers, etc., - for which no provision is made under the Compensation Act", Government will remunerate Companies and LPTB in accordance with the Compensation [Defence] Act 1939 and the sums so secured should be brought to credit in the Control Account. (In which Government shared).
- Regarding the question of "Provision for loss of revenue at the end of the Control period owing to non return of rolling stock, steamers and other assets", this is "Outside the terms of Compensation"!

Government considered it equitable that they should share in excess net revenue.

(No reason was advanced. In contrast, when railways objected to including the LPTB in the War Compensation, the DoT gave a long though irrelevant explanation They did not share in hauliers' profits).

An LMS Memo on the proposed Financial Arrangements read [PRO : RAIL424/15] :

[1] Substituted arrangements [for the 1921 Act] are inadequate.

[a] Increased costs restricted to post 31st August 1939. Increased revenue will offset increases in costs. (Costs had been increasing as war threatened).

[b] Decision on charges increases will be by the MoT, not a Court of Law.

[c] Separate treatment of Government traffic.

The combined effect of the above will seriously reduce earnings and net revenue.

[2] Inclusion of LPTB - which is having a traffic fall off, particularly by road, will be subsidised by rail freight. Statutory London pooling of revenue between main line railways & LPTB, has no bearing. Their inclusion will reduce net revenue.

(The LPTB Act required LPTB and main line railway passenger revenue in the LPT Area to be pooled, and then shared between the five undertakings).

[3] Reduced passenger facilities to facilitate Government and other freight traffic will automatically reduce receipts, costs will remain. Under the 1921 Act, the deficiency would transfer to freight. The proposed system bars this and depletes earnings.

[4] Requisitioning of steamers, hotels, locos, rolling stock and other assets reduces net revenue.

[5] Retention of reserves for future renewals in a Trust Fund outside Railway control will have a damaging effect when prices of stocks and materials rise. Railways will be busier than ever, but earning less, by Government action, and below levels settled by Parliament.

[6] War risk provisions are unclear. (This was probably deliberate, giving the Government an opportunity to renege on the Agreement later).

[7] Payment for lost ships and assets taken over by Government are not to be made to railway companies but thrown into a Trust Fund and be received in the light of "*existing relevant liabilities*". (A phrase which was not explained).

[8] ARP costs are not to be treated as working expenses under Sec. 40 of the Civil Defence Act, but met out of Net revenue - i.e. reduced dividends.

Such reduced revenue is then to be further reduced by a profit sharing scheme with Government which is tantamount to a special tax, and then further by EPT. Each of these reductions is in law, a charge in arriving at net revenue, but Government claim the contrary, thus further depleting earning power. There are many matters of doubt which

Government are not even prepared to agree to, nor to a machinery for settling differences. Standard Net Revenue is already restricted by law to about 4.75% return.

On 11th December the RCA wrote to the MoT [PRO : RAIL424/15]:

1. Base Period: We do not accept inclusion of 1938 - the return was 2.18%, and apart from 1926 - General strike year - and 1932 - severe depression, was the lowest since 1921. Earnings have declined due to unfair road competition.

2. Why should railways alone be subjected to entirely special treatment in a triple limitation of profit:

[a] Statutory 1921 Standard Revenue.

[b] 50% sharing of profits above a certain level, but below Standard Revenue.

[c] by EPT of 60% after [a] and [b] have operated.

This is highly discriminatory treatment.

3. What actually is the "worth" of the minimum guarantee or the real risk and cost of it to Government? Revenue falling below the minimum can arise in only two ways:

[i] Ordinary trading results.

[ii] War damage.

Under [i] if railways have reasonable freedom commercially and are not used to subsidise the other economic activities of the country, and if Government make a reasonable and prompt use of the charging powers belonging to railway companies by Statute, the risk of deficiency is negligible.

Under [ii] War damage can easily be covered by an insurance fund of 5% increase in charges yielding £10m pa which if unused can be returned to the public. The Government are not assuming any risk.

4. Inclusion of LPTB. There are no terminal facilities for freight on LPTB. Railway companies operate all goods trains over their lines. Under present conditions London suburban passenger receipts are in heavy decline. LPTB is entirely dependent on passengers. Railway companies freight will subsidise losses LPTB are now incurring. Whilst joint direction by Government may apply, compensation should be separated. [Government had tried to claim a case for merged compensation because a few goods trains ran over LPTB lines]. Whilst the REC recommended take-over of minor railways, they did not envisage inclusion in main line railway compensation. (Government would have had to subsidise LPTB).

We would accept a fixed rental if it were sufficiently high and subject to a satisfactory settlement of Excess Profits Tax. [LMS Board Minute, 15th December]. [PRO : RAIL424/15].

1940

At a meeting on New Years Day, Milne opposed the take-over of POW's as distinct from making them common user and so far as the GWR was concerned objected to the financial transactions in connection therewith. [PRO : RAIL424/16].

Two weeks latter, Browett told Railways he was prepared to concede 1935-6-7 as the base and add £1m to the 1937 figure. Railways pointed out that they had not been consulted on charges for POW's. [PRO : RAIL424/16].

Had it not been for the farce of the Tribunal procedure, railway revenue would have been £3m higher in 1937. (see page 99).

An LMS Board Minute of 19th January recorded: Propose accepting Government scheme. It is difficult to *publicly* take the ground, that the Government, having now solemnly promised in their scheme to increase rates on lines absolutely agreed by us in order to maintain that revenue and offset increased costs, we disbelieve their bona fides, their intentions or their ability. I like less the prospects of litigation or the tender mercies of the House [of Commons]. [PRO : RAIL424/16].

Five months after sequestration, and three years after talks began, the financial arrangements were published, described as the "Control Agreement", In 1941, this "Agreement" was arbitrarily replaced, and thereafter the 1940 "Agreement", was known as the "First Control Agreement". "Appropriate charges" were to be made for Government traffic - implying on the low rather than the high side, confirmed when Government announced it had "negotiated" reductions of 10-33% for freight traffic, whilst enjoying 50% reductions for military and other Government travel. [PRO : MT47/278].

(Agreed Charges for industry, with high volume, were based on average rates, not average less 33%. The terms contravened the 1854 Act on Undue Preference, and the 1933 Act on Agreed Charges. Goods supplied on Government Account by industry were despatched at reduced Government rates, and charged to Government - this would include goods, which pre-war were supplied by industry, delivery paid).

The Control Agreement [Cmd 6168]

Receipts [excluding railway owned road transport and Irish interests] to be pooled and divided:

1. To be paid average net revenue for 1935-6-7, [LPTB: year ending 30th June 1939] shared: LMS: 34%, LNER: 23%, GWR: 16%, SR: 16%, LPTB: 11%; - Total £40m.

2. Of the balance £3.5m will be paid to them on the same basis.

3. If the Pool exceeds £43.5m, the balance will then be equally divided between Government and railways until £68.5m is reached. Shares of individual main line railway companies will not exceed the 1921 Standard Revenue.

4. Net revenue above £68.5m to go to the Government. At this level, the five undertakings will receive £56m guaranteeing a minimum return on capital of 3.3% and may envisage up to 4.7%".

5. Rates, fares and charges would be adjusted promptly to meet working costs.

6. Costs of restoring war damage, some essential at once, up to £10m pa were to be charged to expenditure [before the net revenue was calculated].

11. The MoT and the Companies may propose a revision for any cause, of a major character, and, ***if agreed***, the arrangements shall be revised accordingly.

Standard Net Revenue should have been the base for railways, which, by law, was £51.4m pa [plus 20% of any surplus], or there should have been no ceiling. An avaricious Government wanted it both ways, having done nothing to justify a share of the cake. They decreed that Railways would only get the Statutory revenue after Government picked up £12.5m [£68.5m - £43.5m = £25m; 50% = £12.5m]. Railways and the LPTB would share £56m. The surplus should have reimbursed railways for 16 years of reduced profits [below those prescribed in the 1921 Act], due to Government inertia over the rates issue, and for handling increased war traffic and traffic diverted to rail from sea and road by the MoT.

At the very least they were entitled under Sec. 59.3 of the Act to 20% of any excess over £51.4m, with the balance returnable to all users, not to the Government.

On 7th February, the MoT described the Agreement as coherent, logical and reasonable. [Hansard vol. 357, col. 222].

By definition, the Second "Agreement" which later replaced it must have been the converse - incoherent, illogical and unreasonable.

On 23rd April, the MoT recapped the "Great War" situation, adding: "In this war, we decided to keep railways solvent. Uneconomic rail rates nearly bankrupted coastwise shipping in the last war. There has been a substantial falling off of LPTB revenue. He itemised price increases of materials [used by railways] of 22-78%. With no White Paper, the RRT would have given an increase in charges to produce the whole of the Standard Revenue. The only function of the RRT abrogated was to see that railways obtained £51m pa. The policy pursued in the last war put off the evil day. [Hansard, vol. 360, cols. 127-165].

Internal DoT Memo dated 6th June: The Control Agreement will have to be approved by the Treasury. Under Government Control the role of the RRT on charges will be suspended. The REC to estimate the quarterly effect of variations in costs and submit proposed increases in charges to the MoT. [PRO : MT47/276].

Criticisms of the Control Agreement

The LPTB will lean heavily on the Pool. It has already suffered from the War, as receipts have fallen due to evacuation and the blackout - a 15% reduction is not inconceivable. They face increased costs of £0.6m in petrol costs [alone]. Participation in the Pool is crucially important to the LPTB. [Economist, 10th February 1941, Page 255].

"Railways were taxed three times - by Government taking 50% of net revenue, by withholding all revenue over the Standard Revenue, and by Excess Profits Tax. No other industry was so heavily penalised". [Lord Stamp, LMS 1941 AGM].

"£2-3m for ARP was repayable when guaranteed Net Revenue [£40m] is exceeded". i.e. It is clawed back from Clause 2 of the Agreement. [GWR 1941 AGM].

In the absence of the Control Agreement, Railways & LPTB would have been earning £55.2m. [Hansard vol. 360, col. 127].

May 10th. Unsigned Internal DoT Memo : War conditions have reduced LPTB earning power. [PRO : MT47/276]

The LMS wrote to the MoT on 11th May pointing out that interest on capital is a cost [The DoT had not included it], and that the word "promptly" was left out of the Draft Control Agreement - on the item dealing with increases. [PRO : MT47/276].

Increases in Charges

The Agreement specified that charges would be increased promptly to match increased costs. In March 1940, the REC asked for a 10% increase in charges. The MoT approved it, from 1st May 1940, but asked the Charges Consultative Committee [RRT in disguise], to advise on the best way to get 10% in LPTB road fares, [short distance fares would be difficult to raise by exactly 10%]. They held a Public Inquiry in May 1940, and made recommendations to the MoT, which he authorised on 26th June for implementation on 3rd July. [PRO : MT47/277].

In August, the REC called for a further increase in charges of 6.8% on existing rates and fares, which with 10% already granted [in April], would make 17.5% over pre-war charges. The MoT asked the Consultative Committee for advice and they held a 10 day Public Inquiry, which concluded on September 11th, attended by 35 local authorities and others, who requested postponement. Objectors included the BI&SF, NFU, Mining Association and the Traders Co-ordinating Committee on Transport. Objectors said that "Government traffic was carried too cheaply. It is arguable that Government is paying less than commercial rates on its traffic". The Committee reported back on September 18th and recommended that fares should increase to $16^{2}/_{3}$% above pre-war - the first increase had lifted them to 10% above pre-war - but that Season and Workmen's rates and all LPTB fares should not be increased. The MoT told Parliament on October 23rd: There will be no increase in Workmen or Season tickets, but a 6% increase will go on all other charges.

Between 1937 and 1946, the only two rail price increases were subject to Public Inquiries - with invasion threatened!.

The provision that [rail] charges may be adjusted to meet variations in working costs is not distinguishable from the "cost plus" arrangement in operation for pricing Government contracts with controlled undertakings or industry in general. The Railway "spiral" is a manifestation of a more extensive spiral. The clamour against proposed fares increases might be more validly and effectively directed against the whole system of Government contracting in which, in effect, every variable element is controlled except the most important. Suggestions that railways have been put in a more advantageous position are not supported by the facts. Their stockholders are no better placed than the proprietors of any other undertaking - controlled or uncontrolled. [Times, 16th August, 8a].

In 1941, the Rates Tribunal sat on ten occasions to consider applications for Exceptional Rates for which its' consent was required, on four occasions to consider requests to alter the GCM and to deal with questions of rebate under the Railway Freight Rebates Scheme. Since Industry could, under the Prices of Goods Act, 1939, increase prices to cover cost increases, applying to reduce rates was unnecessary, but it ensured their post-war position was safeguarded - unlike that of railways.

The Traders Traffic Conference asked the Government to cancel the 1940 freight rate increases. [Modern Transport, 18th July 1942]. (see page 148 for a different attitude on road charges).

Unlike Railways, traders were permitted to pass on increased costs and as the law prohibited greater profits than pre-war, the purpose of objecting was unclear. They did not ask for road rate increases, which were uncontrolled, to be cancelled. [See Chapter 13].

A solemn Agreement broken

On 23rd August 1940, the Railway Gazette wrote of a possible revision of the Agreement. They thought it doubtful that it could usefully be done whilst major items of cost remain uncontrolled. (This indicates a leak in wartime security!).

The ink was barely dry on the "Agreement", before Government became dissatisfied with its first grab at windfall profits - so they reneged and went back for a bigger slice.

"The old policy of encouraging traffic onto the railways had to be drastically modified". [Savage, Page 283]. So Government froze rail rates, whilst competitors' prices rose! A masterstroke. (see pages 128, 133, 139 & 167)

Manoeuvres to reduce the Compensation

On 19th September, LB [Browett] wrote to the Minister [PRO : MT47/276]:

1. The Cabinet has instructed you "To aim at limiting the Pool to £40m, and avoid any increase in railway charges, particularly fares". With the Chancellor, you are to look if there is a case for reducing the Government preference on the traffic rates, subject to no interference with privileges enjoyed by the Armed Forces.

2. It is impossible to forecast Net Revenue for 1940. £48m pa according to Railways, but I suggest it is exaggerated by £3m due to an underestimate for maintenance and should be £44m.

3. Useless to expect Railways to accept a flat guarantee of £40m. They certainly expect to be no worse off. In Railway circles, the Agreement is not regarded as being at all generous in view of the work the railways are doing.

4. LMS & LNER had opposed £42.5m.

5. Railway figures indicate a rate of £78m [Net Revenue] pa, but this could not be considered seriously, due to underestimated maintenance & extra seasonal traffic. *

6. Companies are in a strong bargaining position in view of Revenue being earned as a result of very heavy use of their undertakings. Nothing less than £44-45m is feasible

7. Railways are also entitled [if they accept a flat payment] to increases in costs not yet recovered - some £12m, of which half is payable to Government.

8. There is the question of compensation to be paid at the end of Control if charges are not maintained at an economic level and handed back in an insolvent condition. ***If not handed back***, what is to be Government policy in relation to railway charges. Are they to be subsidised permanently, or is a National system to begin with sudden, unpopular increase in rates and fares? This note is written on the assumption that the Cabinet has definitely decided against any increase in railway charges.

* The average net revenue from 1941 to 1945 inclusive was £76m, although there had been no increases in charges after 1940, so it is clear that the railways' figures should have been taken seriously. This presumption that railways were wrong persisted. (see page 166).

A month later, the Chancellor and the MoT prepared a Memo: Referring to criticism on increases recommended by the RRT and the "vicious spiral". It is our view of the first importance that Railways be maintained in a healthy economic state. The proposed increases do no more than offset increase in wages and other costs, which Railways incur through no fault of their own. Whether, after the War, Railways are brought under Government ownership or returned to their owners, difficult and costly problems will arise, as they did at the end of the last War. If Railways are not run on an economic basis during Control, Government would be faced with a large and continuing subsidy or a heavy increase in charges on the cessation of Control. If railway charges are artificially depressed as in the last war, the effect on other transport may be serious. We have examined the suggestion that the Railways should be tied to a fixed payment based on pre-war earnings with the object of limiting the net Pool to £40m. We think that the principle of the existing Agreement, which recognises that Railways are entitled to a *reasonable and modest* reward for efficient and economic working, is sound. This incentive would be lacking in a fixed guarantee. The detailed Agreement based on Cmd 6168 is practically complete, but needs to be revised due to War Compensation for Utilities which must clearly apply to railways. We recommend:-

[a] Effect should be given to recommendations of the Charges Consultation Committee [RRT]. The longer this is delayed, the greater becomes the "lag". (This indicates that the Committee had already recommended increased charges).

[b] The principle of the Agreement should be preserved, but modified in respect of the War Damage Compensation Scheme. [PRO : MT47/277].

In November, an unsigned DoT Memo referred to First War problems and added: Government decided, this time, Railways should be kept solvent and cost increases met by users. Subsidising railways [to keep charges static] to subsidise industry and travel irrespective of whether they contribute to the War Effort was deliberately rejected. ***It involved the risk of bankruptcy.*** Much additional War traffic is of an urgent character involving special working which seriously interferes with other services with costly adjustments. £6.75m is the increased cost of operations under war conditions, e.g. slowing down movement as a result of the blackout. Increased costs - wages: £20m, materials: £16m, staff in HM Forces: £3.75m. Government agreed railways should make up pay of staff [in HM Forces] on the same basis as civil servants. The guaranteed minimum net revenue - about £40m is sufficient to compensate railways & LPTB up to the ***modest*** level of pre-war earnings, but not for heavy additional traffic. They are not compensated for increased expenditure, which they are obliged to incur to carry increased traffic. Higher charges do not give additional profit, and do no more than reimburse money actually paid out. The Agreement provides for a gradual increase in charges currently and thus avoids the return of their property at the end of the War in an uneconomic condition. When War began, Railways had the ***right*** under the 1921 Act to have charges increased to Standard Net Revenue [£51m], not merely to offset cost increases, but to increase profits. Under the Agreement, this right is surrendered for the Control Period. It is unfair to saddle Railways with increased costs without increasing charges - ***that way lies bankruptcy or subsidy.*** The flat guarantee arrangement in 1914-18 cost the taxpayer £150m. ***Nationalisation of railways*** already dependent on subsidy, will perpetuate dependence on taxpayers, since no Government will willingly increase charges as a first result of nationalisation. It was severely criticised by the Colwyn Committee as failing to provide incentive as to efficiency and economy and after the War, charges had to be increased by 100%. [PRO : MT47/277].

The writer ignores the fact that throughout the period of control 1914-20, Government traffic was carried free of charge! The taxpayer had gained, not lost. The £150m was made up of £90m for the shortfall of net revenue 1914-20 against the 1913 guarantee, and a grossly inadequate £60m compensation for damage, abnormal wear & tear etc. [Hansard, vol. 365, col. 1768]; (see also pages 30-36).

Nine months after Government imposed the First "Agreement", Mr. Strauss, MP asked: "Is it the case that the only change contemplated in the present Agreement is a change arising from the War Damage clause and otherwise the main principle of the Agreement will stand?" Lt. Col. Moore-Brabazon [MoT]: "That is the present situation". [Hansard vol. 365, col. 1771].

His reply is at odds with DoT papers and with his own comments in the House of Lords (see pages 128 & 139).

Hind's Memo of 26th November to Browett Rail charges are only one coil in a vicious spiral and, if removed [artificially by subsidy] the spiral will continue so long as wages and prices rise; and the railway subsidy will increase accordingly. [PRO : MT47/276].

1941

Internal DoT Memo dated 5th January, by Hill: Railways are the world's largest owners of docks, hotels, and in the UK of road transport, steamships [130], canals [1,000 miles], factories, land, houses, property. Mergers of the main line railways & LPTB were being considered for implementation [during the War] to reduce profits to stockholders from £40m to £29m. In the First War, Government took possession, in this [War] they took control. [PRO : MT47/275].

Five days later, Browett wrote to the MoT "Railway charges are dragged in at the tail of the spiral rather than contribute to it". On the same day, Sturgess suggested returning the share [of net revenue] due to the Exchequer to railways. [PRO : MT47/277].

A Memo dated 15th January, [PRO : MT47/277] endorsed for use of the Minister, was passed forward with a covering note by LB [Browett]:

> "Railway increases are less than general price levels and much less than coal, iron, steel and timber", [which are 60% -100% compared to a proposed rail increase 31% over pre-war]. Government "liabilities for the LPTB and requisitioning of POW's* has been carried by the Pool [main line railway earnings], saving the taxpayer millions of pounds". Once the economic stability of railways is interfered with, it will be difficult to restore. This means: if they revert to their owners after the War, a substantial lump sum payment, plus compensation for loss of earning power and big increases in charges; or if they pass into public ownership, a severe and unfair handicap on the new Railway Authority. Advantages of a flat guarantee are illusory and there are certain inherent objections:-
>
> [1] Taxpayers will be prejudiced and railways ruined economically.
> [2] Disincentives to management and staff.
> [3] Less responsible use of railways by Government Departments.
> [4] Repercussions on other transport.

(* During the war, they were paid £38m and £85m respectively from the Pool).

Browett's covering Note read: I advocate maintaining the present Agreement, [subject to amending for War Damage]. If that is politically impossible, (identifying the real motive), the only alternative is a flat guarantee and I suggest it should apply from 1st January 1941. [PRO : MT47/277].

At the end of January, the Treasury wrote to the MoT: Railways should be told the Agreement needs revising due to War Damage. [PRO : MT47/277]. (More duplicity).

On 11th March, LB [Browett] wrote to the MoT : Told Hopkins [Treasury], the continuing state of uncertainty with the railways is deplorable. Railways had put in a claim two months ago for a further increase and we were not able to do anything about it. The position is really becoming impossible. [PRO : MT47/277].

Despite his personal views and recommendation, (see page 128), in his Budget Speech, the Chancellor publicly stated that railway prices would be pegged:

"The aim of 100% Excess Profits Tax was to ***take the profit out of war and .... that the increased production required by war would not become the means of enrichment as it did in the last war.*** 20% of the net amount of EPT paid at 100% will be refunded after the war for essential reconstruction and adjustment. The objective of a post war refund was for it to be spent on replacement of obsolete or unsatisfactory machinery etc. It would be treated as trading receipts and subject to income tax. To stem inflation it would be necessary to counteract a further rise in the cost of living, continue and extend the policy of stabilising, by means of subsidies, the cost of essential goods & services in order to prevent any further rise in the cost of living index, apart from minimum seasonal charges, above the present range of 125-130 in terms of the pre-war level. Consequently, the Exchequer would take over increases in shipping charges, including freight rates & insurance premiums and as transport costs were an important factor in determining the general price level, he was examining the question of Exchequer help in averting further increases in railway rates and fares. The general policy of restricting increases in prices to a minimum would apply to coal, gas, electricity, and articles in general use. "The burden on the Exchequer would be increased to minimise the impact of transport costs". Further essential goods and services are to be subsidised". [Hansard vol. 370, cols. 1297 & 1331).

Railways were impoverished in the Great War by Government, not enriched. Railway charges were subsidised by railway companies, not the Exchequer, and were 8-12 points below the level he quoted! Throughout the war, the Exchequer's "help in keeping rail fares and rates down" consisted of not paying a penny to railways, but drawing huge profits. Railways did not benefit after the war from EPT refunds. He made two inexplicable leaps: general prices to transport, and thence railways! No change was made in charges paid to owners of POW's, which affected rail traffic, nor in road haulage charges which were unrestricted. (see pages 144, 173, 152-156 and Chapter 13).

On 9th May, the Ministries of Shipping & Transport were merged into a Ministry of War Transport under Lord Leathers. [Keesing 4606B].

Hill wrote to Hurcomb on 18th May: The original view was that war damage costs should be passed on to users. Now the Exchequer will make them good after the War. [PRO : MT47/277].

On 4th June, the MoWT told Railway Chairmen: "Railways had given splendid help". On war damage, all public utilities should be dealt with in same way - and there are no exceptions for controlled undertakings. Holland-Martin said the existing Agreement had not been liked by Railways nor honoured by Government, which was going back on its word. The MoWT said it was not a fair way of putting it. [PRO : RAIL424/18]. DoT Meeting Notes referred to Railways' rejected proposals for compensation based on a percentage of gross receipts. Such a scheme was not excluded from consideration, but was not attractive to Government. (The underlined phrase was crossed out). [PRO: MT47/278].

On 17th June, Railways submitted proposals for a new Control Agreement of £50-55m. War Damage to May 18th totalled £13.25m. [PRO : MT47/278].

Three days later, Hurcomb led Rental discussions with the RCA, supported by Browett & Hill. Browett said it was agreed that the present Agreement should terminate. Wood [LMS] said it had not been agreed, and pointed out that the first 20 weeks of 1941 were a 100% improvement on 1940. He said that Government proposals on maintenance were unsound, and if Government was trying to subsidise users they should pay the Pool for it, as suggested by the Chancellor a couple of days ago. This was not favourably received by the DoT. (DoT representatives did not refute these comments nor produce evidence to the contrary). [PRO : RAIL424/18].

On 11th July, a Paper, WP [41] 158, was presented to the Cabinet:

"Future of Railways"

Need to revise the Present Agreement:

[1] Railways & LPTB guaranteed £40m. If another £3.5m is earned, they kept it, plus half of the additional Pool receipts over £43.5m up to £56m.

[2] Rates & fares to be adjusted to meet costs arising from the War.

[3] Cost of restoring War Damage up to a maximum of £10m in any full year charged to revenue expenditure and charges revised to meet such costs.

[4] After the end of 1940, either party might propose a revision of these arrangements for any cause of a *major* character, and if agreed, the arrangements should be revised accordingly.

Revision is inevitable by two developments:

[1] The Chancellor said in his Budget, as part of a policy of Stabilisation, he was considering how he could help avert further increases in rates & fares.

[2] The Chancellor's proposals for compensation for War Damage to Public Utilities provide for the State and the undertaking to pay half. For these and other reasons, my Committee agreed the Control Agreement must be revised. The Policy of stabilising railway rates involves substituting fixed remuneration. Under the Present Agreement, railways have a financial interest in securing efficiency and economy. If the new Agreement is made - how can efficiency and economy be obtained? One group declare in favour of post war unification, the other group favour more effective control. The MoWT was opposed to a post war statement - which would hinder the war effort, because the 1923 Amalgamation caused uncertainty among staff which caused chaos. There is no real evidence that managers pay regard to the interests of individual companies [rather than the national emergency].

War Damage was a minor cause, affecting one clause of the Agreement. Moreover, the Chancellor said: "The need to fight inflation and transport costs were an important factor in determining the general price level". Attention was directed on rail, the only sector already rigidly controlled, not on road, industry or canals, all free to increase, nor on the owners of POW's, so this was not a major cause. Government did not share profits of other Utilities, hence the reference to them was irrelevant. The effect of a new Agreement on efficiency and economy was unanswered.

"Stabilisation" of railway rates was embraced in the 1921 Act which required the Railway Rates Tribunal to reduce rates if the 1913 Standard Net Revenue was exceeded. This was a really a reduction which applied to no other industry, all of which were able to increase prices - otherwise the RPI and Industrial Price Indices would not have outstripped railway rate indices during the War. (see pages 131, 164, 167 , 186 & 187)

On 16th July, Col.. Llewellin: In view of Government's decision not to allow an increase of fares and freight rates, a modified agreement has become necessary. Asked to take into consideration the need to co-ordinate road & rail to promote the war effort, he said "That is a different matter". [Hansard vol. 373, col. 595].

Five days later, the MoWT spoke to the Cabinet on the review of the Agreement. "The [new] terms proposed represented a reasonable payment to the railways during the Control Period. Railway Chairmen agreed that new policies made it necessary to modify the present agreement as from January 1941". (They had not agreed - see page 132).

"When told that Government proposed to substitute a fixed payment for the existing Rental, Railways called for compensation not less favourable than under present terms. Arising from the Present Agreement with no charge for war damage and no 'lag' between increased costs and increased charges, there is an unbridged gap for 1940 of £11.8m plus £2m in 1939. Under that Agreement, this [gap] could have been closed. There can also be attributed £3.5m in 1940 to delay by Government on implementing an undertaking to increase charges promptly. Government failure to act on the Agreement to raise charges had cost the Railways about £13m and in 1941, Railways could earn under the existing Agreement as much as £57.2m". "Salient data is as follows:"

A	Standard Revenue under 1921 Act [now including LPTB].		£55.3m
B	Existing Minimum Guarantee		£39.4m
C	Current Net Revenue [Total & Railway Share]	Total	Railway
	[a] Pool earnings 1940 after charging £1.4m for War Damage	£42.3m	£42.3m
	[b] 1940 [notional] if War Damage excluded and increased costs		
	properly recovered by increased charges. *	£55.7m	£49.4m
	[c] 1941 on the same basis as [b] and if :-		
	[i] Net Revenue for first 20 weeks continues	£52.7m	£47.8m
	[ii] Increase in Net Revenue of first 20 weeks over		
	corresponding period of 1940 is maintained	£61.3m	£52.2m
	(* this was the basis enjoyed by all other industry)		

D. War Damage: "War Damage is to be treated as Capital, not working expenditure. [Treated as working expenditure, charges were raised accordingly]. Companies were told Government did not accept their view that whatever the scale of Damage, Government would continue to bear the first £10m in any full year, instead of a half as envisaged in the new Scheme. Companies pointed out that if the existing Scheme is kept, the economic stability of railways would be maintained by a continued adjustment of charges - this will cease if charges are pegged.

"Government regard £39.4m as appropriate. Railways were losers in 1940, due to delay in increasing charges - whilst the old Agreement was in force. (***It was still in force***). Government would be prepared to go to £42.3m, the profit shown in 1940 Accounts under the old Agreement, but may have to negotiate as far as £43m, which under the old Agreement, Railways are entitled to retain in full [without surrendering part to the Exchequer] if they earn as much".

(They were limited to £56m by the First Agreement. Note that his predecessor had supported retention of the existing agreement as ***reasonable and modest,*** and the MoT before his immediate predecessor had said it was logical and reasonable. The £10m War Damage was coming from increased railway profits. This change would increase Government's immoral share).

Having imposed an "Agreement" giving Railways & LPTB a maximum Rental of £56m in 1940, "Government [now, in 1941] regard as £39.4m as appropriate and favourable to Railways". The facts were known in 1940, hence it does not explain abrogation of the First "Agreement", which was less than Railways' legal entitlement under the 1921 Act. Laws, it appeared, were to be obeyed by Railways, not by Government The Agreement could be altered if both agreed there were major changes - but the Railways did not agree. (see page 132).

An Internal Memo dated 22nd July to Browett stated Railway rates for Government traffic would be below Standard Rates by 10% for Coal & classes 1-6, 15% for Classes 7-10, 20% for Classes 11-20, 33% for Explosives, and 33% for Motor spirit.
[PRO : MT47/278].

On 24th July, A Memo from the MoWT to the Cabinet said Net Pool profit in the first half of the year was £27.5m (despite static charges and rising costs). It might make it difficult to reach a settlement [on the fixed basis proposed]. [PRO : WP-41-173].

Incredibly, in the light of his Memo of 24th July, the MoWT told the Cabinet: Future revenue may be inadequate to pay the current minimum Rental of £40m. * The Cabinet wished to persuade Railways to agree, rather than impose a new Rental. The MoWT had told the Railway Companies that the Government proposed to substitute a fixed rental for the existing Agreement, because there were (unspecified) "major changes" affecting it. Government made it clear that the Agreement would be changed. Railways asked for £55m: Standard Revenue of £51m plus £4m for LPTB. "The Treasury would not go above £41.7m". This was raised to £43m, which the MoWT had told the Cabinet he was prepared to offer.

(* If there had been an inadequacy, it was due to Government's decision not to increase rail charges, contrary to the "Agreement" and contrary to principles which applied to all other industry But there was no inadequacy, net revenue for 1941 would exceed £43m by August).

At a meeting on 28th July between the MoWT, Civil Servants and Railway Chairmen, Royden recorded: that Government's intention to drop the previous Agreement and negotiate a new Agreement had no regard to the past or obligations already incurred. In these circumstances one could have little confidence in entering into any Agreements with the Government. Hurcomb was obviously embarrassed and uncomfortable when the terms were put to us. Royden said Railways would have to consult Stockholders. Llewellin was dismayed at the need to consult Stockholders and obviously did not relish the prospect. [PRO : RAIL 424/18].

The DoT Memo of the meeting records that Hurcomb told Railway Chairmen, Government may consider amalgamation or reorganisation after the War. (It was a clear warning to toe the line on Rental or face nationalisation). [PRO : MT47/278].

On the next day, Browett wrote to the Treasury : 50% of £2.9m paid as Grants for ARP, up to the end of 1940 under the Act, are to be repaid by the railways. [PRO : MT47/278].

An LMS Memo dated 30th July stated: "Understand Government reserve the right to revise the Agreement at any time. We need to query whether the railways will be handed back in an unimpaired physical condition". [PRO : RAIL 424/18].

RCA Notes of informal meeting on 7th August with Hurcomb, note that he decreed that the meeting was for "elucidation purposes - not bargaining" :-

Q: What is meant by "Control to end one year after the termination of the War?"

A: It means "A general armistice followed by cessation of hostilities. Government would consider a minimum period of two years thereafter.

Q: Are ARP payments affected.

A: "Payments for ARP will not be disturbed. Will be charged as a working expense". (That was changed retrospectively).

Railways told the DoT a minimum of £47.5m was justified but they would settle for £45m. [PRO : RAIL424/18].

LMS Memo dated 12th August:

- Under new proposals for War Damage, Companies are required to assume additional liability not exceeding £5m pa. The War Damage already incurred would impose an additional liability of £5m for the current year. This equals £2.5m to the Companies, hence we are being asked to accept a minimum of £38.5m against the present guarantee of £39.4m.
- The offer of £41m is £1m less than the net revenue for Companies for 1937 and less than 1940, [excluding War Damage].
- The additional cost of wages and prices is £4.25m. [PRO : RAIL 424/18].

The MoT had said on 23rd April 1940: In the absence of the First Agreement, Railways & LPTB would have been earning £55.2m, and the Rates Tribunal would have been bound to sanction the increase. Any trade or business is at present entitled to earn up to the amount of its average profits of 1936 & 1937 before it becomes liable to 100% Excess Profits Tax. Before the War, Railways were making sub standard profits, and would not have been liable for that Tax unless revenue was well above 1936/37. The new figure ought to be above the 1940 figure, not between that and existing minimum guarantee. Railways are otherwise subject to a double limitation on Revenue "unique and inequitable" to quote the late Lord Stamp. [Times, 15th August 1941]. (see foot of page 124).

A Memo for the LMS Board dated 15th August 1941 referred to a Draft RCA letter to the MoWT, recapitulating the situation:

1 The [Existing] Agreement followed lengthy negotiations and was embraced in a White Paper [Cmd 6168]. The Agreement had been unsigned pending passing the War Damage Act.
2. The Paper was debated in Parliament on 13th February 1940, and approved. It was endorsed by the Stockholders.
3. The Agreement by its terms, was not open to revision at the instance of any one of the parties against the other. Revision can be made for any cause of a major character. No revision can be made without the assent of all parties.
4. Browett told Railways on 16th January: that we: "Need not assume that any new arrangements will be any less favourable". Railways had agreed on 24th January that Government proposals for War Damage entitled the Government to propose ***some*** revision.
5. The former MoT, Lt. Col. Moore-Brabazon said in Parliament on 13th November: "The only change contemplated was in respect of War Damage, and that otherwise the main principles of the Agreement would stand". Railway Companies & LPTB have never agreed the proposals constitute a major cause entitling Government to propose a further revision of the Agreement. We are prepared to accept £43m with misgivings. It does not represent existing or potential earnings capacity. It is an accommodation in view of Government representations on the grounds of a National Emergency. We require an assurance that Government will afford time for charges to be adjusted under the 1921 Act and that records be kept to show what real earnings would have been under the First Agreement. [PRO: RAIL 424/18].
(I have found no trace of such records).

"The railways are doing a good job - due to railway foresight and maintaining a good system. The nation should be grateful. The moral is that after the War, railways should be put back in a position where they can earn enough to carry on the good work. If their efficiency has a strategic value, Government should recognise it in the appropriate way. Stabilisation of charges means a Subsidy, the consequences of which will come home to roost sooner or later. Authorities will have a problem after the War if they are to avoid an abrupt and highly damaging jump in transport charges. We warn of the need for action to overcome a difficulty - this subsidy will bring in its train - for the trains".
[Financial News, 18th August].

Railways, as we now know, were not put back into such a position.

On 22nd August, the RCA wrote to the MoT: Railways have never agreed that the present proposals constitute a major cause entitling a revision of the Agreement. 1940 Pool receipts before war damage were £44m; and the long time lag between cost and price rises was equal to £13.8m. The Net Revenue of Pool Receipts for six months to 30th June 1941 was £2.7m in excess of 1940, despite increased costs of £4.25m. Government proposals for £42m are inadequate and only equivalent to the net revenue of 1937, and £2m less than 1940 before allowing for the £13.8m. In the first six months of 1941, Net Revenue was £23.5m, which, if continued, gave £2.5m to Exchequer, but the RCA expected it would be more. They forecast an average Net Revenue not below £47.5m, if no increase was made in wages, prices or charges. We are only willing to accept [a fixed Rental] because of the

National Emergency - but did not expect to be in a worse position. Railways sought at least £47.5m. Railways and LPTB could not accept £43m as in any way representing the existing or potential earning capacity of the undertakings. We regard it as an accommodation to meet the urgent representations of the Government in time of National Emergency. They would recommend Boards' accept £43m if the MoWT increases to that level. [PRO : RAIL 424/18 & MT47/278].

On the same day, Milne met Hurcomb, who said the Government meant to revert to the ***political scheme*** if their latest offer was rejected. The six months wrangle which would follow would not be in the public interest. [PRO : RAIL 424/18].

The meaning of the "political scheme" was not recorded, but it could only mean nationalisation.

An undated Memo by Hill stated : At the last meeting, [22nd August], the MoWT told the railways that before the end of Control, Government would step up charges and the criteria for stepping up was recovery of current increases over pre-war levels of wages and prices, not the attainment of a particular level of Net Revenue. This is very different from adjustment under the 1921 Act. [PRO : MT47/278].

The "particular level", by law, should have been £51m pa, plus 20% of any surplus. .

On 25th August, Haselgrove wrote to Hurcomb, Browett, Hill, Page and Hind

"Charges of Public Utility Companies"

At a meeting of the Lord President's Committee on 22nd August, it was stated that Stabilisation precludes an increase in gas prices, so that a levy would have to come from the profits of the more prosperous undertakings. A levy is unacceptable to the industry. It is impossible to freeze all at the level on Budget Day. The Chancellor said that Departments have discretion to allow gas, electricity and water prices to rise by 30% or more in exceptional cases. Gas companies had been prevented from increasing prices since December. [PRO : MT47/278].

Rail charges had not increased since August 1940; the current rejected rail increase was 31% over pre-war. (see page 130).

The Second Control "Agreement" [Cmd 6314]

On the same day, the MoWT told the Cabinet that negotiations with the Chairmen of the four main line railway companies & LPTB had reached a conclusion. They had agreed to recommend to their Boards, acceptance of a revision of the existing settlement on the lines set out below:-

> The First Agreement had a minimum guarantee of £39.4m with full profit participation therefrom up to £43m, and a 50-50 split with Government beyond this figure. (Not so, there was an upper limit to railways participation in their own profits, but no ceiling for Government). It also provided that fares and charges should be advanced to cover increasing costs and because these had not been able to be sanctioned by the Government, following the Chancellor's announcement on stabilisation, the railways had a fair claim of lag up to the end of 1940 of some £13m. The special War Damage compensation in the present Agreement would have to be withdrawn and the Government's War Damage Scheme, as applied to public utility undertakings

generally, substituted. This was much less satisfactory to the railway companies and they estimated the adverse difference to them at not less than £2.5m pa. In place of the foregoing, the Companies had now agreed to accept a fixed payment of £43m pa subject to confirmation by their Boards. This was exclusive of interest on capital issued or redeemed since the base period. [Cabinet Minutes].

On 27th August, the MoWT wrote to Sir Wm. Wood: War Damage cost to date is £14m. The Railway proportion is £7m, [of which] the LMS share is £2.5m. Companies to repay shares to Government according to the percentage of the Pool. [PRO : RAIL424/18].

An LMS Board Minute of 28th August recorded: The Chairman explained the ***political considerations of the settlement with Government***, which was then approved. The MoT had told Parliament that but for the restrictive effect of the First Control Agreement, Railways would have earned the Standard Net Revenue. The RCA said the First Agreement provided for passing on increased costs to users. Railways and LPTB could not accept £43m as in any way representing the existing or potential earning capacity of the undertakings. We regard it as an accommodation to meet the urgent representations of Government in time of National Emergency. [PRO : RAIL 424/18].

The Minutes do not amplify the meaning of "political". The inference is that it refers to nationalisation.

On 30th August, the MoWT implemented, backdated to 1st January, a fixed £43m Rental [later inappropriately named the Second Control "Agreement"], which included £4.73m to the LPTB, leaving £38.27m for main line railways - £13.13m below the 1921 Act figure.

DoT files include a copy of LP 41/60, "Copy No. 24" of the Second Railway Control Agreement endorsed "SECRET", and stamped: "To be kept under lock and key". (The word "Second" on the file is significant, as Ministers later tried to pretend that there was only one Agreement, and that the 1941 edition was merely adjusting the 1940 edition to incorporate War Damage provisions). [PRO : MT47/277].

The Railway Stockholders Union wrote to "Modern Transport" in March 1944: We "had been assured that the Second Control Agreement would not place railways in a more unfavourable position than the First Agreement. The only reason advanced for change - to bring railways into line with industry in respect of War Damage risks" - was given in the Parliament on 13th November 1940. "During the currency of the present Agreement, £80m of stockholders' capital will receive no dividend". [Hansard, vol. 374, col. 1837].

In March 1944, the MoWT was asked to back his claim that the Control Agreement was fair, by publishing correspondence and records of meetings. He refused, saying they were confidential and it would be contrary to public interest. He declined to release them nor undertake to do so after the war, 'even if both parties agreed'. [Hansard vol. 398, col. 847].

Clearly Government realised that if the papers were released, railway Chairmen would be free to speak openly and deny that they had agreed there were grounds for a savage cut in compensation terms. He did not say it would jeopardise State security.

After the war, Hurcomb and Hill, key Whitehall players in holding down the amount paid to railways out of their own revenue for sequestration, were appointed to top nationalised transport posts. Hurcomb became Chairman of the BTC at the age of 65. Hill, aged 60, became Chairman of Inland Waterways. Both were career Civil Servants.

The records of RCA, LMS and DoT files clearly refute claims that Railways had accepted all too readily the uncertainty of war profits for security of guaranteed net revenue and maintenance level. It is unambiguously clear that railways did foresee a traffic and revenue increase.

Government gains & Railway losses from the "Agreement"

War damage ceased to be a charge; the railway share of war damage was to be 50%, [estimated £2.5m pa], to be met from the Rental, giving £40.5m net, instead of between £43.5m and £56m. Net revenue for 1941 was £65.1m, [£42.8m for 1940]. By August, it would have reached £43m leaving four months revenue to be seized by Government. Railways had said in 1939, "there was no risk of loss, if they were not used to subsidise other activities, Government having solemnly promised to increase charges to maintain revenue and offset increases. War damage could be covered by a 5% increase in charges, returnable if unused". The real reason for replacing the original ungenerous terms by the more miserly ones, was not that publicly advanced - a stabilisation of prices. Government was playing to a gallery of traders and others protesting about rail price increases - all of whom were legally increasing prices to cover increased costs. The new "Agreement" skimmed £22m overtly in 1941 alone, whilst hidden gains were far greater. Railways were used to subsidise industry and Government. (see Economist view of industry on page 161).

In October, Llewellin told Parliament: We have been able to get a good Agreement from our point of view. Railways do not accept £43m as representing existing earning capacity. We can congratulate ourselves that we have made a good bargain for the taxpayer. Sir G. Court Hope: Railway companies were assured the new Agreement would not be less favourable - it is less, ***much*** less favourable. He also said "No praise is too great for everyone from the General Managers down. [Hansard vol. 374, cols. 1815, 1839 & 1840].

On 25th October, the MoWT said: "Government had assumed the risk of profit and loss in exchange for £43m pa Rental, receiving any surplus, making good any deficiency, and determining rates, fares and charges without obligation to adjust them to working costs". [Keesing 4844G].

In November, the PS to the MoWT could not say how many free warrants had been issued. [Hansard vol. 374, col. 2077].

On 1st November, the 1939 ARP Agreement was modified. Each undertaking had to refund sums paid to it under the Civil Defence Act 1939, Sec. 40. In respect of emergency repair stores, sanction for purchase was given for a cost not exceeding £1.4m. The refund will not be a charge on expenditure for the purposes of Net Revenue Account. After deducting £1.4m from the grant of £4m, which the MoWT was prepared to make under Sec. 40 - the balance of £2.6m will be paid. [PRO : RAIL424/18].

In October, 1943, Lord Brabazon [former Tory MoT]: We have hired railways at the arbitrary figure of £43m and they have earned a great deal more than that. Are we going to hold onto them until net receipts fall below £43m and then hand them back. It seems like a very immoral piece of sharp practice to hire them at a price decided by yourself, to hold onto them until earnings fall and then hand them back. [HoL Hansard vol. 129, col. 366].

This confirms his disagreement and disquiet when asked to look at the arbitrary and high handed abrogation of the First Control Agreement.

A 1944 Select Committee Report, Para 7: The revised Agreement had proved favourable to the Exchequer. Para 18: Paid tribute to the immense contribution to the National effort which Railways have made in increasing measure, and that no corresponding financial advantage is accruing to them or to those who invested their savings in Railway capital. In contrast, it criticised the Road Haulage organisation set up in 1943. (see page 150).

The increased rail traffic was a disbenefit, as assets were worn out faster.

1942

The Ministry of Information praised railway achievements, and highlighted their problems, including:-

Page 20: The blitz crammed London's rush into one hour instead of two and a half hours.

Page 44: A huge war effort of Railways has had to be made, without the help of new rolling stock. Indeed, there have been sacrifices. By the end of 1941, engines & wagons were being sent out to Persia to hurry supplies to Russia. We had to leave some in France earlier. 90,000 railwaymen joined HM Forces.

Page 45: The first winter of the war was the worst for 40 years - 1,500 miles of track was blocked by snow.

Page 51: The full story of what railwaymen did during the Blitz will be an enormous one when it is written. ["Transport goes to war"].

On 5th May, Noel-Baker told Parliament that "profit from railways was going to the Exchequer". [Hansard vol. 379, col. 1206].
He made no reference to fears of any loss to be subsidised by the Exchequer, which the Chancellor had forecast, nor that the profits were needed to cover future railway losses.

The MoWT announced a new scheme for road haulage, envisaging the transfer of as much traffic from road to rail as possible. [Economist, 7th November, Page 570].

This was a compelling reason for Government imposing a fixed Rental on railways, because they were planning to reduce road transport to economise on fuel, transferring the traffic to rail at nil cost, achieving a further reduction in war transport costs. Meanwhile, road hauliers could continue to adjust prices to ensure that their profits were not below pre-war levels! Rail assets would wear out faster. A piece of very sharp practice.

1943

Keenlyside wrote on 3rd August, to Hurcomb, Page and Hind: Government need railways in wartime and should contribute to their upkeep. [PRO : MT47/275].

In December, the MoWT said: "Few people seem to realise the extent of railways' achievements. The density of traffic is probably greater than that of any other system in the world. Mr. Holland-Martin replying, said: When victory is won, we shall expect Government to hand us back our property. ["Coming of Age", Page 53].

At no time did transport congestion threaten the war effort. [Savage, Page 255]

Further Revision of Agreement Justified by Major Changes

Materials and labour for the construction of factories, airfields and military camps added to the load. [Savage, Page 220]. (These were mostly in rural areas, where rail transport was normally at minimal levels).

In 1941, Parliament was told : Railways are working under heavy pressure owing to :-

[1] increasing production of munitions and coal,

[2] we have sent abroad a substantial number of ***our*** best locos to assist Russian armies. [Savage, Page 512]. This reads as though the State, not the private companies owned the locos.

The REC made a survey in 1942 of passenger travel in three test months, taking January as 100, February: 119%, March: 129%. In each month, about 38-39% was at Government traffic. In 1942 & 1943 passenger journeys were up 8%, but passenger mileage was 70% up on pre-war. [Savage, Pages 511 & 513].

One of most serious problems facing railways was a rise in passenger journeys: August 1942: 114.7m, August 1943: 123.6m, partly due to an influx of USA troops, but partly the larger number of civilians taking holidays. [Savage, Page 570].

Railways were carrying 50% more freight and 100% more passengers than pre-war by late 1943. [Savage, Page 589].

In November 1943, the MoWT said Railways are carrying 50% more traffic than pre-war and still rising without additional rolling stock and with staff depleted by the claims of the armed forces. In addition to normal traffic there are 2,000 Government specials per week carrying troops & war stores, 6,000 extra trains for workers in Government factories and 1,100 extra block trains of coal direct from collieries to consuming areas. In the last six months the number of such trains has been steadily increasing. He warned of the part to be played in the gigantic military operations planned next year [D-Day]. In the two months before D-Day, there were 24,459 special trains - with troops, ammunition and stores. 1,000 trains directly linked to D-Day carried 230,000 men. ["Coming of Age", Page 53].

By 1944, passenger mileage was 68% up on pre-war, whilst the availability of coaches was 8.6% down. [Smith Page 151]. (Railways gained nothing from it).

By 1944, there was a huge increase in travel by HM Forces who were allowed four free leave passes pa and also cheap fares. [Savage, Page 512]

Noel-Baker told Parliament that, excluding season tickets, passenger journeys were up 20% in 1943, and passenger mileage by 60%. Merchandise traffic was up 86% on pre-war, mineral traffic 68% and coal 13%. Average hauls of freight traffic are also longer. [Economist, 13th May, 1944, Page 653].

Traffic by rail, compared to 1938, increased by 49.5% in 1943, 50% in 1944 and 35.3% in 1945. [Committee on Inland Transport, 31st July 1947, PRO: MT6/2830]

All these substantially increased costs, and wear and tear with no increased revenue to compensate. (see also diversions from canals : page 157, and sea : page 158)..

The RCA wrote to the MoWT on 19th April 1944: The Minister will be aware that in the original Railway Agreement, provision was made by which he or the Railways could propose a revision of the arrangements for any cause of a major character and, if agreed by all parties, the arrangement should be revised accordingly. While this provision could have no legal significance, and was for this reason not embodied in the Second Agreement, it was made clear during negotiations that the Government did not wish to depart from this understanding as, if new circumstances arose they might again require the Agreement to be amended. Since the revised Agreement was made, two new circumstances have arisen. On December 9th, 1941, war was declared upon Japan and two days later Germany and Italy declared war on the USA. These resulted in a far greater burden upon railways than anticipated at the time the Agreement was negotiated. The Minister will remember that although the railways, in the national interest accepted the revised agreement as a wartime measure, without regard to the ordinary commercial considerations which would have to be taken into account in determining the amount of compensation to be paid for the use of the undertakings under normal conditions, they made it clear that the minimum guaranteed sum annual payment was the lowest which could be accepted without grave injustice to the proprietors. Although charges have not been increased to cover enhanced costs of labour and materials profit to Government has far exceeded anticipation. For the last three years net earnings of the four main line railways and the LPTB have been in excess of the £43.5m payable by the Government under the revised Agreement as follows:- 1941: £22m, 1942: £46m, 1943: £62m. Increased earnings are undoubtedly due to circumstances not contemplated at the time the Agreement was made and therefore the new arrangements have proved to be more unfavourable to the proprietors than would have been the case had the original Agreement still obtained. The Chairmen have hitherto not submitted a request for a revision of the agreement, but as strong representations were made at all the recent AGM's that the present arrangements inflict a grave injustice on them. For the reasons outlined the Chairmen request that :-

[1] The guaranteed annual payment should be increased, and

[2] The basic figure for maintenance should be adjusted to cover the intensified user of maintainable assets.

The expansion of traffic has caused more intensive use of the assets employed and it is inequitable that the basic figure for maintenance should in these circumstances be limited to the levels of the years 1935-6-7. [Modern Transport, 8th June 1944]

If this was not a "Change of a major character" as set out in the original Agreement, it is unlikely any "major change" could ever take place - since MoT files show they had dismissed rail forecasts of any increase. It certainly eclipsed Government's concept of a "major change" in 1941. (see page 132).

Two months later, the Minister replied to Lord Royden, [RCA Chairman]:-
Your request took the form of asking for an increase in the guaranteed annual payment and adjustment of the basic figure for maintenance to cover intensified user of maintainable assets and it was suggested that the extension of the area of war which occurred at the end of 1941 constituted a case for revision. Government do not find themselves able to accept this suggestion, and I feel bound to point out that the revised arrangement into which we entered in the course of 1941 was such as to relieve the railways of any uncertainty as to

the effects of the war upon their net revenues*. As my correspondence with Sir Ronald Matthews shows the companies' acceptance of the fixed annual payment of the agreed amounts was for the period of control. The Government have given the most careful consideration but regret that they are unable to agree any increase in the amount of the fixed annual payments. We must adhere to the agreement but I may remind you that it makes provision for an allowance for abnormal wear and tear of maintainable assets, if it is agreed to be justified over and above the figure for maintenance. While I cannot commit myself in any way until the matter has been fully investigated, I am prepared to examine it fully with you without delay. [Modern Transport, 8th June 1944].
* This was absolute nonsense as his own Department's files revealed. The files contain no evidence that his staff reviewed the matter. He did not accept a "major change", but in the preceding November, he publicly stated that railways were carrying 50% more traffic! One cannot believe that if the area of war, and hence the workload and revenue had declined, Government would not have been back at the double to reduce the payment on the grounds of a major change. Moreover, Railways had never asked to be "relieved of any uncertainty". They had no doubts that net revenue would increase.

Two weeks later, Lord Royden wrote again: Railway Company Chairmen have had an opportunity of discussing your letter regarding their request for a revision of the terms of the agreement. At the AGM's of all companies this year, stockholders passed resolutions calling on Boards to express to you and the Chancellor of the Exchequer, their opinion that the Control Agreement is inequitable and should be revised in such a manner as shall enable the companies to receive the Standard Revenue under the 1921 Act. You will, I feel sure, appreciate the disappointment which the Government's decision will cause not only to the stockholders but also to those who represent them. The Railway Chairmen welcome your assurance that the question of allowances for abnormal wear and tear of maintainable assets will be fully investigated. [Modern Transport, 8th June 1944].

Curiously, this correspondence is not enclosed with PRO files on Rental. However, there are references to the "correspondence with Sir Ronald Matthews", but no copies of that either. The references take the form of debating whether the reference to him in the original draft of the MoWT's letter should be deleted. Questions were raised about the matter in Parliament, but MP's were fobbed off with refusals to publish, because the correspondence was confidential. [PRO : MT47/279].

On 26th November 1945, the MoWT was asked in Parliament if he would consider increasing the Rental so that railways receive some benefit to correspond with the reduction of EPT upon industry. He replied: "No, Sir". [Hansard vol. 416, col 1022 The MP was misinformed - railways paid EPT in addition to having profits milked by Government. **(see page 124).**

Some Consequences of Control

Railway earnings are below Standard Revenue due to inaction by Governments on a fair system of rates & fares. Noel-Baker, PS to the MoWT thought control would continue for two years after the war. [Modern Transport, 1st January 1945].

Up to the end of 1945, Government took £197.6m, overtly, from net railway profits, ***before tax and EPT***. Due solely to its inept policy - having frozen only rail, but no other industry prices - net revenue in 1946 and 1947 fell below the Rental, and under the terms of the "Agreement", Government had to repay £70.1m of its immoral gains. If charges had been increased to cover increased costs, as applied to every other industry, and as set out in the First Control Agreement, there would have been a surplus for 1946 of £154m, and a similar sum for 1947 for Government to skim off. Their covert immoral gains in the form of frozen rail charges and discounts on Government traffic increased their total gain for eight years of Control to at least £1 billion at wartime prices. (see page 173).

Railway net revenue was held below potential by frozen charges and because, due to a lack of materials and war damage, railways had to reduce train speeds and cut public services. Passenger services were curtailed by the MoWT to give preference to war [passenger & freight] traffic. In 1942, HM Forces and dependants made 10m journeys per month, rising to 15m in 1943 and in 1944. Their journeys were mostly twice the distance of civilian passengers, [hence, costs of movement were higher], and at fares which were either free or at half the standard rate. [Bell, Page 65].

People on Civil Defence, Home Guard or Fire Guard duties had return tickets for single fare. Cheap Day tickets for civilians were withdrawn. Munitions workers transferred from their homes had special concessions. A typical munitions factory had 426 trains each week for 222,500 passenger journeys. Nearly 6,500 workmen's trains ran each week to Government factories - workmen's were the lowest fares of all. (Their fares had been pegged since April 1940, unlike their wages - they were among the highest paid). In 1943, railborne coal was up by 12.5% over pre-war, and other freight traffic, which included all war materials, was up by 79%. [Bell, Page 18].

There were other Government employees enjoying free travel - at railway expense. I learned from a personal contact that employees of the Health Department were given three free tickets pa! Doubtless, this was common to all Departments.

Due to the iniquitous Second "Agreement", all extra traffic was carried free of charge, and much other traffic at sub standard charges, whilst costs and wear and tear increased. From 1944 public services, and hence revenue, were further reduced due to demands arising in advance of D-Day and for long thereafter due to the constant flow of traffic to Europe. In 1944, railways ran 178,263 freight trains with war materials - one third of the total for the whole war - all at depressed Government freight rates. [Bell, Appendix 12].

With railways struggling to cope with a 50% increase in workload, Government did all it could to discourage civilian rail travel, leading to long term transfer to road operators who could obtain new buses - even during the war. Fuel rationing did not seem to have much effect. (See page 146).

Paradoxically, Government allowed horse racing to continue, and required railways to provide transit for both horses and race-goers. [Bell, Page 67].

There was heavy travel to Ascot races a month before D-Day, and serious congestion at Liverpool Street with travel to Newmarket. It is difficult to understand why racing continued when the public was asked not to travel. Government attention was drawn by the REC to the wasteful use of resources arising from the continued conveyance of cut flowers by rail. Government tried (?) to prevent their conveyance by rail, but growers used subterfuges to disguise produce - e.g. labelling as vegetables - so that Government gave way, lamely arguing that flowers were good for civilian morale, [Savage Pages 503-5 & 599].

It is highly improbable that flowers were purchased by factory or mine-workers and bombed out East Enders, where morale really needed lifting, rather than that of the well-to-do who could afford the luxury of flowers.

"Political, TUC and Social conferences were allowed to continue, creating heavy railway demands". (Whilst civilian travel was discouraged). [Savage, Page 518].

"A main cause of current railway insolvency is undoubtedly obsolete equipment. The main problem is that the modernisation programme is 20-30 years late".
[Draft DoT Paper, Page 5, for Cabinet on 23rd May 1956, - PRO : MT132/32].

Perhaps the most incredible consequence of the Control Agreement was that the MoWT demanded that the five undertakings must seek his approval to appointments from September 1941, to the positions of General Managers and Chief Officers. Although the companies initially objected, they had to give way. [PRO : RAIL1098].

Given the vastly increased workload handled by railways without additional rolling stock and with fewer staff, they should have emerged from the war in a wealthy condition, instead they were penniless - entirely due to Government policy and practice. An MP alleged that railways had charged Government 75% more for carrying traffic than civilian customers. [Hansard, vol. 431, col. 1830]. Unarguably, Government traffic was carried at up to 33% *below* the frozen level of freight rates, and Government also helped itself to an immoral share of railway profits, before tax. Some civilian customers had no doubt that Government traffic was carried too cheaply. (see page 127). Perhaps he was thinking of road hauliers. (see page 147).

Government favoured road transport before and during the War, when it sequestrated four railways "to co-ordinate them in the national interest", but not 60,000 "A" & "B" licence hauliers, with 150,000 vehicles, nor 350,000 "C" Licence vehicles operated by 140,000 traders. A year after the War, hauliers were freed from a half-hearted superficial control never properly implemented, despite nationalisation plans, whilst Government control of railways continued a further two and a half years.

1939

A Pool of 1,241 road vehicles was formed by the Wholesale Meat Transport Association, which became the Road Haulage Section, Meat of the MoT. As far more were required for imported frozen meat, Government pooled all Road and Railway insulated units. The Railways contributed 6,317 vans, plus 2,354 containers on flat wagons. [Bell, Page 97].

Hauliers were paid. Railways, up to the end of 1940 paid half to the Government and after 1940, gained nothing, due to the fixed Rental.

The MoT told Parliament: 316,000 Road Transport vehicles had been organised in 700 regional groups! 441,000 vehicles [89% of UK] had registered under a census to prevent overlapping. [Keesing 3634A].

Government could not liaise with four railways! Evidently, Government had not been unduly interested in gathering information on road transport using public roads, whilst it had gathered far more detailed information about railway owned rolling stock using privately owned railway tracks under the 1911 Act,

"The majority of road operators have provided the MoT with ***their record*** of fuel consumption in 1938". [Economist, 8th July, Page 62]. (This was tailor made for anyone to inflate figures, to ensure that rationing would create no problem),

"A", "B" & "C" licence conditions are suspended, any vehicle having an identity certificate from a Licensing Authority can operate for hire or reward as well as for "C" licence traffic. [Modern Transport, 9th September].

Payments for requisitioned road vehicles were suggested by the MoT after consultation with Road Transport industry representatives. [Modern Transport, 30th September].

Unlike railways, where Government had ***dictated*** its terms.

Government warned road operators that if the present voluntary system of pooling was unsuccessful - they would have to come under Government control. The present system involved free issue of fuel. Instead of having 10-12,000 carriers to deal with, the South Scotland Regional Transport Commissioner, wanted to organise them in 300-400 groups. [Modern Transport, 21st October].

"The detailed management and operation of all [road] services is in the hands of professional transport men". [Modern Transport, 12th December]. (As on the railways).

Regional Transport Commissioners [RTC's] had power to requisition vehicles but not drivers. [Savage Page 154]. (Government had given itself such powers over railways).

On 4th April, the MoT was told of motor coaches running seaside trips from Leeds and Hartlepool. [Hansard vol. 359, col. 595].

Many civilians were unable to use rail for such pleasure trips due to Government exercising priorities for Government and military traffic. To discourage civilian travel by rail, stations were adorned with the Government message :

Is Your Journey Really Necessary?

1940

The MoT told Parliament: There are in road transport, 500,000 vehicles and 200,000 operators. [Modern Transport, 16th February]

(No problems were envisaged in liaising with these huge numbers!

The Commercial Motor Users Association wrote to hauliers that rates increases of 10-15% to cover overheads and running costs, and an additional percentage to cover increased wages was justified. [Commercial Motor, Vol. 71, Page 31].

"Hauliers are complaining of loss of traffic to rail and called for co-ordination". [Modern Transport, 10th August].

The Road Haulage Consultative Committee was set up in August 1940, to facilitate discussion between the MoT and the road haulage industry. It had no executive powers and did little to organise the industry. [Economist, 29th November, 1941, Page 655]

The MoT drew attention of a tendency of road haulage rates to increase. He has power under Defence Regulations to control rates. [Modern Transport, 26th October].

"By December, Government produced a scheme for operational control of trunk haulage which was ***acceptable*** to the road haulage industry"! [Savage, Page 314].

Whereas railways had to fund most of their snow clearance work in the winter of 1940/41, with occasional military help, road transport was able to rely almost wholly on hundreds of thousands of men from the unemployed register who were paid - by the State - to shovel it into lorries for dumping into rivers.

1941

In January 1941, as a first step towards direct control, the MoT introduced a scheme to hire vehicles to carry Government traffic. The scheme never grew to full stature. [Economist, 29th November, Page 655].

Transport pools formed at ports have forced rates up. The MoT drew attention to high rates. He could issue an Order for the control of rates - but to prevent the necessity for that, he appealed to all concerned to refrain from making increases without submitting proposals to RTC's. The machinery [through RTC's] does not seem to have checked the general tendency on the part of hauliers to increase rates and further action ***may*** well be necessary. Large volumes of traffic pass under the ownership of Ministries of Food and Supply [using hired transport] and steps may have to be taken to combat the inclination inherent in human nature, to take advantage of Government Departments. Government will hire vehicles to carry Government traffic. Running and maintenance will remain in the hands of owners, (as with railways). Financial aspects were still to be discussed with a Road Haulage Consultative Committee. [Modern Transport, 1st February].

This was in stark contrast to Railways, where assets were sequestrated, not hired and Government dictated how little they would pay for Government traffic, froze rates in 1940 for the duration and took a large slice of the profits, before tax!

Payment for vehicles hired by Government to give the same net revenue per ton of payload capacity as that earned in a Standard Year - twelve continuous months selected by the haulier! [Modern Transport, 1st March].

A Government Road Haulage Scheme [under the MoWT] was announced. It was a scheme for voluntary entry. There have been lengthy negotiations - since 22nd January. [Modern Transport, 22nd March].

The TCCT was perturbed at recent increases in road haulage rates. Cases have been brought to light where rates have doubled between June 1940 and January 1941, whereas costs could not have soared to this degree. Apart from this, loading is better and return loads not so difficult to obtain. Until a few weeks ago, it was considered that 20% increase was reasonable. During recent times, many thought that this was too conservative. The MoT recently issued notices that he had powers to control rates. This rule has not, so far, been enforced. [Commercial Motor, Vol. 73, Page 239].

Traders were only *perturbed* by haulage increases which had *doubled,* when with railway rates frozen at *16% above pre-war* since August 1940, they asked Government, in July 1942, to cancel that August 1940 rail increase! (see page 127).

The National Director, Association of Road Operators urged hauliers "to keep rates at a reasonable level". [Modern Transport, 3rd May].

A Standing Joint Committee was set up comprising eight Road Haulage organisations - to represent rather than amalgamate. "It would ***negotiate*** rates on behalf of members with Government Departments and other bodies". Positive safeguards were needed against unreasonable rates. "Road Haulage pools have not hesitated to push up rates to an undesirable degree". The Rates Division of the MoWT was preparing a review. Control remains in the hands of Operators, not the Joint Committee. [Modern Transport, 19th July].

In contrast railways were told that Government would pay two thirds of rail rates frozen at 1940 levels!.

The Association of Road Operators had suggested that rates should increase by 15%, but others say it should be up to 18%. [Commercial Motor, Vol. 74, Page 234].

In July the MoWT introduced another Committee - the Road Haulage [Operations] Advisory Committee. [Economist, 29th November, Page 655]

By the Autumn, progress on a new scheme was disappointingly slow. By October, a ***compromise*** plan was developed. [Savage, Pages 319 & 320].

The existence of thousands of hauliers cannot be cited as an excuse for further delay in bringing vehicles into the scheme. [Economist, 25th October, Page 500].

In October, the MoWT announced a new scheme to provide the Ministry with 4,100 vehicles, including 1,600 already chartered to carry meat. [Economist, 29th November Page 655].

The MoWT again drew attention to a tendency of road haulage rates to increase. [Modern Transport, 26th October].

Road haulage rates were to be increased to reflect Sunday working costs for drivers [Modern Transport, 23rd November].

No similar allowance was permitted for Railways which had had to increase Sunday working and extend weekday hours of all staff to handle an increased volume of traffic.

"By the end of 1941, Government had requisitioned 3-4000 out of 50,000 buses". (Compared to 100% of rail assets in September 1939!). "The biggest single grievance of workers was the inadequacy of bus services". "There was some diversion to local trains to help buses". [Savage, Pages 325, 335 & 336].

Railways did not gain a penny from these diversions.

1942

Road Transport is not yet organised into any comprehensive groups. Agreement is not even in sight. [Economist, 13th January, Page 832].

The rise in road rates was often out of all proportion to increased costs. Under Defence Regulations, the MoWT made the Road Haulage & Hire [Charges] Order 1942, for vehicles defined in Sec. 1 [2] of the Road & Rail Traffic Act 1933, [viz. road goods vehicles]. The Charge for Carriage of goods on roads and Hire of vehicles, including detention charges shall not exceed such charges as would have been fair and reasonable in October 1940, with an addition of a percentage to that charge reflecting increases in costs since then. Any question as to whether a charge conforms with these conditions will be decided by MoWT or a RTC (no mention was made of public hearings packed with objectors as applied with railways). What is fair and reasonable, is charges actually made in that year, and in the absence of proof to the contrary, the appropriate percentage to be added shall be 7.5%. The Road Haulage & Hire [Charges] Order 1942 dated 12th February came into force on 23rd February. [Modern Transport, 28th February].

Rail rates were pegged by the MoWT from 1940, and Government was taking a rake-off from rail, but not road revenue. Railways were not allowed to increase charges to reflect increased costs.

The MoT had announced the Government Road Haulage Scheme in January 1941. It was not until March 1942 that the first chartered vehicle turned a wheel under the compromise partnership scheme evolved between him and the Haulage industry. [Modern Transport, 29th August]. (Three years after sequestrating railways, and overriding the 1921 Act, a year after reneging on its original enforced so called "Agreement" Government was *compromising* with Road Transport).

By August, only 475 road haulage vehicles had been chartered. The Government scheme was a compromise, it failed and was abandoned. [Savage, Pages 533 & 538].

In November, the MoWT said that the new haulage scheme supersedes the scheme whereby the MoWT had hired a few thousand vehicles. The new scheme will enable as much traffic as possible to be transferred to rail. [Economist, Page 570].

The effect of this transfer to rail would be to have more Government traffic carried free of charge, as a result of the fixed Rental whilst hauliers continued to be paid, whether their vehicles were used or not. If vehicles stood idle or under-used, when the war ended, they would be in better condition than railway rolling stock.

1943

The origin of the 1943 haulage organisation was 90,000 vehicles on journeys up to 60 miles & 25,000 on long distance. The first step was limited to the latter. The problem was how to induce hauliers to offer undertakings or vehicles for Government services. Financial arrangements attracted hauliers in. [Savage, Page 538 & 541].

The war was beyond the midway point!. The Government was threatening the railways with nationalisation and bribing hauliers to contribute to the war effort. (see pages 137 & 138 and below).

The haulage industry rejected the MoWT pooling scheme involving 300 firms as 'controlled undertakings'. [Keesing 5873A].

1944

The Select Committee, which praised railways, (see pages 140), was very critical of Government's road haulage scheme, and of hauliers. Para 25: The MoWT intention was to keep the Road Haulage Scheme voluntary. Para 32 [f]: Attention was drawn to complaints by industry of unexplained increases in road rates. Protesting firms said charges were absolutely ridiculous.

The Committee criticised the Road Haulage Organisation set up in 1943 for:-

Para 35: Higher prices, and recommended immediate re-examination and adjustment of road freight charges.

Para 37: Uneconomical use of vehicles.

(Unlike railways, hauliers were able to financially exploit the increased wartime demand).

Rates for War Office road vehicle hire rates are increased. The MoWT allows for depreciation on Road Transport. [Modern Transport, 13th May & 15th July].

1945

Road haulage was able to obtain new vehicles during the war. [Hansard, vol. 408, col. 2017].

The Fawkner Committee rejected as impractical, a railway style classification and rates structure for road transport. [Modern Transport, 24th November]. (see also page 116).

Salter said in 1932, that a common structure was vital to co-ordination. (see page 83).

By the end of the war, more buses were being operated than pre-war - 2,000 came onto the roads in 1943, and again in 1944, compared to 1,000 in 1942, and 500 in 1941. [Savage, Page 525]. (This compared with a dramatic fall in building railway coaches).

"Higher road rates often proved the only way of getting operators to carry essential traffic". "The control of fuel did not stop hauliers seeking the best paying traffic, rather than the most essential". [Savage, Pages 311 & 313].

1946

In February, the MoWT told Parliament that the demand for guard rails between front and rear wheels of lorries had been fully reviewed in 1938, by the TAC, who said "it was not likely to effect a contribution to road safety which would justify its imposition". There was no new evidence for the Committee on Road Safety to re-examine.
[Hansard vol. 218, col. 181]. (It had first been raised in 1919 - see page 60).

Side-guards did not become mandatory on articulated vehicles until 1983; even later, on rigid vehicles!

On 27th July, Modern Transport contained an illuminating example of unfettered increases by road transport. The Eastern Area RTC made a decision on an application under the Road Haulage & Hire [Charges] Order 1942 in respect of the removal of the same household effects which cost £7.25 in 1940 and £29.50 in 1945. The 1942 Order authorised a 7.5% increase. The charge was eventually reduced to £15.75 by the RTC. (That was a 100% increase against static rail charges!).

The Government Road Haulage Organisation, (which had far less control over road than rail), was disbanded on 17th August. The Road Haulage & Hire Charges Order 1942 was amended to reflect current costs in relation to pre-war. It had been a half hearted control, not worthy of the name. Railway charges having been frozen for five years were not increased for a further year. 100% Control of railways, on the cheap, did not end for a further eighteen months.

The marked differences between Government control of rail and road transport included :-

	Railways	Road Transport
Assets	All sequestrated in 1939	Some hired - halfway through the war
Manpower	All taken over in 1939	None taken over
Charges	Controlled from 1939, frozen in 1940	Virtually without control and encouraged to increase to cover increased costs
Profits	Government took a large slice	Government took no share
Traffic	Had to accept all	Free to pursue better paying traffic
Control	Ended in 1948	Ended in 1946

Chapter 14 OTHER TRANSPORT & INDUSTRY IN WAR

The wartime treatment by Government of other transport and of industry was generally more favourable than railways.

Privately Owned Wagons

Privately owned railway wagons [POW's] were those owned by companies which did not own or operate railways. They were for historical reasons, used for most coal traffic, often on short hauls. This concept was fostered by the Railway Clauses Consolidation Act 1845, Sec 92: Owners of engines and carriages or wagons are entitled to use any railway on payment of [State] controlled tolls.

During the "Great War", Government did not requisition Privately Owned wagons because their designs - unchanged by 1939 - made them unsuitable for other than their primary purpose - coal and mineral traffic. Government accepted railway advice that these wagons could best help the 1914-18 war effort by issuing a Government Order permitting them to be used for "Back Loads" where railways considered it beneficial - which was about 20-30% occasions. The balance would have to return empty either because there was no back load to the originating area or because of wagon unsuitability. They were no more suitable in 1939 than 1914.

PRO file MT6/2611 contained letters, meeting notes and Memos relating to the requisitioning of POW's. The PRO Index said the file was "Open 1972", but the File was originally endorsed "Closed until 1991". The last item in the file was dated April 1948. Why was such an innocuous subject to be kept from public view for so long? Certainly, shareholders of the former railway companies would have been aggrieved to read how much more generously, owners of private wagon companies had been rewarded by Government for the use of what was later described as "wretched little trucks" - however, when the papers were released, no prominence was given to them in the media, and the shareholders have probably all passed away by now. (see page 156).

The text in respect of POW's is drawn from MT6/2611 except where shown.

Internal DoT Memo, undated, on the arrangements for Common Use of Privately owned railways wagons in the Great War: "Shall be paid such amount as may be agreed or as may be determined in default of agreement by the R&CC or arbitrators appointed by the R&CC". An entitlement legally shared by railways, but denied to them. (see page 32).

1938

Internal DoT Meeting, 29th March: The take-over of POW's is essential, and to be by Railways on a hire basis, hire to cover the cost of replacement. This involves assumption of the War Risk by Government. Allowance should be made for this in the rates of hire. (Assets were to be ***hired***, not sequestrated. At this stage, no consultation had taken place with railways in regard to this responsibility. Government did not accept the war risk for railways' assets, after 1940. (see page 133 & 135)

July. Committee of Imperial Defence, Sub Committee on supplies of coal in War for Public Utilities - Para 16: Difficulties anticipated in ensuring a sufficient supply of hoppers for gas coal. Beckton Gas, Light & Coke Company need two wagon tipplers with necessary conveyor belts at a cost of £50,000. They expect the Exchequer to pay.

Estimate railways may have to move 240-250m tons pa (an increase of 20-25%) in wartime. The total wagon fleet including POW's is adequate subject to the imposition of demurrage charges.

Demurrage did not apply to POW's in peace-time. In discussions with Railways, Civil Servants who had read these - and following papers, which forecast extra traffic, and did not dispute the forecasts - later pretended that they did not believe that rail traffic would increase in wartime. (see page 120).

The MoT wrote to the REC on 27th September: No decisions have yet been made on the take-over of POW's. (They had decided six months earlier - see page 152).

The next day, the Mines Department [of the BoT] wrote to the MoT, dealing with the implications of War on coal movement. They forecast a diversion from Coastwise shipping to rail. Railways are now conveying 200m tons pa, would be required to move an extra 15-16m tons. The Committee said Pooling of POW's was essential. The DoT accepted the Mines Dept view that railways could cope with diversions from coastwise shipping of 17m tons of coal from the North East to London, without taking account of other demands. The MoT failed to see the effect on wagon utilisation. [Savage, Page 70].

On 21st December, Meredith sent an internal DoT Memo on POW's to Stedman: There are powers in the 1919 Act, Sec. 13 to purchase these wagons. Ownership of 640,000 wagons is as follows:- Collieries: 400,000; Merchants & Factors: 125,000; Coal Trade: 64,000; 90% are used for coal traffics. There were 5,000 owners. The value of wagons is put by the DoT at £48m, [600,000 at an average of £80 each]. Chas. Roberts, Wagon Builders, Horbury say that in 1929, the cost of a new 12 ton wagon was £130. A census of wagons was made on 28th July 1937 and was required at short notice by Committee for Imperial Defence. (In contrast, the Government had been supplied, by law, every year, since 1911, with a complete census of railway wagons and all other assets).

1939

Railway Managers wrote to the MoT on 24th February pointing out that there were powers in the 1919 Act for Government to purchase these wagons. [The DoT said there would be strong opposition from powerful interests! - see page 154].

Internal DoT Memo from Page to Hill on 6th April: A Meeting with the Mines Department had agreed financial responsibility should be upon Railway Companies who should pay for the hire of POW's to the Owners and take the receipts and that any loss or gain would be reflected in the general revenue position of the railways and so dealt with under the general terms of compensation for control of railways. War Risk to be covered by Government. Railways became responsible for maintenance - carried out in peacetime by Private Wagon Repair Companies. Work would be allocated to those companies by Railways, who must keep records of receipts and expenditure on repair and maintenance. (Railways were not consulted, but were to do the work, and Government would scoop the profit).

A Meeting at the Treasury, on 14th April of Sir Alan Barber, Tribe, [both from the Treasury], Hill & Page [DoT] noted that POW's are half of the total wagon stock. (The rest were owned by Railway Companies).

Three days later, at a Meeting at the DoT between Wedgwood [LNER], Deacon, Hill, Page, Faulkner [all from the DoT], Wedgwood said the most suitable course is for Government to requisition the POW's, compensate owners and hand to railways to use for the benefit of the Government. (He was not told that the MoT had already decided and it involved railways compensating owners, not the Government).

On 20th July, Page [DoT] wrote to the Mines Department [BoT]:-
The alternatives are:

1. Purchase POW's at an estimated cost of £30-£50m. Economies of £2m are possible [reduced railway shunting and empty haulage etc]. This alternative would be opposed by *powerful interests.*
2. Requisition. The final settlement of compensation could be left to the end of the War, but it would be necessary to make interim payments.
3. Hiring by Government.

I favour the second alternative. The basis of compensation proposed is that in the Compensation [Defence] Bill for requisitioning of vessels, vehicles and aircraft which is a fair rate of hire, together with the cost of making good any damage. To be decided by a special Tribunal. This would seem appropriate for POW's. (But not for railway wagons or other railway assets!). Railways should keep records of receipts and expenditure on repair & maintenance. I propose to seek authority in a major emergency to requisition POW's and hand them over to the railways.

DoT Memo, dated 8th August: At their 338th meeting on 17th November, the Committee for Imperial Defence dealt with coal supplies to Utilities. They stated, Para 7: We have no doubt as to the desirability of abolishing the POW system.

On 1st September, [two days before war began]. Government requisitioned over 600,000 privately owned wagons [POW's] under the Emergency Powers [Defence] Act, September 1939, (at the same time as it sequestrated all railway assets).

In October, the MoT appointed a Committee to advise on questions arising from the requisitioning of POW's, having two Sub Committees with representatives of the Owners and Repairers, to deal with Compensation & Repairs respectively.

Government's policy placed an extra burden on railways, who had to allocate wagons to private repairers, hitherto the responsibility of owners, and check repairs had been done as ordered. For this purpose railways had to employ additional staff. The average annual workload of repairs was 2m wagons, which meant that requisitioned wagons were in repairers' works 3-4 times each year. They were not fit for long hauls on which many were used [in lieu of coastwise shipping], had frequent breakdowns and were so slow that they occupied tracks for almost twice as long as other freight trains. [Bell, Pages 102-3].

1940

13th January. DoT Memo from Hill to Bailey :-

"Committee on National Expenditure"

Compensation on the basis of simple hire plus repair costs will be paid to owners for the use of wagons. Railway companies will charge users for the use of those wagons. Negotiations proceeding with the Owners, Repairers and Railway Companies as to the amount of compensation to be paid, meanwhile owners & repairers are receiving *substantial* payments on account.

Hill wrote to the Minister on 27th April: You appointed a Committee on 11th October to advise on questions arising from the requisitioning of POW's. Two Sub Committees deal with Compensation & Repairs respectively. On 12th April, the main Committee had before it scales of weekly compensation agreed by the Compensation Sub Committee ranging from 3s.3d [16p] for 8 & 10 ton capacity wagons to 5s.9d [29p] for 12 ton wagons built between 1933 and 1939. These cover 97% of the fleet. Scales covered pre 1904 vintage wagons. The scale for 12 ton wagons would be reviewed and adjusted at the end of December 1941. The Mining Association own two-thirds of the wagons and they wanted to delay finalisation until a dispute was resolved with railways regarding the cost of short haul traffic, which mainly affects South Wales. [Hill said] this is irrelevant. We are writing to Owners; meantime interim monthly payments were continuing.

The DoT wrote to 5,000 Owners giving these proposed scales and adding that Government would deal with the matter of interest on the balance of compensation over and above payments already made on account. The Owners agreed the terms. The DoT estimated that £5.75m pa would be payable in respect of compensation for requisitioning of POW's, to which must be added liability for repair & maintenance of about £4.5m pa.

The Wagon Repair Sub Committee stated that "the estimate of £4.5m was an increase compared with pre-war, when the standard of maintenance was lower due to shorter journeys, and to reflect increases in costs of labour and materials". Information indicates costs will be 20% higher by April 1940 than on 3rd September 1939. Some firms said it was 20% higher by January 1940.

These principles relating to longer journeys and repair costs applied to, but were denied to railways. Railways were allowed 10% increase in April, Repairers were claiming 20%.

The DoT letter was sent to Owners' Associations, viz: Association of Private Owners of Railway Rolling Stock; Mining Association of Great Britain; Scottish Wagon Owners Association; Railway Carriage & Wagon Builders & Financiers; Association of Wagon Repairing Companies; Hirers Ltd.

Undated DoT Paper on POW's: Under the terms of the Agreement for the control of Railways all payments arising out of requisitioning will be met out of the Pool of Railway receipts. (see page 125).

An undated DoT Memo on the Compensation Defence Act provided for wagons of later build than those in the Memo dated 27th April. (see above).

1942

An undated DoT Memo said £5.95m was paid to Wagon Owners in 1942.

1943

80,000 POW's were under and awaiting repair - 60% above the 1940 position. (Owners were getting a bigger rate of return from their inferior wagons than railways were paid for their assets, many of which were more modern).

DoT Paper, "Planning for Post-war Reconstruction : 606,000 POW's belong to 5,000 owners. 248,000 were built since 1911, 212,000 in 1901-1911, 115,000 pre 1901. Railway companies say wagons should be scrapped after 40 years. [PRO : MT47/275].

It will be noted that POW's of less than 20 ton capacity were built after 1932 despite the recommendation of the RCT. (see page 80).

1946

"British Wagon Builders will not get foreign orders when all they show in the shop window are their present wretched little trucks". [Modern Transport, 22nd June - reader's letter].

Roberts [wagon builders] replied : Old wagons are not necessarily uneconomical and said the 1926 Samuel Commission recommended railways should give wagon companies an inducement to build bigger wagons by rate reduction. [Modern Transport, 27th July].

In fact, the GWR offered a 5% reduction in freight rates for traffic conveyed in 20 ton wagons on the GWR. Felix Pole pointed out that two 10 ton wagons cost 50% more to build than one 20 ton wagon. [Pole, Page 72].

An MP said that his company could build 1,000 20 ton wagons and pay for them out of the savings on repairs of old wagons. [Hansard, 1929, vol. 231, col. 664].

They expected to get a multiple benefit from investment - reduced maintenance costs, increased utilisation and lower railway rates before considering investment. (see page 88].

During the war, POW owners and repair companies were paid £85m from main line railway revenue - 8.25 years at £10.25m. (see page 130).

Post-war

Government nationalised 544,000 POW's - but not with Exchequer funds. They were acquired by the BTC for £43m Redeemable Loan Stock, the burden of redemption and interest fell on the BTC, and through the allocation of Central Charges, debited against BR, creating artificial losses. BR had to make best use of these ancient wagons, until they were progressively replaced over the next ten years by modern wagons. So poor was the condition of POW's that within twelve months, 55,000 were scrapped whilst 347,000 required repairs. Government had considered ending the right of non-railway companies, including some who did not produce any coal, to own and hire wagons to convey coal and other products. The 1919 Act provided powers to buy the wagons up, but Government shied away from the problem. Their excuse was set out in DoT files. (see page 154).

Inequitable allocation of essential materials by Government ensured that BR had to keep these museum pieces in service. About 27% were still in use 10 years later. They frequently broke down in service causing disruption and delay. Inevitably, industry blamed BR for delays. An analysis of the vintage of POW's in 1943 showed that 115,000 were built before 1901, and 212,000 between 1901 and 1911. (see page 155).

Hence, about 255,000 were over 40 years old by 1948. Railway policy was to scrap wagons of such vintage. By scrapping only 55,000* in 1948, railways had been obliged to keep 200,000 in use simply because Government denied the railways adequate materials to build modern replacements. (* see BTC 1948 Report, Para 246).

Canals

1939

On 1st September, 34 railway owned canals [995 miles] passed into Government control. Discussions on making the best use of railways in wartime began in 1937. Three weeks later, the MoT told Parliament: "To ensure the best use of canals, an Advisory Committee has been set up"! [Modern Transport, 23rd September].

The MoT was reluctant to take control of canals. In the 1914-18 War, control from 1917 to 1920 cost the Treasury £3m in compensation. [Savage Page 82].

1940

The MoWT wrote to Railways: Government has decided to pay canal carriers a subsidy of 50% of canal tolls paid by them, and to allow canal companies to increase tolls to cover costs with effect from 1st June. [Savage, Page 172].

This must have hurt the Treasury. It helps to explain the replacement of a coherent, logical and reasonable Rail Agreement, enabling them to find funds to subsidise canals. the LPTB and POW's.

1942

On 1st July, the MoWT took control of other canals and certain carriers under Regulation 69 of the Defence (General) Regulations 1939. [Keesing 5224A].

18 Canals were taken over by the MoWT, who received the income and paid a fixed annual sum equivalent to the average revenue in the last three pre-war years, plus outgoings considered necessary for war purposes. [Hadfield, Pages 258-9].

The Treasury agreed the cost of new warehouses and boat repair depots could be paid for by the MoWT, and also grants to maintain canals. [Savage, Page 445].

Control of canals from 1942 to the end of 1945 cost Government £2.4m. [Savage Page 85]

1944

"On the whole, canals came out [of the War] financially, better than railways, as the annual payment can be increased upon an increase in efficiency of working". (Only Government gained from improved railway efficiency). [Modern Transport, 5th May].

Canal traffic had fallen from 13m tons pa in 1938 to 10m tons pa by 1946, of which half was coal. [Hadfield, Page 260]. (The balance had transferred to rail - effectively free of charge for Government traffic, at frozen rates for industrial traffic).

Whilst Government creamed huge profits from railways, averaging £45m pa, plus tax and Excess Profits Tax, it had to subsidise independently owned canals - which would explain the two year delay in take-over. Railways subsidised their own canals, which they had, by law, to keep open for traffic. The difference between the fixed sums paid to canals and railways, is that the former was carrying, a declining volume of traffic, whilst the latter was carrying 50% more.

Shipping

Coastwise Shipping was protected long before the War, against lower rail freight rates and also subsidised from the Railway Freight Rebates Fund. (see page 92).

1939

Shipping requisitioned or chartered, was paid all working and maintenance costs, compensation for lost ships and Government "would return them to owners in the same good order as when taken over". [Bell, Page 174].

These terms contrast with the lack of Government action to restore railway assets to the condition in which they were taken over.

By mid September 1939, coasting tramp rates were 50% over pre-war, by November they were 100-200% higher. The Ministry of Shipping did not control coasting tramp rates. [Savage Page 183]

1940

All regular passenger and cargo ships will be requisitioned as from the date they complete their first discharge after 1st February. The Scheme is similar to 1914-18. Companies manage and operate ships, but account to Government for receipts and expenditure. All profits and losses to go to the Government. [Modern Transport, 13th January].

A White Paper on requisitioning of ships was issued. The rate of hire will cover owners' costs, provide an adequate allowance for depreciation, and give a reasonable return on capital. For liners, the return will be worked out for each ship at 10% pa on an agreed basis of value. This will allow 5% return on capital and 5% for depreciation. Under the shipbuilding loans scheme a total of £4.8m was approved. If a ship is lost, the pre-war value of the ship will be paid in cash and any "increased value" credited to the owners when the ship is replaced. [Cmd 6218]. (Thrice the return which railways were allowed. Government made railways pay half the cost of war damage from the 3.3% return on assets which they were allowed!).

Cabinet agreed to requisition some coastal liners in August 1940. Owners received reasonable remuneration whether ships were employed or not and the Exchequer bore the loss. [Savage, Page 349]

The subsidy paid to shippers to convey coal by sea to avoid it being forced onto overloaded railways cost £103,048 in the 1940-1 winter. [Savage Pages 185/6]

1941

By early 1941, tramp rates were 300-400% over pre-war. [Savage Page 185].

The MoWT accepted ship requisition terms were low and made allowance for higher building costs. [Modern Transport, 8th November].

Nothing similar was paid for railway assets. Indeed, Government had just reduced the railways' requisition terms. Three years later, the Government refused to accept irrefutable evidence that railways had been subjected to a 50% increase in workload, and assets were being inadequately maintained, and refused to concede better terms.

Post-war

Charges approved by the MoWT for coastal shipping, was up 200-300% on pre-war rates. [Hansard, March 1947, vol. 434, col 14].

This contrasted sharply with increases approved by the MoT for railways which were only $16^{2}/_{3}$% above pre-war until July 1946, thereafter 25-33% above pre-war. (see page 164).

Payment for lost railway ships [130 were sequestrated] were to be thrown into a Trust Fund and received in the light of "existing relevant liabilities", [a clause, which was not clarified]. [PRO : RAIL424/18].

The requisitioning of or transfer to other duties of coastwise shipping placed an extra load on railways, for which they gained nothing, but ran from 1940 to the end of the war in August 1945, 46,000 "Convoy trains" of coal from East coast collieries. [Bell, Page 83].

Airlines

Aircraft were, initially, hired by the Air Ministry to transport men and supplies, because they had failed to provide enough transport aircraft for military use.

1939

On 1st September, the Air Minister ordered Air Operating Companies to place their aircraft at his disposal. They have fulfilled a number of charter duties for the Royal Air Force and Government. These charters have not interfered with the running of regular services overseas. [Modern Transport, 1st September].

1940

The Air Ministry listed 11 internal routes to continue to be operated, [e.g. Northern Ireland, Scottish Islands - often carrying military personnel]. As from 1st March, companies serving other routes or engaged in private hire or charter will be called on to hand over their machines at valuation. Over 100 aircraft handed over at valuation. [Modern Transport, 2nd March].

Government did not offer to take railways over at valuation.

The Independent Airline Operators [nine companies], owned aircraft valued at £200,000. They had flown 1m miles on Air Ministry duties in five months. [Modern Transport, 9th March].

It will be noted that they were paid normal hire or charter rates, not rates imposed a third or more below normal commercial rates as applied to railways. Unlike railways, during the period 1938-1949, airlines were subsidised. [Hansard vol. 466, cols. 109-110].

Industry

Correlli Barnett reveals poor industrial management before and during the War, and an example of a return on capital in the steel industry nearly tenfold the return allowed to Railways which were subsidising them. [Barnett[1], Page 94].

"Already in 1914, the British industrial firm was too small and unit too traditional in methods, clinging to products and techniques successful in the past. Britain did not retain initiative after fundamental inventions. Industry failed to appreciate that it was entering a new highly technical phase". [Barnett[2], Page 191].

The General Council of the TUC criticised large profits being made out of rearmament in May 1938. [Bullock, Page 625].

1939

The Prices of Goods Act 1939 permitted businesses, but not railways, to increase prices to reflect cost increases. The "Permitted Price" was the "Basic Price" [that on 21st August 1939], plus the "Permitted Increase": increases in costs of materials, manufacturing & processing operations, wages, salaries, pensions, benevolent & welfare schemes, ***transport***, administrative & establishment expenses, premises, customs duty, advertising, interest on loans and bad debts. Independent arbitration would hear appeals.

Compensation Defence Act 1939: Sec. 2: Tribunals to decide compensation for war damage - Sec. 12: Railways were excluded from arbitration.

1940

By early 1940 the increase in average profit per ton of coal over pre-war was 33%. [Supple, Page 518].

No thought had been given to rationalising coal movement although it had been done in the 1914-18 War. [Savage, Page 139].

No other major industry [than coal] carried so many unsolved problems into the war, none brought more out. [Court Page 391].

Bevin criticised Britain's failure to achieve economies of standardisation in car design and their failure to produce for export, and attacked the steel industry for inefficiency and artificially high prices. [Bullock, Pages 386 & 389].

Industry did not respond to Government calls to improve wagon turn-round. Vastly increased traffic, in lieu of imports [timber, iron ore etc.], inland diversion of former exports [especially coal] plus war materials, demanded better wagon utilisation, by faster turn-round, since, apart from retaining 50,000 wagons due for scrapping, few new wagons were likely as Railway Workshops were put on war production. POW's - were designated as "available for general use", but poor design and longer journeys carrying coal, due to replacement of coastwise shipping by rail caused more defects in these poor quality wagons, and created little margin for other traffic. Moreover, they were not designed to carry general goods, and being impregnated with coal or other minerals, were unsuitable.

Railways unloaded wagons on Sundays to speed turn-round, but Industry did not. The MoT doubled detention charges, and reduced the "free period" for unloading or loading to 24 hours. In December 1939, traders would not pay saying free periods were inadequate, (they did not get 24 hours to unload a lorry). The MoT capitulated, increased free periods, and waived all charges from December to February 1940. Traders were still dissatisfied and refused to pay on the new basis with £5m unpaid. The Government backed off, and introduced a "List of Circumstances" for claiming reduction in detention charges, which continued long after the war. They were really ***excuses for not releasing wagons***. By the end of 1940 the REC and Government complained of a conspiracy to avoid paying demurrage charges. Government Departments were not guiltless. Amounts unpaid by September 1941 was £4.5m, and by September 1942 £5.2m. [Savage Page 111].

Investigations revealed blocks of 50-100 wagons to consignees who could only unload 3-4 per day. The Ministry of Supply said a consignee who could unload 25 per day, held up for 3 days could not handle 75. [Savage Page 213].

This was an infantile defence for apathy. It is highly unlikely any consignee's sidings would ever be empty, given the appalling turn-round times. If they were able to deal with 25, it was unhelpful if 200 were in the pipeline. He was playing with figures. No expert would accept such an infantile hypothesis for an unnamed location. The hypothesis relates to locations with ***up to 25 days*** of traffic in the pipeline! Moreover, "Transport problems did not threaten the war effort". [Savage, Page 255].

Railway Docks rates and charges increased by 20% from 1st November 1940. After 1940, Government policy [of price freezing] applied to railway docks, which did not increase charges, but at docks managed by Public Boards dues were increased by higher percentages, in at least one case by 100%. [Bell, Page 152].

In November 1940, a Departmental Committee [of the DoT] found that Port Movement Officers were ignorant of cargoes expected or their planned destinations or ability of consignees to receive and unload promptly. [Savage, Page 235].

This lack of knowledge did not facilitate expeditious transport.

In November & December 1940, 90,000 wagons were underload at destinations. Traders & coal merchants were reluctant to break peace-time habits. [Savage Page 238].

In September to December, average steel imports were 1.16m tons against 50,000 tons pre-war, requiring long wagons of which there were few. Pre-war, industry had reduced production capacity to increase profits. This was applied ruthlessly in the shipbuilding industry, berths of 1m ton capacity being destroyed. [Taylor, Pages 546 & 340].

Railways had not had to cater for such imports before the war, due to Government's protectionist policy, and UK industry needed few wagons of the now required length.

1941

In July 1941, The Exchequer subsidised some industrial coal. It is not clear why Government gave way to owners. Some collieries which did not need help were given Grants. [Court, Pages 187 & 194]

The Lord President's Committee concluded on 22nd August, [LP41/138]: Stabilisation precludes general increases in gas prices, so that a levy would have to come from the profits of the more prosperous undertakings - a levy is unacceptable to the industry. It is impossible to freeze all at the level on Budget Day. The Chancellor said Departments should have discretion to allow electricity and water to rise by 30% or more in exceptional cases. London gas companies had been prevented from increasing prices since December (Railways last increase was in August. The rejected level of rail increases was 31% above 1939. Railways opposed a levy to subsidise the LPTB - but Government ignored them).

Cabinet Minutes for 29th September 1941 refer to reports in newspapers of inefficiency in production matters.

The Board of Trade blocked the collection of statistics by the Coal Commission in 1941 to avoid upsetting coal owners. [Supple, Page 499].

The President of the Board of Trade said the coal industry was notoriously inefficient and recommended Government should requisition it in return for a rent for the duration. [Supple, Page 522].

Industrial attitudes were described as "The cynical spectacle of suppliers of materials, at increasing prices to railways, complaining of consequential increases in railway charges". [Economist, 2nd August, 1941, Page 140].

1942

The Restoration of Trade Practices Act was passed to secure co-operation to improving industrial productivity. It promised restoration of restrictive practices after the war.

Government established dual control of the coal industry. Collieries were left in private hands. Ministerial control proved inadequate. [Cmd 6364 & Supple, Page 544].

Government decided that Nationalisation of mines was politically impossible during the war. Bevin's proposal in May 1942 was to requisition the mines by a compulsory lease for the period of the war and six months thereafter, paying an annual rent equal to average net profits for the last five years. It was rejected. [Bullock, Page 169].

Rail nationalisation was considered during the war. Railway "production" rose 50%, mines fell. Coal industry rent was to be based on five years earnings, including the profitable war and rearmament period, whilst railways rent was frozen with production rising continually. There were widespread coal strikes in 1942 and 1943, despite a ban, losing three times as much production in 1943 as 1941. Government didn't do anything. Coal mining was the one major industry in which production fell instead of rising. [Bullock, Pages 259 & 261].

1943

In October 1943 the Minister of Fuel & Power said the only solution was for the State to take ownership of mines for the duration of the war. Government avoided the ownership issue and established a cumbersome system of dual control. Owners remained in possession of their property and continued to be responsible for finance. The Fuel Minister recommended the temporary elimination of the coal owner, and Government renting pits for the duration of the war, Government declined. [Supple, Page 553].

It would have been similar to the railway "Rental", but doubtless, Government feared "powerful interests" in the mining industry, as they did in the wagon owning industry.

1944

Unofficial strikes and go slows in industry had by 1944, lost working days which were three times 1938 levels. [Deighton, Page 416]. Industrial disputes compare unfavourably with railways, where, for example in 1939, on the eve of war, ASLEF did not proceed with a threatened strike over pay, when the Government appealed to them that they would be needed to evacuate the children from cities. (see "Blueprints for Bankruptcy", Page 198).

British rolling mills could not meet minimum railway needs for rails. The gap was filled by 161,000 tons of American 39ft rails, which had to be welded into UK lengths. [British Railways in Peace & War, Page 46].

A 1944 Report on British mining by American engineers was too critical to be made public. They were astonished at the atrocious state of industrial relations, poor morale and lack of urgency on the part of miners, managers and owners. The Coal Charges Account [Government's subsidy to the coal industry] was in deficit between June 1942 & December 1944 by £26m which was met by the Treasury. [Supple, Pages 561 & 585].

In contrast, American rail experts made three visits to the UK, and were so impressed with railway operations, they had no suggestions to make. [Hansard, vol. 431, col.2065].

Coal production fell throughout the war and threatened all production. The peace-time attitude had been to restrict output in the interests of a higher price. [Court, Pages 109 & 182]. Coal owners had called for lower rail wages in peace-time to increase profits. **(see page 76).**

1945

From June 1942 to December 1945, the Exchequer subsidised the coal industry by £22.78m. Despite this, and frozen rail rates, coal prices increased by 125% between 1938 and 1945. Little was done to facilitate transport rationalisation : one depot received 500 tons per week from fifty collieries, another depot 195 tons per week from six collieries, and to a gas works, 750 tons per week from fifteen collieries. [Court, Pages 340, 347 & 369].

Post-war

Whilst Government was planning "rail nationalisation on the cheap", and planning to deny railways essential materials to restore the system to pre-war standards, they gave the cotton industry 25% of the cost of new spinning equipment to replace their outdated equipment, but rejected nationalising that industry. [Economist 21st December 1946, Page 1007].

The Government subsidy to agriculture, had reached £400m, in 1948. [Cairncross, Page 62]. Agriculture was subsidised by railway rates until 1957, and by Freight Rebates until 1951. Between 1938 and 1946, the price of coal had risen 130%. [Chester, Page 1054].

The MoWT criticised the disparity between rail and industrial inflation. (see page 165).

PART V

THE KNOCKOUT

The original White Paper proposed total freedom.
Churchill told his Cabinet: he "would not accept the BTC should be free even with the approval of the Tribunal to adjust rates without intervention by Government or Parliament".

[Cabinet Minutes, April 1952]

Governments do not learn from history. Throughout the "Great War", they kept railway charges virtually static, but in 1921 to avoid railways becoming bankrupt, Government had to authorise average increases of 112% over 1913 freight rates compared with increases of 200% in the price of materials (see page 44). Pursuing a similar policy in World War II, but not taking similar post-war action, they expressed surprise when railways began to lose money.

In contrast, Government wasted no time in helping other transport to resume normal activity. Road transport was released from pseudo control in 1946, leaving railways which unlike road had contributed vast sums to the Exchequer, controlled for another 18 months - two and a half years after the War ended. The reason could only be, the expectation of further unearned income for the Treasury, directly or indirectly from controlled rail rates, and free travel for HM Forces. It was not a consequence of Government's intention to nationalise railways, because it intended also to nationalise road transport. The BTC had to negotiate terms to take haulage into State control, and these, unlike railways, were subject to independent arbitration.

In August 1946, the MoT told Parliament: ten railway ships were still under requisition, of which four were undergoing reconditioning to return to commercial service. In contrast, the SS Queen Elizabeth ended war transport duties on March 6th and by September was back in civilian service. [Modern Transport, 10th August]

After the Essential Works Order was lifted in August 1946, nearly 5,000 footplate and over 13,000 permanent way staff left in six months because wage rates in other industries were 68% above August 1939, whilst railway wage rates had been restricted to 54%. [Select Committee, PRO : MT47/276].

So much for Stabilisation of costs in other industry. Government had kept rail wages lower because RSNT arbitration decisions on wages were binding.

Rail Charges

Despite rising costs, no increase was made after 1940. Charges should have increased in 1941, by 31% over pre-war. (see page 130). Had charges kept pace with the unremitting rise in costs, as applied to industry, there would have been a surplus of £154m in 1946.

In 1946 Government forgot it had "assumed the risk of profit *or* loss" *. Clearly, they had expected no risk of loss. In May, the MoT said that railway revenue did not cover the Rental, due to costs being 70% above pre-war whilst rail charges were only 10% to $16^2/_3$% above pre-war. (Because Government had determined charges without obligation to adjust to working costs). The MoWT said "It [this uncommercial situation] had been made possible by the large volume of war traffic including Government traffic. With the rapid decline in Government traffic rail receipts had fallen sharply. The MoT estimated that a £19m surplus in 1945 over fixed rental would, in 1946, become a deficit of £40m. An increase in charges is a first and urgent step and would produce £30m in a full year". He authorised, with effect from 1st July, an increase in fares from $16^2/_3$ % above pre-war to $33^1/_3$%, workmen & season tickets from 10% to 25%, goods from 10% to 25% with a yield of £30m. [Hansard vol. 423, col. 1168]. (* see page 139).

Government conveniently forgot the MoWT's promise in August 1941: "Before control ends, time will be given for the operation of any machinery governing the level of charges". (see page 137). Reinstatement of suspended powers of the Railway Rates Tribunal, under the 1921 Act would have obliged it to increase charges to produce net revenue of £51m, not the wartime main line railway Rental of £38m.

Government also ignored the statement by the MoWT in 1943 : "If railways are deprived of higher grade traffics by road transport competition, they must increase rates in other traffic or sink into oblivion. The railways must be returned in full efficiency". [HoL Hansard vol. 129, col. 383].

Government amnesia also extended to the pre-war problems which gave rise to the "Square Deal" campaigns. Despite all the evidence put before them publicly and those advanced secretly, Ministers obsessively clung to the concept of controlled railway rates based on what the traffic (they assumed) would bear. And, lo and behold, freight traffic resumed its drift away from railways.

The period August 1945 to December 1947, marks one of few occasions in peacetime when Government refused to implement the provisions of an Act which had not been repealed. It is not without significance in a review of the "Square Deal Denied" that there were two other notable occasions - both of which were to the disadvantage of railways - in 1920 and in the 1930's. (see pages 32 & page 63).

On August 3rd, 1946, the MoT asked members of the Railway Rates Tribunal acting as a Charges Consultative Committee to consider railway charges, and to hold a public inquiry at which local authorities and other representative bodies would be given an opportunity of being heard, [i.e. "objecting"]. Their Remit was:

> To advise on the best method of adjusting charges to equate to the fixed annual sum payable under the Rental Agreement. [Hansard vol. 423, col. 1168].

Their 579 page verbatim SECRET Report to the MoT of a 25 day Public Hearing, held between 16th September and 23rd October was dated 15th November. There was a panel of three, and 26 KC's and other advocates appeared before them, representing local authorities, traders and industry. The Report was "Closed to 1997". [PRO MT6/2704]. Another non security jeopardising file kept under wraps for 50 years!.

Heald, KC for Railways said: Government did very well out of railway control securing over £200m between 1940-45. (These were the overt profits. Hidden discounts raised the gain to £1 billion - see page 144). The Emergency Powers Act had expired 23rd February 1946, but Control was retained under the Supplies & Services Order 1945, which allowed Defence Regulations 56 & 69 to continue. In 1944, Government traffic amounted to £150m and the whole of railways traffic in 1938 had been less than £200m. He noted that the MoT had told Parliament on 29th May: "that railway costs are up 70%, charges only $16^2/_3$%. If every other commodity and service in the country had an increase of only $33^1/_3$% or 25%, [comparable to railways], we should be in a much happier position than we are today". The Railways' submission showed costs had increased for all materials expenditure. Steel & timber by 50%, all stores had risen, some had doubled.

The Railway companies stated that total railway expenditure was estimated at £317.3m and estimated receipts were £340.2m

Despite the disparity between expenditure and receipts, Industries, Local Authorities and others objected to ***any*** increase. The LCC said that receipts were under-estimated by £10m. Southend, Barking & Essex local authorities objected to fares increases.

Over the next 22 years these local authorities vociferously and successfully achieved the retention of sub standard fares - trailing well behind the RPI and fares elsewhere on BR - and then criticised railway management for not providing improved services from negative profits! (See "Blueprints for Bankruptcy").

Objectors, including the Traders Co-ordinating Committee on Transport, said that low freight charges kept down prices, assisted full employment and helped industry to maintain their position. Much of the "last five and a half days [of the Inquiry] was devoted to the interests of Coastwise Shipping". "The separate Report on Coastwise Shipping referred to was not published" by the Consultative Committee Report on Fares & Charges. [Ford, Page 194]. It could not be found in the PRO.

The Committee concluded that at present level of charges, gross receipts can be expected to be substantially more than the Railway estimate of £340m for 1947. At existing wage and price levels, the Committee forecast gross 1947 expenditure at £329.97m, and receipts at £359.42m, a surplus of £29.45m, or £9.2m less than the £38.6m payable by Government to Railways (excluding LPTB). The proposed increases would bring net revenue to £38.5m, £132,000 less than the Rental. The Committee reported that "All parties contend Railway estimates of 1947 receipts were too low, and that no increase was necessary". (Events proved them to be hopelessly wrong - see page 167).

The Committee recommended lifting fares and parcels rates by 35% over 1939, freight rates by 30% over 1939, from January 1947. "Differentials in Workmen and Season ticket fares should not be increased - due to a critical period ahead for industry", there should be no change in these fares. [Keesing, 8469C].

This would have maintained the wartime subsidy by privately owned railways for inefficient industry, which had been free to increase prices to cover increased costs throughout the War. Perhaps herein lies the reason for hiding these papers away for 50 years. It is incredible that the only estimates which were dismissed were those of railway companies, who were subsequently exonerated by the facts. It is tragic that there were no public inquiries in which railway managers, and their barristers, could challenge the estimates of UK industry and prevent the savage increases in costs which railways had to suffer. UK industry had become so dependent on uneconomic rail charges for basic materials to enable it to compete with foreign companies, that it was blind to the alternatives of modernisation of methods or of thinking.

The Report, dated 15th November, was not made public until 24th February 1947. Government sat on it. The MoT told Parliament that in view of the uncertainty of the level of railway traffic in the current year, Government had decided not to take action until the end of March when the position will be reviewed. [Hansard vol. 438, col 1672].

Government made a knee jerk reaction to the demands of those who expected that rail charges alone should remain below the RPI, whilst they pushed their own prices and wages up and up. There was only one way rail traffic would go from the wartime peak and that was down. The MoT had drawn attention to the decline in traffic. (see page 164).

On 5th August - ten months after the Committee's recommendation - the MoT told Parliament that railway charges will be increased on October 1st by 16.25% for fares and merchandise by passenger train, and by 24% for all other rail traffic equivalent to 55% above pre-war. He said that the Pool fell short of the main line companies' Rental by £37m in 1947 and £28m in 1948. With wages increased by Government's Court of Inquiry, the shortfall would be £59m in 1947 and £65m in 1948. The 1947 yield was estimated at £15.5m leaving the Exchequer to meet a balance of £43.5m. He said that the deficiency arose because charges had not been adjusted during the war to the upward movement of prices making an immediate adjustment necessary. The question whether the ***relationship*** between the various types of charges should be varied would be left for decision by the Transport Tribunal. (This did not envisage that their decision would determine total revenue - which is how they subsequently acted). [Hansard vol. 441, col. 1297].

The MoT said adjustment of rates and charges to present levels arises because they were not dealt with by Government during the war. [Hansard vol. 441, col. 1299].

1947 Revenue was £355m, after an increase yielding £17m, confirming railway forecasts. It is notable that the MoT made the same error as was made in 1920, pushing up freight rates more than passenger, and thereby encouraging further creaming-off. Government also repeated its' 1919 interference in wages with a public Inquiry.

Compensation for War Damage

The first Paper on War Damage [Cmd 6136], in 1939, stated that Government has undertaken to pay the highest compensation possible at the end of the war. The basis of reinstatement will be the value as between a willing seller and a willing buyer. In 1940, another Paper [Cmd 6197] was issued for agriculture. In 1941, a third Paper [Cmd 6403] was issued covering Public Utilities, "which are now excluded from earlier provisions as they were not appropriate". Government reduced its' share from an inferred 100% to 50%, and then told railways to pay their share of War Damage from the "Rental" - not from the working costs, whilst Government covered its share from the fat sums they gained. In contrast, compensation for other industries was to be decided by independent Tribunals.

15th January 1943. Internal DoWT Paper on Post-war railways: It is estimated that war damage at the end of 1942 was £19m and is forecast to be £25m by the end of the war. (The date of which would be pure speculation). [PRO : MT47/275].

The passenger fleet was reduced by 3,000 due to war damage. (BTC 1948 Report, Para 243).

By Treasury Order in June 1949, the Government, as its share, paid £24.8m, ostensibly 72% of the Railways claim for wartime damage, based on an inflationary uplift to reflect the decline in money values. DoT papers show that, as at 1948, the claim was to be uplifted by 118%, amended in 1949 [when the claim was paid] to 100% - as prices were still rising the factor should have increased, not decreased. [PRO : MT47/263].

The cost of commodities in general use had risen 145% over 1939 - applying this rate brings the payment close to 50%. [BTC 1949 Report, Para 200].

Government blocked the repair of some war damage for up to ten years, by which time money values had fallen even further, so that less was achieved from it. (see page 179).

Payments for Abnormal Wear & Tear

During the war, Railways appealed in vain to the Government to review the "Agreement" in the light of very much heavier traffic levels, and to introduce charges based on fair competition [with road transport]. The claim for abnormal wear and tear was settled in 1949 by the MoT and BTC for £46m - some media reports said this was not generous. Little opposition to the MoT was likely from Sir Cyril Hurcomb, Chairman of the BTC, who had led the DoWT deputation in the Rental talks and was duly rewarded.

Coaches

At the outbreak of war, new railway coach building - but not road vehicles - was suspended. Many railway coaches were modified for war use, as ambulance trains and trains for top military leaders. Within two months, 82 vehicles had been converted by railways for use as ambulance trains at home and abroad. Later, 66 ambulance trains were converted for use in Europe for D-Day. In 1945, another 22 trains of 14-15 coaches were sent to Europe for military use. The Government were advised that the transfer, when 25% of coaches were under repair would cause great difficulty, but they insisted. The conversion cost was £1.8m. [Bell, Pages 196-8 & 201].

In 1944, railways needed 1,200 new coaches, but were compelled to send twelve trains of coaches, and 3,000 wagons to help the French Railways. [Savage, Page 626].

Compared to 1939, there were 2,650 passenger carrying vehicles and 1,478 non passenger carrying vehicles less. Plans to build 3,000 were cut [by Government] to 1,200. 389 coaches due for scrapping had to be refurbished at a cost of £188,000. The average age of passenger vehicles increased from 18 years in 1939 to 21 in 1948; 21.5% were over 35 years old. [BTC 1948 Report, Paras 243-4 & 271]. Intensive use equated 35 to about 50 years.

There were 1,000 coaches more under repairs than pre-war. (BTC 1948 Report, Para 243).

Locos

In July 1939 the War Office had demanded 800 locos for service overseas, and were initially given 100, some were left behind in France in 1940. Another 343 locos were later handed over for the duration of the War, plus many others hired to Government. [Bell, Pages 110-111]. (The term "hired" is a misnomer, as the effect of the Fixed Rental was that Government had their use, free of charge).

138 locos were lost in France. Pre-war, railways built or bought 600 locos pa. In the first two & half years of war they could build only 359 for their own use. [Savage, Page 402].

The MoWT cut plans for loco building in October 1942 - instead of 229 by the end of 1942, it was reduced to 185. Of 455 for planned in 1943 only 246 were expected. The loco repair position was forecast to be worse - dangerously so. The Ministry of Production said labour for loco building was more important than shipbuilding. [Savage, Page 406].

By the end of 1943, the loco build was 1,900 less than the pre-war rate, without allowing for excessive numbers under repair due to the 50% overload they were handling and traffic was still increasing.

Wagons

Up to the end of 1943, the annual build of wagons was less than half that of pre-war, which had been 21,000 pa. Private owners built less - to the end of 1943, 3,000 compared to 9,000 pa pre-war. In 1943, 40-50,000 wagons were in service which would have been scrapped pre-war. They required heavy uneconomic repair. [Savage, Pages 411& 412].

Arrears of Maintenance

The railway companies had largely re-equipped themselves before the war. They had laid new track, loops, sidings & exchange junctions. A good deal of this was done for coal traffic and £2m went on this alone. ["Transport goes to war" - Page 46].

Hill wrote to the MoWT and Hurcomb on 23rd July 1941: It is acknowledged that maintenance is deteriorating through lack of a stitch in time, with workshops being engaged on war munitions etc. [PRO : MT47/278].

At a meeting in September, Hill [DoWT] said removing glass from station roofs had reduced maintenance costs. Wood [LMS] said there was a greater contra due to rain falling on floors not built to resist and drain it away. [PRO : RAIL424/18].

This was a nit picking attempt to justify cuts in compensation. A prudent non professional would have asked *if* removal of glass had reduced maintenance costs.

September [circa] 1941. Undated Internal DoWT Memo :

> **Arrears of Maintenance**
>
> Railway companies point out that they are likely to end the Control Period with complete renewals of permanent way and rolling stock more heavily in arrears than repairs. The cost of executing renewals in the post Control period will be higher. [PRO : MT47/279].

Hill wrote to the Minister & Hurcomb, on 10th October, on the subject of Maintenance: The original offer limited maintenance to pre-war standards. Costs over that standard, after adjustment for prices and wage levels, to be borne by the companies from their own funds. There was provision for a review at the end of the Control period, in the light of "relevant liabilities". The Railways objected strongly. It was eventually agreed to deal with maintenance on a broad basis during Control, ruling out abnormal wear and tear, uneconomic repairs, allowing railways to retain sums brought out by the arrears formula without attempting to assess the actual expenditure to be incurred in making good, physical arrears of work. Up to the end of 1940, the formula showed arrears of £20m, this will be substantially increased in 1941. [PRO : MT47/279].

Internal unsigned DoWT Memo, 30th September: Railway arrears are estimated to be £90m at the end of 1943 and in competition with current work, could hardly be disposed of in less than 8-10 years [after the war]. [PRO : MT47/275].

In 1935-6-7, track renewals averaged 1,366 miles pa. In 1938 & 1939, renewals were, in total 249 miles above average. However, in 1940-42 inclusive, renewals were 1,215 in arrears. Relaying of sidings was heavily in arrears. The permanent-way deficiency was 30% pa compared with pre-war. [Savage, Page 572].

This is the deficiency at pre-war traffic levels. However, "Traffic increases of 50% more freight and 100% more passengers by 1943", meant that arrears were much greater. Railways had 20,000 route miles, comprising 35,000 track miles, plus 14,000 miles of sidings in 1938/9. Post-war arrears were phenomenal.

By September 1942, the LNER had 19.87% locos out of use in sheds plus 8.59% in shops - a total of 28% against the target of 15%. [Savage, Page 406].

The 1944 Report of the MoWT's Chief Inspecting Officer of Railways stated: "The cumulative effects of longer hours in traffic, heavier loads and insufficient staff to repair and service engines had a marked effect on their condition and the consequent increase in failures in traffic adversely affected operating efficiency".

At the end 1944, 1,000 coaches were in use for ambulance trains, arrears of repairs on coaches was 44% of 1944 stock. [Savage, Pages 512 & 625]. 14.45% of coaches are under and awaiting repairs. [BTC Report, Pages 243-4 & 271].

By October 1945, 12% of wagons were Under & Awaiting Repair - three times that of 1940, due to retention of over age wagons, poor supplies of materials and scarcity of labour. [Bell, Page 100].

The Maintenance Trust Fund

In 1940, Government decreed that maintenance was to be charged to the Control Account on the basis of the average expended in 1935-7 allowing for the increased cost of carrying out the work ***during*** the war - but not for heavier wear and tear. The Government established a Trust Fund in 1941 into which was paid money chargeable to expenditure which would have been spent on maintenance had materials and labour been available. It was not a gift, but part of chargeable expenditure before Government was left with £1 billion of discounts and profits, (see "Blueprints for Bankruptcy" Page 27).

It was to be paid out at the end of the Control period, when prices would be higher and, hence, its' value lower.

By 31st December 1946, the Fund amounted to £147m plus interest of £5.26m. [Keesing 9283A]. Average maintenance costs in 1935-7 were £42m pa. £147m was 3 years expenditure at pre-war levels - a formidable backlog to arise from seven years of Government Control. Little wonder that, in 1956, the MoT said that "railways emerged from the war with most of their equipment out of date and all of it run down". [Cmd 9880].

Having sequestrated railways, Government had a moral (even a legal), duty to return infrastructure and assets to the condition in which they found them. Had they repaid gratitude voiced by Ministers, (see below), they would have put them into better condition as a reward for wartime efforts. In contrast, road competitors obtained new vehicles in excess of Government policy, (see page 178), funded by wartime profits. (see Chapter 13).

Ships returned to owners were restored to pre-war condition. Words of gratitude were no substitute for restoration of assets worn out by excessive war demands and war damage, and which should have been replaced by Government using the vast sum skimmed out of railways. (see page 144).

Gratitude for Railways' Wartime Efforts

After the First World War, Ministers and military leaders expressed praise and gratitude for the vital part played by sequestrated railways in the conduct and winning of the war.

The 120 separate Railways were then forcibly amalgamated into four companies, and the rates which they could charge thereafter subject to detailed legal control. Their profits were, uniquely, to be held, in perpetuity, at 1913 levels! In 1939, Government swept this aside to reduce profits to a lower level. In 1948, they went further, abolishing profits altogether, by a new Statutory requirement, merely to break even.

There was a stream of praise for Railways during the 1939-45 War for Civilian Evacuation, Mobilisation, Dunkirk, North African campaign, D-Day and afterwards. The number of civilians evacuated from London was greater than the population of Leeds.

In June 1940, the War Minister and MoT thanked Railways for the part played in the Evacuation from France of 319,000 troops requiring 820 special trains. [Bell, Page 74].

In November 1943, the MoWT said "Railways have earned the gratitude of the country. No other transport agency could have moved the masses of men and materials required by modern warfare". ["Coming of Age", Page 53].

A month later, the Prime Minister wrote: "I should like to take this opportunity of expressing to Railway Management and to every railway employee, the Nation's thanks for the highly efficient manner in which they have met every demand made upon them during the last four years of our desperate struggle with Nazi Germany. Throughout the period of heavy German air raids on this country, the arteries of the Nation, the Railways, with their extensive dock undertakings, were subjected to intensive attacks. Yet the grim determination, unwavering courage and constant resourcefulness of the railwaymen of all ranks have enabled the results of the damage to be overcome very speedily and communications restored without delay. Thus, in spite of every enemy effort, traffic has been kept moving and the great flow of munitions proceeds. Results such as Railways have achieved are only won by blood and sweat, and on behalf of the Nation, I express gratitude to every railwayman who has participated in this great transport effort, which is contributing so largely towards the final victory". ["Coming of Age", Page 60].

The Admiralty, War Office and Air Ministry stated: During the war, railways excelled themselves. The magnificent service rendered during heavy air raids was a triumph of organisation, devotion to duty and outstanding skill. That they have been able to handle the vast military traffic and still provide the civilian population with a train service on the present scale, despite depleted and diluted staffs is a great tribute to those who are giving devoted service on railways and to the capabilities of directing staff. The rapidity with which damaged tracks were reopened to traffic at the time of air raids proved that the engineering staffs are second to none. We are grateful to all for the response to calls made upon them. They played a proud, praiseworthy part in victory. ["Coming of Age", Page 60].

That gratitude was never repaid. The "Square Deal" was abandoned. The industry was taken away from the owners who were criticised by Government for the poor state of assets, which had been put into such condition by Government policy and the heavy war workload for which railways had been grossly underpaid. (see page 180).

During the war, the MoWT refused to acknowledge the detrimental effect the increased workload was having on under maintained assets. Given Government's anti-rail polices, it is inconceivable that Government's post-war assessment of the amount due for Abnormal Wear and Tear approached what was really due.

Wartime Planning for Post-war Railways [PRO : MT47/275]

Internal DoT Memo, 15th October 1940 to A.T.V. Robinson :-

Draft of Proposals for a National Transport Corporation

Para 38: All railways to be transferred on the Appointed Day. Lorries bought up in stages. POW's to be acquired.

Para 43: POW value to be based on present market value at so many years purchase of present hiring rates.

Para 46: Corporation to be self supporting - no subsidy. Uneconomic requirements imposed by the State should be paid for by Government. (A pious hope!).

Para 47: The Rates Scheme prepared by the Corporation to be submitted to the Advisory Committee for their Report. The Corporation to consider their Report and implement without further sanction. Revise as necessary. (Another pious hope!).

Conclusion - Para 80: A Bill rests on four pillars :-

[a] Financial independence

[b] Commercial freedom to fix universal non discriminatory tariffs.

[c] Complete monopoly, except for Traders vehicles.

[d] Wise staff and labour policy.

If any one is broken, the whole fabric of the Bill will collapse.

Post-war legislation completely ignored this conclusion - see Chapter 16.

DoT Memo dated 23rd December 1940, "Railway Mergers, including LPTB" states "these mergers were being considered for implementation during the war to reduce profits to stockholders from £40m to £29m.

R.V.N.H. wrote to Sir Henry Wilson [Treasury], on 21st March 1941, that "the MoT accepts unification only after the war". [PRO : MT47/277].

War Cabinet, 24th July 1941. Memo from the MoWT: WP [41] 173: One matter which may have to be dealt with was the basis for post-war reconstruction [including reorganisation of the national transport system - road transport as well as rail. This was a Tory Government envisaging nationalisation].

At an internal DoWT meeting on 18th November 1941, Hurcomb advocated determining post war requirements. "Care to be taken not to divulge to the outside world". [PRO : MT47/275].

Government Gains from Sequestration

In 1938, the strength of the HM Forces was 0.3m. The wartime average was 4.12m. In 1946-47, it averaged 1.75m, falling to 0.75m until 1958, and gradually decreasing until by 1990 it was back to the pre-war level. [CSO].

It peaked at 9m in 1945, from 1.27m in 1939. Releases from the Forces were- 1945: 1.5m, 1946: 2.8m, 1947: 0.6m. [Statistical Digest, Table 10 & 13].

These all represented a huge increase in traffic for railways both during the war, and during demobilisation, for which railways effectively received not a penny. During the war and since, railways had to subsidise HM Forces travel from other sources.

Had the Square Deal been implemented, rail charges should have increased under the 1939 Prices of Goods Act. Wartime costs were £2,266m. The "Permitted Increase" would have been £2,266m less £1,268m (eight times the average pre-war cost of £158.5m pa), giving £998m additional revenue, to which must be added £127m Government took from the Pool. Even had the LPTB been paid 11% of this greater sum, this would have left a balance of £1 billion, for main line railways. This covert gain comprised profits and discounts to Government from holding down prices it paid to industry through frozen rail rates and by traffic diverted to rail from other modes, free of charge. Revenue would have been higher had Government traffic been charged at rates reflecting the excessive wear and tear which it caused. If costs were adjusted to reflect the war traffic increase of up to 50%, the maintenance cost of £2,266m would be about £3,000m, increasing Government's immoral gain by a further £770m. This £1.77 billion was worth £1,330 billions by 1990.

Government did very well from railways, having its traffic carried at up to 50% below frozen public charges and then creamed off £127m. The total "Rental" was £301m [£43m pa for 1941-47 inclusive], plus £42m for 1940, a total of £343m. Of this, 11% went to the LPTB and £0.5m pa to minor railways, leaving main line railways with £305m for eight years sequestration instead of a Statutory minimum of £411m, [Standard Revenue of £51.4m pa plus 20% of the excess], which the law entitled them to earn. Running assets into the ground, Government gained enough to buy railways outright, leaving BR free of debt. Then the State would have been able to claim that it owned BR. Instead, they decreed that BR should buy itself, but prevented them from doing so by holding prices below the RPI, whilst costs soared above the RPI, due to Government interference inflating railway wages, and inertia on the prices of other industry. Government's discriminatory price policy left BR behind the start line as the post war inflationary spiral took off. BR effectively began life in 1948 with 1941 prices and 1948 costs. Other industry had 1948 prices and 1948 costs - some probably had 1949 prices!

Factors leading to resumed traffic losses

The worn out state of the assets and excessive arrears of repairs, together with speed restrictions imposed by wartime damage not properly repaired by Government directive, and continuing military priorities were at the root of resumed traffic losses after the war.

In November, 1945, the MoWT was told of overcrowded trains and asked to bring back rolling stock from abroad. He said that about half had returned (in unspecified condition) and the rest would come as soon as possible. [Hansard, vol. 415, col. 1604].

In December 1945, the MoWT told Parliament that passenger miles were 70% above 1938, and train miles were 24% less than 1938 (causing severe overcrowding), due to shortage of coal and coaches, (arising from wartime sequestration). [Hansard vol. 416, col. 2708]

In January 1946, trains were being run for the military over Christmas - totalling 806 on the GWR alone. [Modern Transport, January 12th]. (Priority had to be given to such traffic, on free warrants or at sub standard rates, further alienating civilians).

In 1947, railways asked for 3,070 coaches and were supplied with 1,200. Inferior coal led to heavier consumption and reduced efficiency. [Chester, Page 726].

The President of the Board of Trade said: "Transport is to be the basis of a 10% cut on passenger services as compared with last year and the introduction of the summer services will be later - 1st June 1947 instead of 1st May". He confirmed "serious arrears of railway maintenance due to the wartime workload. Coal and industry will take priority over passengers this year especially next winter". [Hansard vol. 434, col 964]

He was not really referring to transport in the full sense, but to railways, which were to bear the brunt of Government's post-war economy measures, although the result would be a further denial of a Square Deal. Existing and potential passengers would inevitably turn to road transport, both private and public - where bus and coach operators were finding no real difficulty in obtaining new vehicles. (see page 178).

Retrospective Assessments

Assets were not fully maintained during the war and kept in service as long as possible without replacement. There was excessive wear and tear arising from minimum maintenance standards since 1939. The Summer service was operated with 4,000 fewer coaches than pre-war - 3,000 smaller fleet due to war damage losses etc, plus 1,000 more than pre-war under repair after excessive wartime usage. Wagons Under & Awaiting Repair was 16.62% in September 1947, due to wartime material shortages.
[BTC 1948 Report, Paras 48, 146 & 150].

War damage losses includes some sent to war zones by Government acting as though they owned the assets.

The MoT said that "During the War, the railway system, its equipment and rolling stock was subject to workloads well in excess of design and kept in use long after normal renewal dates. It was impossible to provide resources to maintain railways except to the very minimum to keep them running, whilst they were subjected to the increased strain imposed by heavy war traffic and wartime operating conditions". [Cmd 9880].

He claims it was "impossible", but new buses and lorries were built in the war. The word for which he was searching was "expedient". Road haulage, from the higher rates they had imposed on industry and Government Departments or "negotiated" with the MoWT, bought a new post-war fleet. (see page 178).

A major cause of arrears was that, during the war, much of railway workshop capacity was deployed on building tanks, aircraft, guns, etc. This soaked up resources which would otherwise have been employed in building locomotives and rolling stock. Whilst motor manufacturers produced military transport, when they were no longer needed, they could be sold for civilian use. Likewise, aircraft had a post-war civilian use. Tanks, guns and aircraft made in railway workshops were useless to post-war railways.

Reduced availability and poor condition of freight rolling stock, led to a decline in standards. Coupled with the unimpeded build of new lorries, and the retention of Government's pack horse rates system, the creaming-off of freight traffic quickly resumed after the war. Wartime losses of rolling stock and arrears of repairs resulted in overcrowded trains, which alienated the public and initiated the drift to road blessed with a surfeit of new buses and cars.

Rolling stock had not been replaced because railway workshops were heavily engaged on producing war weapons and ammunition - 32% of workshop labour was deployed in this way. No railway coaches were built for use in the UK. [Nash, Page 4].

Was it wise to starve railways of capital equipment and manpower so seriously during the war? Railways, the most important branch of wartime transport suffered heavier wear and tear than most essential industries and were not allocated nearly enough resources to maintain their capital intact. [Savage, Page 637].

The end of the war found the country short of railway facilities required for expanding production. During the war, railway workshops were diverted to production closely connected to the war effort. The overtaking of arrears of maintenance and production will have to be gradual. Wagons and locos will be given priority [over railway coaches, not road vehicles of any kind]. It will be some years before railways can catch up on replacement of rails and sleepers. 300,000 tons of rails pa are required for some years to come to catch up on arrears. In 1948, only 250,000 tons can be provided, safety will continue to make some reduction in speeds of trains necessary and this will accentuate the shortage of wagons. [Cmd 7344].

In fact, steel supplies fell way below these levels. (see page 179).

Inefficient, demarcation ridden UK industries could not produce the essential materials in quantities needed, nor at reasonable prices, to enable railways to be restored to pre-war condition, like their competitors. The motor manufacturing industry was given such a huge leg up, that they were quickly equipped to produce on a scale surpassing pre-war. The main beneficiaries were, of course, railways' main competitors. Their resumption of pre-war activity was again facilitated by post-war commercial inequality.

Government had the powers to regulate the supply of cars through raw material controls, but "felt unable to use them". [Plowden, Page 419].

If railways had been returned to their rightful owners in 1945 and not seized in 1948 like the Suez Canal in 1956 - an act which caused this country to go to War - owners would have again demanded equality. If Government had then continued its anti rail policy to maintain rail subsidies to industry, the slide to bankruptcy would have accelerated. Swingeing closures and mergers of competing lines would have been inevitable - some areas would have been without public transport. It is a common fallacy among towns-people that buses would take up the displaced passengers. Some rural areas had no bus service, and some only once weekly. BR was compelled by Ministers to subsidise buses put on to replace closed rail services. Had railways been returned to their owners after the war, subsidising such bus services would never have been tolerated by railway companies.

Had Labour not won the 1945 election, the Tories would have been bound to nationalise railways. To return them to their rightful owners would have required Government to pay substantial compensation on a scale far higher than the overt sums they had skimmed out of railway profits during the war. No privately run business could have survived with its prices held so far behind costs. Under private ownership, fares and freight charges would have had to increase beyond the timid levels approved by Government, in 1946/7 after public hearings, to bring them into line with industrial inflation. These scenarios were quite clearly spelled out during the war. (see pages 128 & 129).

In an attempt to suggest that the privately owned railways were not profitable, an MP stated that "After World War 1, Government gave railways a subsidy of about £30m". Sir Arthur Salter explained that this was part payment for war services. [Hansard vol. 493, col. 306]. (see also page 35).

Chapter 16

INEQUALITY IN THE PUBLIC SECTOR

When the BTC took over railways, they were running at a loss due, to Government's unrealistic, infantile and discriminatory pricing policy, whilst costs continued their unremitting rise - because industry, had been free to increase prices to reflect costs. Government created losses, in a situation in which making a profit was child's play. Nationalised railways were treated less favourably than other transport. BR was saddled with the purchase cost of £43m for 544,000 outdated POW's, instead of the MoT under the 1919 Act, and of maintaining them until they could be replaced by modern bigger wagons.

Marshall Plan [PRO : MT6/2830]

The Marshall Plan, was developed post-war, to enable European countries, including the UK, to obtain aid from the USA.

The Railway Maintenance Division of the DoT wrote on 9th July 1947 to the DoT: Arrears of Railway maintenance in connection with the Marshall Plan are as follows:

> Rails 400,000 tons; sleepers 10m; Locos 1000-1500; wagons 150-200,000*; Carriages 6000. Signalling £10m. It should be emphasised that any imports from America should be in the form of raw materials and not finished locos or rolling stock.

*This could have taken no account of POW's, which alone had 255,000 wagons overdue for scrapping. (see page 156).

A letter from the REC dated 14th July, referred to a 5 year programme. The annual requirement includes 4.7m sleepers & 32,250 tons pa of steel for bridges. A further note on 18th July added : It has been assumed that arrears will be overtaken between 1948-51 inclusive.

The Committee of European Economic Co-operation on Inland Transport wrote on 31st July:

I. Railways

1. Causes of Strain - During the War, output of Railway workshops was diverted to building locos & wagons primarily for armies in the field and to building other types of equipment and armaments : 1943-5, of 2,482 locos built, 66% were sent overseas. The annual intake of new locos should have been 600. Of 72,000 wagons built, 16% were sent overseas. The UK intake should have totalled 105,000.
2. [a] Additional traffic: Net ton miles - compared to 1938, 1943 was up by 49.5%, 1944 by 50%, and 1945 by 35.3%.

   [b] Effects: Of over 1m units of rolling stock - 300,000, or 24%, are over 35 years old and overdue for scrapping. (35 years old, adjusted for increased wartime user equated, in reality, to 50 years old).

   During 1944-46, Abnormal repairs were 1,480 locos, peaking at 1,625, under and awaiting repair. Wagons under and awaiting repair averaged 118,000 in the same period, peaking at 140,000.

Action taken to reduce the strain, were hampered by: -

[a] A shortage of raw materials, power and fuel.

[b] The necessity to build locos & trains to help other countries who have also suffered in the War, e.g. in 1946, out of 725 locos built in UK 376 exported. (Help them to get their industry and railways restored at the ultimate expense of the UK).

D. Conclusion - Railways have been flogged to win the war, and it needs exceptional efforts to get them back into good condition again. The Committee forecast 1948-51 exports as a percentage of UK production - locos: 45.5%, lorries 39.8%, PSV's: 33.3%, lorries plus PSV's: 39.0%. (More evidence of discrimination in favour of road transport). The REC said that not less than 700 locos pa should be scrapped in the next five years and replaced by 600 pa.

II. Road transport

The annual requirement of lorries for normal replacement is about 80,000.

Annexe to the Report. With a full availability of materials [1948-51]:-

			Average
Locos	Production	870-1,200	1,100
	UK market	470-700	600
	Exports	400-500	500
Wagons	Production	59,000-76,000	72,000
	UK market	55,000-72,000	64,000
	Export	4,000	4,000
Lorries	Production	142,000-155,000	152,000
	UK market	84,000-95,000	92,000
	Export	63,000	63,000
PSV's	Production	11,000-12,000	12,000
	UK market	7,500-8,000	8,000
	Export	4,000	4,000

(Had a corresponding 39% of locos been kept for the home market, it would have come close to the 700 needed as specified in "Conclusions". A better situation would have prevailed if the percentage of locos exported had approximated to the percentage of commercial motor vehicles which were actually sent overseas - which would have meant 737 locos for the home market, but the rail "lobby" was not as powerful as the road lobby).

"Under Government direction, 33% of commercial vehicles were sent overseas".
[Modern Transport, 3rd August 1946]. (see also page 178).

REC to Maintenance Division of DoT. Under the five year plan [For restoration of permanent-way and rolling stock to pre-war condition], it is estimated that traffic will be about 1946 levels up to 1952, but coal will increase from 200m tons [1947 target] to 250m tons by 1952.

"Annexe to Minister" dated 6th July 1948: The BTC said that they take no account of a 35 year life of locos but scrap according to condition. 8,000 [40%] are over 35 years, which [DoT] say requires a scrapping rate of 975 pa to catch up in 20 years. The REC recommended not less than 700 be scrapped pa. During the next five years, Railways require 3,700 locos, that is 740 pa. An MoT paper says the UK can only build 566 pa, with existing resources. BTC are therefore only planning to scrap 450. At the Paris meeting emphasis was given to the arrears of 400,000 tons of rails and 10m sleepers, plus current renewals.

In July 1948, 39%, [7,940] locos were over 35 years old. In July 1949, 41.2%, [8,209] locos were over 41 years. (The position was worse when adjusted for the 150% wartime workload. How could railways compete, if they took 20 years to recover the pre-war situation, when road transport had achieved pre-war parity by 1946 - see below).

Memos dated 3rd & 4th August 1949 from Walter to Wilson : There is no prospect of getting 10m sleepers. The requirement of 10m sleepers was calculated from the average wartime replacement compared to 1936-8

Discriminatory Control of Materials

Government's road-rail discrimination policy was apparent in the control of materials which affected the provision of new assets.

Government Economic Surveys: Road transport:

1948 [Cmd 7344], Paras 140/1: The Goods vehicle fleet was 500,000 in 1938, 450,000 in 1945, and 650,000 by 1947. 100,000 vehicles were supplied to UK transport interests in 1947. This should be limited to 50,000 in 1948.

1949 [Cmd 7647], Page 53: 85,000 goods vehicles were supplied. in 1948. To be limited to 50,000 in 1949.

1950 [Cmd 7915], Page 43: Goods vehicles were delivered in the second half of 1949 at an annual rate of 100,000. They should be reduced to an annual rate of 65,000 in the second half 1950.

1951 [Cmd 8509], Significantly, no statistics and no limitations on supply.

The Surveys also revealed that PSV operators were also over supplied against target by 29% pa. Hauliers and PSV operators must have made huge wartime profits to afford so many new vehicles. Paper Government restrictions were blatantly ignored.

Government Economic Surveys: Rail transport.

1948 [Cmd 7344], Para 132 : Overtaking of arrears will have to be gradual in view of the steel shortage. Para 134 : Against 300,000 tons of rails required, can only have 250,000 tons. Ensuing track speed restrictions will accentuate wagon shortages.

1949 [Cmd 7647], Page 51: Arrears of track renewal to be overtaken only to the extent necessary for safety. (speed limits would cause delay and lose traffic).

1950 [Cmd 7915], Page 42: Restrictions on railways will be severe. Since the war, maintenance expenditure on BR has been severely limited. It has not been possible * to carry out a programme for overtaking wartime arrears. (* really means expedient).

1951 [Cmd 8509], Para 70: Increased traffic placed a severe strain on BR - due to a shortage of labour & materials. To ease the strain, coal and other traffic was diverted to road #. Para 72: BR will have substantial cuts in the programme for replacement of locomotives and rolling stock, and work on stations, bridges, tunnels must be severely restricted and track renewal curtailed. (# Government policies restricted materials to railways, whilst competitors poached traffic with their excess vehicles! Railways had to make do and mend).

Cabinet

In March 1951, the MoT told the Cabinet: "Government refusal, to allow Railways to carry out much of the Capital investment which they thought to be necessary, resulted in an accumulation of higher costs".

BTC Annual Reports

1948. Para 46: It is not possible within [Government] limits to construct modern wagons which are the first requirements, without it, uneconomical expenditure on out of date rolling stock must continue. The investment level Government prescribed has been governed by the availability of the principal controlled material - steel. Allocation and delivery are matters for grave concern. Para 48: Assets were not fully maintained during the war and kept in service as long as possible without replacement. Para 146: Excessive wear and tear arising from minimum maintenance standards since 1939. Para 150: Wagons Under & Awaiting Repair were 16.62% in 1947, due to wartime material shortages. Para 271: Hopes of overtaking arrears within a short time were 'modified' by the 1948 White Paper on Investment that supplies of materials for the permanent way must be reduced to current needs, about the same as pre-war without overtaking arrears. Plans to build 3600 coaches had to be cut to 1200.

1949. Para 22: It has been possible to do little more than keep pace with current maintenance and to overtake to a very modest extent [rail] arrears accumulated during and since the War. Steel allocation to BR for 1949 was 1m tons. It proved impossible to obtain more than 810,000 tons.

1951. Para 2: Control on expenditure [for renewals & maintenance] by Government continued, and control on supply of materials. Para 68: Until BR can be assured of sufficient steel to carry out maintenance & renewals no return to pre-war speeds is practicable. Para 71: Only two thirds of bridges in the programme repaired due to steel shortages. (Causing speed restrictions, increased costs and reduced reliability).

1952. Para 1: Steel shortage affecting replacement of rolling stock. Government allocated 20% below BR needs. Deliveries did not reach the reduced allocation, hence output was at half of workshop capacity. Compared to 1951, new building by workshops and contractors was down 12% on locos, 24% on wagons.

1953. Para 125: Arrears of development is due to past restrictions and shortages of materials. The position is more serious in relation to railways than road transport. A complete post war re-equipment of road fleets, passenger and freight, but on BR, even arrears of maintenance due to the intensive use made of Railways in the war have hardly been made good. Para 126: Shortage of steel & other materials. Discouraging and disruptive effects of constantly changing limits upon capital investment combined to hinder progress. Still having to "make do and mend".

1954. Para 113: War arrears still not cleared by the end of 1953. Para 116: Old rolling stock and structures are outdated and over expensive to maintain. In the first nine months of 1948, 710 locos were exported despite serious shortages. BR allocated less materials than needed, but the supply of road transport exceeded Government limits.

Wartime arrears of road transport, if there were any, were made good by 1946 - see Cmd 7344 - whilst those of railways were not cleared until after 1955. Pre-war investment averaged £22m pa. With 50% more traffic from 1939 to 1947, investment needed to be at least 50% above pre-war: £5 billion at 1996 prices.

Co-ordination through Nationalisation

In 1946, the Labour Government announced plans to nationalise key industries, including transport. DoT files at the Public Record Office clearly show that the wartime, Tory dominated coalition Government had similar plans. (see page 172).

The alternative to Nationalisation agreed by traders, canals, coastwise, railways & road haulage was a continuation of Square Deal discussions with all to be common carriers and have a related GCM and rates, for rail and road to accept non discriminatory rates. Traders to have the right to both "C" Licence and to object to railway rates! Railways & hauliers submitted a scheme for integration, including freight wagons used solely by hauliers for express long distance services. [Modern Transport 4th July].

The 1947 Transport Act nationalised railways and some other transport. Railways objected, pointing out that the dividend and interest in 1946 was £42m, and between 1928-38 averaged £35m, the interest from British Transport Stock would pay £23m. They asked for independent arbitration as in 1921. Government refused, although it had applied for coal nationalisation. A Select Committee dismissed share value as a basis for coal nationalisation, opting for "Net Maintainable Revenue", but as arbitration for coal took so long, it scared Ministers from using that basis for railways. [Chester, Page 222-256].

In "The Great Railway Conspiracy", Henshaw said that S.W. Hill had arbitrated in the nationalisation of railways. It is clear that there was no arbitration.

The London Stock Exchange said share prices were not a fair basis for acquisition, as they were not related to the value of assets. Railways objected to Nationalisation and said the BTC would be merely a servant of the MoT in view of his wide powers. Protests were made by stockholders and others. [Keesing 8365A].

In a normal acquisition, share prices would probably have risen.

In November, the MoT announced terms of compensation for nationalisation. Valuation for railways and the LPTB was £1,019m compared with the nominal amount of securities on the Stock Exchange of £1,142m. During the debate on the Nationalisation Bill, the Chancellor said "the permanent way is badly worn, rolling stock in a state of great dilapidation, railways are a disgrace, railway stations and equipment a disgrace to the country". [Keesing 8267A].

It is incredible that a man who was a wartime Minister was blind to the excessive wear and tear of railways, which were not maintained properly due to Government policy and for which railway companies were not recompensed. The Opposition criticised the compensation terms. They had no room to do so, after their wartime treatment of railways!

Railway critics claimed that world-wide evidence of nationalisation proves that railways are unprofitable. In 1920, Parliament was told that they were nationalised in Belgium & Switzerland to rest ownership from foreign capital, in Japan to end concessions which were preventing fares reductions, in Austria & Prussia to provide railways with proper capital because private capital would not invest, and in Germany after 1870 and Russia for military reasons. [Hansard vol. 130, col. 2454]

Railway dividends were low in the inter war years, in some years zero, due to Government refusing to treat rail and road equally. However, contrary to current supposition, they were still profitable, otherwise they would have been liquidated.

More Anti-rail legislation

Transport Act, 1947

Railways, still under Government control, were nationalised without arbitration. Road haulage, released from pseudo "control" eighteen months earlier, would, if operating more than a 25 mile radius, ***subject to arbitration***, be bought up piecemeal by the BTC. The Act contained principles, which continued pre-war discrimination. By not implementing the Square Deal, the Act ensured that freight by rail would continue to decline and that prophecies by Ministers and Civil Servants would be fulfilled. (see pages 128 & 129).

The effect of the Act on freight traffic was to perpetuate, indeed, exacerbate, the inequities which the Square Deal campaign had sought to end :-

1. Directing integration without regard to problem areas. Pre-war Railways sought equality, not integration. Government Inquiries had said co-ordination was impossible, given different rates systems whilst road experts said that a common classification with rail was impractical. (see pages 83 & 150).

2. BR to obtain authority to increase charges, initially from the MoT and thereafter from a Law Court - the Transport Tribunal. Without corresponding price control on suppliers, it could only lead to insolvency. No other State Industry prices were similarly controlled, and neither were those of State owned BRS, a subsidiary - like BR - of the BTC. (see "Blueprints for Bankruptcy"). It goes without saying, that the prices of the private sector were ignored completely by Government.

3. BTC to prepare Charges Schemes. Until a new Charges Scheme based on different principles could be drafted, considered and implemented, the lethal 1928 system had to be perpetuated. This enabled road haulage to resume creaming off traffic from post-war railways lumbered with over-age war worn wagons to compete with post-war built lorries. (see page 178). This inflated road transport profits, and hence raised the ultimate cost of compensation of road companies nationalised over the next 4-5 years. The BTC would not have a freight monopoly, as some public haulage would remain and the pre-war growth of "C" Licence vehicles - carrying goods for the owning company - was set to accelerate. No reason was given for having "Charges Schemes".

4. The Railway Rates Tribunal was replaced by the Court of the Transport Tribunal, Sir Wm. Bruce Thomas being appointed its President, at the age of 70. The new Tribunal would hold Public Inquiries and had greater powers, whilst railways' rights were reduced, as there was no requirement to ensure that a Standard Net Revenue or a profit was to be earned - the new Statutory objective "to pay its way" effectively meant "break even"- a policy undermined by Government. (see "Blueprints for Bankruptcy").

5. Trade organisations and major industries could object to Freight Charges Schemes.

6. Competitors could object - Sec. 78 [3]: "Any body representative of persons providing services comparable to services for which the Schemes relate", may object if Schemes provide for charges which are unduly low. (Road hauliers, canal carriers and coastal shipping could object. In no other industry did this apply).

7. Pending introduction of a Charges Scheme - Sec. 83 permitted increases of an Exceptional Rate which was unduly low by reason of the competition of road haulage, canal carriers or coastal shipping, up to not more than 60% of the Standard Rate. Any trader aggrieved may appeal to the Tribunal. (Competitors offering a rate below rail rates could increase their rate to narrow the margin of undercutting, BR was prevented from doing likewise. Customers and competitors could force BR to hang on to unprofitable traffic! This prevented prompt commercial action to reduce losses). **8.** Directing the BTC to "pay its way taking one year with another" - break even - prolonged Tribunal hearings into applications to increase BR charges - exploited by objectors, who increased their own prices to BR and others! [Butterworth's Legislative Service: "It was not clear over what period Accounts must balance"].

Objectors argued to defer and reduce proposed increases on the grounds that the future may be brighter. It never was! Tribunal and Government actions prevented viability.

"There is a single buyer, which for the past seven years has fixed the revenue of the Railways, and now determines its current value. It is nationalisation on the cheap and comes near to expropriation". [Economist, 23rd November, 1946, Page 836].

Draft Transport Policy [Amendment] Bill, 1952 [PRO : MT62/138].

Following a change of Government, in 1951, a new policy was drawn up for inland transport. Co-ordination was abandoned and road-rail competition resumed.

The Secretary of State for Economic Affairs wrote to the MoT : The Draft Bill envisages an MoT representative on the BTC reporting to him. This would destroy any semblance of even semi-independence. (confirming that the BTC was not independent). He referred to the proposal to amend Sec. 4 [1] of the 1947 Act to enable the MoT to give Directions of a "general or specific character", pointing out that the original limitation to "general" was intended to protect the Minister from Parliamentary pressure to give Directions to maintain or establish uneconomic services.

It did not prevent specific Directions to retain uneconomic fares, nor to retain loss making services. (see "Blueprints for Bankruptcy", Pages 100-104 and Chapter 2 - IV).

Internal DoT Memo, undated and unsigned: The main principle is that road haulage should be allowed to expand to the extent that may be justified by demand and railways should effect such economies to offset the resulting loss of traffic. (This prophecy could only be fulfilled if Tory Ministers, now abandoning their pre-war policy of co-ordination, refused to give the Square Deal sought by railways before the war). The Memo included the sentence: The policy which the Commission [BTC] would like is not necessarily the right policy for transport as a whole. It was endorsed in ink: "Better left out" of the White Paper - and it was. (It would have exposed whose hand was really on the tiller).

Internal DoT Memo on the Transport Bill, 23rd June: Charges Schemes - Not only to provide for maximum BR charges giving flexibility, but are to contain provisions precluding "unduly low charges" designed deliberately to undercut competitors and drive them out of business. (Flexibility is achieved by having no maxima - as always applied in any industry except railways even when privately owned. There was no provision to prevent road haulage undercutting BR to drive them out of the freight business). Draft Bill Clause 21 - BTC power to make temporary increases must be of the same percentage across the board, not discriminatory - i.e. totally lacking in any commercial flexibility.

The BTC had written to oppose the clause on "unduly low charges". In the New Draft on 2nd July: "Unduly low charges" was replaced by the right of BTC's competitors: road, coastwise shipping, canals; to object to the Transport Tribunal of uneconomic undercutting. Why Government was obsessed with this angle, when BR had not yet become debtors to Government's ill conceived 1956 deficit financing policy is not apparent. Without that, there could be no uneconomic undercutting. Either undercutting must be profitable or the BTC could not pay its way, and the BTC was opposed to being subsidised. (see "Blueprints for Bankruptcy", Page 49).

On 8th July, Hurcomb wrote to the MoT : The BTC was not consulted on your road haulage intentions. We have barely completed take-overs of road haulage under the 1947 Act. (Clearly, pre-war Tory Government talk of co-ordination of transport to avoid giving railways commercial freedom, was a ploy to play for time). The BTC letter also drew attention to the 19th century legislation surviving from which competitors are free - while a new disability is introduced.

An internal DoT Memo dated 18th July to the MoT refers to an "Economist" article criticising the fact that BR are not being relieved of common carrier obligations, and states: "But do these obligations bear so hardly upon railways? They would not, in any case, turn away traffic, just as hauliers do not, although they have no common carrier obligation". (It clearly reveals he did not realise that hauliers refused empty crates, and traffic to remote rural areas. Government had been told of this before the war - his predecessor reported to the Cabinet on this very issue. BR could neither refuse it, nor price up to cover costs in such areas).

Ten days later, the MoT [Leathers] wrote to the Prime Minister: Had talked to "Economist", who said the Bill is unjustifiable unless we are prepared to relieve railways of all obligations - common carrier, prohibition of undue preference, and see out-and-out competition. This would lead to outlying, sparsely populated districts paying far more for railway services than towns. (This can only be true if road haulage did not serve such districts, leaving railways with no competition because the traffic was uneconomic).

1952 "Transport Policy" [Cmd 8538]

"The BTC will be given latitude to vary Charges Schemes so as to improve the ability of railways to compete with other transport. Within ***prescribed limits*** they will be free to raise or lower charges with subsequent approval by the Tribunal, ***subject to the overriding power of the MoT***". (A unique form of freedom. not shared by suppliers or competitors. What was totally illogical, is that having set out to devise a strait jacket to prevent BR from offering charges which were too low, the Government enacted legislation to determine maximum charges. Surely, they should have specified minimum charges! Obviously, they planned a concept where road would expand on main routes, leaving railways to serve fringe areas at a loss. This was railways' reward for war service and a blunt rejection of anything remotely resembling a "Square Deal". If Tory Ministers could not foresee that the end product of their "Unsquare Deal" was railway insolvency forecast by their predecessors, there is little wonder that the UK has gone downhill.

The original White Paper proposed total freedom, but in April 1952, Churchill told his Cabinet: he would not accept the BTC should be free even with the approval of the Tribunal to adjust rates without intervention by Government or Parliament, and that BR should not be obliged to cover all costs, including investment from revenue. This was no surprise - Government had a few days earlier blocked a legal judgement by the Tribunal. Needing Tribunal approval was not "free". ("Blueprints for Bankruptcy", Pages 47, 66 & 100).

1953 Transport Act

The Act retained restrictive concepts: "operating as one undertaking", (which legally precluded making railways independently viable), "paying its way taking one year with another" and "Charges Schemes": ritualistic appearances in a Court of Law to beg permission to increase prices when suppliers made unfettered increases. Maximum charges were still controlled "in the Public interest". The Act perpetuated and expanded 1921 Act provisions to protect shipping and canals from "unfair competition" by BR - not by road - and gave no protection to BR against unfair competition by any other transport. It gave protection against "unreasonable charges" to traders desiring to send merchandise by rail "in circumstances in which that merchandise cannot reasonably be carried by other means of transport". Interpreting "reasonably" must have been a lawyer's dream.

BR had no protection against unreasonable charges by suppliers. Blee wrote in 1951 of "Price rings being abundantly apparent whenever BR went out to tender". [PRO : AN6/10].

It is a common belief that BR took seven years to prepare a Freight Charges Scheme. The first, based on integration, was ready to submit to the Tribunal in 1951, when the BTC was told to consult Coastal Shipping who were fearful of losing statutory protection. The Act required the BTC to create a new scheme based on competing with denationalised road haulage. In this unique form of competition, one side was totally free whilst the other still had its hands firmly tied! Government should have given BR independent status and the commercial freedom sought by railways before the war. It was another nine years before BR gained basic freight rates freedom - 40 years after the first complaint to Government of inequality. Coastal shipping retained protection until 1980. Regrettably, heavy industry, on which Government's rates system had made railways dependent, was entering its death throes by the time railways were given belated freedom.

When plans to denationalise road transport emerged, a pressure group called for railway denationalisation. Government responded only to the road haulage pressure group. So ended the Tory commitment to co-ordinated transport . [Railway Gazette, 21st July 1950].

The 1953 Act gave railways what Lord Stamp opposed - 'a little relief to continue the unequal battle for another round'. It took four years to implement and the round lasted five years - ironically, the trial period that the TAC had envisaged in 1939.

1957 Freight Charges Scheme

Blee proposed on 16th November 1951 that a new Freight Charges Scheme should be based on a maximum charge for the sparsest load from the greenest field area for each class. He had preferred no classes, only one sparsest load from one greenest field, but was told that the Tribunal would not agree to either option. [PRO : AN6/10].

To secure a pale image of the freedom which road haulage had always enjoyed, BR submitted a Freight Charges Scheme to the Transport Tribunal in 1955, who, 18 months later, after a Public Inquiry, spanning from July 1955 to March 1956, watered it down, reduced existing rates, when the object was to create headroom, and continued protection for coastwise shipping to object to "unfair" rail [but not road] rates! It retained controlling power over maximum charges - just as the President of the Railway Rates Tribunal had urged in 1939. The Scheme ended Classification [GCM]. (see Blueprints for Bankruptcy).

Private Sector road haulage could alter rates at will. So, paradoxically, could the BTC in respect of its residual road fleet, which had not been sold off. Hauliers and Traders with "C" licences, were legally enabled to "cream-off" profitable traffic. Legislation prevented BR from retaliating or protecting its commercial position.

The MoT admitted in 1956, that railways were not free to secure freight traffic on equal terms. Para 74: The Charges Scheme [supposed to give the same freedom as Road Haulage], was "appreciably restricted by the Transport Tribunal". [Cmd 9880].

It was an under statement of some magnitude. The Tribunal reduced some existing freight rates and retained control over others. (see "Blueprints for Bankruptcy").

In February 1949, Sir Gilmour Jenkins Permanent Secretary, DoT, told the Institute of Transport : "To be successful, transport had to be run on commercial, not on Government lines and given a large measure of freedom of action free from Ministerial control on its day to day administration". (Regrettably, no one in Government was listening).

Beneficiaries of the "Unsquare Deal"

Government

The major beneficiary of low rates and delayed increases was Government. Delayed increases, and charges below the inflation rate, kept down the cost of its traffic. The BTC told the Transport Tribunal in its 1950 Freight Charges submission that Government traffic receipts were 1947: £47m, 1948: £40m, 1949: £35m. On that revenue, over the three years Government's self imposed preferential discounts would be worth £60m. The covert gain in these years was really around £100m, since BR rates should have been 145% above pre-war like industry, not 55%. (see pages 167 & 186).

Control of charges held the cost of military travel at sub standard levels. Large gains continued to about 1960 when HM Forces and military freight traffic were back to pre-war levels. Buses did not have to give them cheap travel. (see "Blueprints for Bankruptcy", Page 46).

The Exchequer gained by dumping the financial burden of the loss making Caledonian and Crinan canals onto the BTC. "These canals were non transport bodies - deficits were formerly carried by the Exchequer". [BTC 1951 Report, Para 30].

Government gained by avoiding subsidies to inefficient industry in lieu of uneconomic rail charges, from holding down official travel costs, and commuting costs of Government employees which would reflect into lower salaries.

Industry & Agriculture

Until 1962, inefficient agriculture and heavy industry continued to gain, as they did before and during the war - by being effectively subsidised by uneconomic rail rates. This inflated private sector profits and gave scope for higher wages. (see page 73).

Industry gained by being able to use rail for under-priced low value goods. "The Obligation to carry includes:-

[a] Obligation to operate services regularly even though not financially profitable in certain cases;

[b] Users given equal treatment;

[c] Offer uniform tariff which does not reflect cost of individual services whether in areas with low or high volume". [BTC 1951 Report, Page 29, Para 60]

Road Transport

Road transport gained by not paying bridge costs. "The total burden [of bridges and canals] was £1-2m". [BTC 1951 Report, Para 30]. (Almost certainly under estimated, see Chapter 6).

Shipping

Coastal Shipping gained from Government directives, as well as from the Charges system. In 1964, the MoT reminded BR that they were still subject to coastal shipping objections to "unfair freight rates", when he compelled BR to increase freight rates for china clay from Cornwall to Kent following an objection by shipping interests, which customers paid rather than divert to sea. [Fiennes, Page 128].

That was not in the national interest. Government had never compelled road haulage to increase rates when railways objected to unfair competition. Protection continued to 1980.

Passengers

Passengers, and consequently their employers, gained from fares held below the rate of inflation from 1941 to 1982. (see "Blueprints for Bankruptcy", Page 63).

Renewed calls for the Square Deal

BTC Annual Reports

1948. Para 43: It is not possible that any undertaking which is to pay its way should submit to constant increases in costs of commodities which it needs and yet refrain indefinitely from raising prices to customers. Para 291: Higher prices of commodities above pre-war vary from steel up by 80%, to linseed oil up by 633%.

1949. Para 28: Draft Principles for a Merchandise Charges Scheme were published on 15th December. [The Tribunal had not approved it by 1951 and a new Government told the BTC to begin a completely new Scheme]. Rail charges were still at 1947 levels, which were below 1938 in real terms. Para 200: Prices of the index for selected commodities in general use were 145% above pre-war.

1950. Para 46 **No system of transport can absorb shocks of this nature without at least some increase in charges it makes to customers. But the increases do not come into effect until long after the need for them has become manifest.** Para 47: The Commission is practically alone in having little latitude for adjusting its own charges. Para 49: We began without reserves and have not secured any margin to accumulate them. Para 50: Any organisation working under these limitations [price control and no reserves], is bound to be chronically in deficit. Para 57: An Application to increase freight charges was submitted to the MoT in November 1949, but it was not until May 1950, that an increase became effective. The delay cost £11m. Para 71: Prices continue an upward trend, without pause or warning. By contrast, charges made by the BTC can only be altered after formal and public hearings which involve preparations and investigation over a considerable period of time. Para 74: **Even after freight rate increases, there was no change in volume.** (Contradicting the myth that ***only*** rail price increases lose volume). Para 99: We asked for a method of effecting quicker changes in prices to avoid deficits. Para 101: Where BRS charge less than the [statutory] railway charge, traffic will flow by road, where BR's charge is less than road and perhaps well below actual cost, (due to Statutory Rates based on cross subsidies), the traffic may go by rail. Remunerative is lost to rail, only the unremunerative remains. (The BTC could not prevent this iniquity begun in the 1920's even though it controlled

BRS and BR. BRS rates had to allow for the fact that, at the peak of the BRS fleet, 110,000 "A" and "B" licence, and 800,000 "C" licence vehicles remained in the private sector). Para 226: By December, BR freight rates were 81% and fares 75% above pre-war levels whereas, prices for steel rails had doubled, copper plates & tubes trebled, sleepers quadrupled, brass & tin quintupled, general timber 3.5 times, oil and coal tripled, motor spirit & diesel up 2.5 times, uniform clothing quadrupled.

1951. Para 25 : Only when co-ordinated charging arrangements exist for both rail & road can true costs compete. Para 29 : The present deficit occurred in the late 1949 when waiting approval for delayed increases on freight charges. Four years deficit is less than the profit accrued to the Government in any single one of the late years of the war.

1954. Para 6: With no margins in charges to meet rising costs until readjustment is possible, a deficit is inevitable. Para 27: It is imperative to have a free system of charging and to adjust rates to attract traffic to rail which is suitable. (Freedom trumpeted by the MoT in 1953 was illusory, they had to submit a new Scheme).

1955. Para 5: BTC's road haulage rates are varied according to circumstances. It would benefit BR if they had equal liberty to adjust charges, and assist them to attract to rail, goods for which that medium is suitable, whilst transferring the rest to road. Para 22: BTC is still without that greater freedom to charge, and hence to compete, which Parliament intended them to have. Para 36: Another factor is the growing volume of competition from privately owned transport, coupled with unequal terms on which BR are expected to meet competition, being hedged about with restrictions and obligations not shared by competitors, leaving the BTC providing many types of services at controlled charges that fall short of the individual cost of providing those services.

BTC Minutes, August 1958: The BTC approached the MoT on the "Reasonable Facilities" law. (It was both costly and very unreasonable so far as BR was concerned). May 1960: They "would prefer to be free to run the business as they judge, but doubted whether such freedom would ever be accorded".

British Transport Review, April 1952, Page 20: Rail freight charges at 120% over pre-war compares with a level of wholesale prices which is 225% higher.

BTC Chairman: We were promised freedom of charging on railways and release from restrictions on rates which they may quote. Because of the cumbersome procedure which has to be followed before approval can be had to a new Freight Charges Scheme, railways have not yet achieved the flexibility in charging which the Act promised, meanwhile the competition of privately owned road transport grows daily.
[Paper to the Royal United Services Institution, February, 1956).

Reappraisal of Modernisation Plan [Cmnd 813] July 1959, Para 6: Freedom to compete on less unfavourable terms with other transport was sought. Also relief from statutory obligations which bear unfairly on railways such as costs incurred on public level crossings, and maintenance of bridges over railways. Towards this end, it was agreed that £2m for 1959 will be made towards such costs, £1m for the second half of 1958. (This overdue, inadequate payment for road traffic, was soon withdrawn).

Appendix A, Para 10: It is critical that BR should be free to settle charges they make to their customers in the light of normal commercial considerations of the market. Appendix B, Para 6: Wagon modernisation - problems arise such as sharp curves in industrial premises.

MoT's Special Advisory Group was appointed by the MoT in 1960 and reported secretly to him. Its findings were kept secret until 1991. The Group criticised Government for the unitary nature of finances; statutory restrictions on operations; losses caused by the Tribunal; having to prove costs had increased to be allowed to increase prices; that road haulage was free to charge and carry as it will whilst BR was under an obligation to consult coastal shipping about charges and be under a risk of reference to the Tribunal; statutory prohibitions on the use of land and property and the lack of powers to develop car parks. DoT officers told the Group that it opposed removal of restrictions, notably on rates for bulk freight - the field in which BR had volume, and were concerned about freedom on Season rates for commuters because of "a possible effect on road congestion". [see page 6 for source].

In the light of my findings of the "Square Deal Denied", I was surprised to read: "When railways were nationalised in 1947, the pretence was maintained of controlling their rates, but before many years had passed, they obtained everything they had originally demanded in the 'Square Deal' campaign". [Dunbar, Page 120].

How could the FBI and ABCC be advocating to the secret Special Advisory Group in *1960* that railways should be given commercial freedom, and that Committee - composed of private sector businessmen - be making that same recommendation to the Government, if railways already had commercial freedom?

From nationalisation freight rates were controlled by a new Court of Law working to more penal restrictions than pre-war, there being no requirement to ensure a railway profit, their proceedings occupied three years in aggregate alone for freight rates and a further nine for fares. Railways' demands were, with the exception of protection for coastwise shipping, not removed until 1962 - 15 years after nationalisation. Shipping protection ended in 1980. Neither can hardly be classified as "not many years".

Anyone believing there was a "pretence at controlling rail rates", before nationalisation, will find ample evidence to the contrary in this book. Post nationalisation evidence will be found in "Blueprints for Bankruptcy", which contains a summary of 6,000 pages of verbatim evidence of the Hearings of the Court of the Transport Tribunal covering the years from 1948 to 1962 for freight, and to 1968 for passenger fares. .

Whilst the "Square Deal" campaign arose from the iniquitous disparity between policies applied by Government to rail and road public transport, post-war Government policies, particularly in regard to materials allocation created a situation in which disaffected passengers could also transfer easily to private cars, to escape overcrowding and old coaches, the continuance of which was due entirely to inequitable Government policies. Government set export motor car targets and allowed allocations of steel to motor manufacturers on that basis. "The gap between promise and performance grew steadily". [Plowden, Page 315]. Clearly, the road lobby was as powerful as ever.

Chapter 17 EPITAPH

If Lord Stamp had not been killed in 1941, and had been put in charge of the BTC - and it is inconceivable that Government would not have asked him, with his business and transport experience to run nationalised transport, in preference to the commercially inexperienced Sir Cyril Hurcomb* - he would have demanded rail freedom simultaneously with Government's 1953 denationalisation of road transport. There is no reason to suppose that Government would have removed their heads from the sand. It is a paradox, that Governments had called on Stamp to be a member of, or to lead inter-war domestic and international investigations, and was acknowledged to have a brilliant brain, yet on one issue they would not listen. On the railways' need for statutory equality, they remained intransigent. (* see Elliot, Page 90).

There was no justification for those who transferred easy deliveries to road, objecting to BR increasing charges, based on averages of good and bad paying loads, to compensate for being left with residual awkward loads to remote corners of rural UK. One can imagine the political and public outcry if BR had refused rural traffic, from 1948, and concentrated on trunk routes. Statutory control prevented BR increasing rates to an economic level, refusing traffic or adopting private sector practice of pricing uneconomic business up or out of the market. Suppliers increased prices but objected to BR doing so.

The inadequacy of industrial and commercial premises persists. Juggernauts delay other traffic whilst they make several shunts, or arrogantly use the highway to unload. Those who advocate converting railways into roads would do well to ponder the implications as such roads would be narrower than existing roads. The concept was dismissed as impractical by road experts, including a spokesman for the BRF, and by new statistical evidence confirming its impracticability. [see "Blueprints for Bankruptcy" Chapter 13].

Political Ineptitude

BTC Reports, 1948-61 show that Merchandise (vulnerable to competition) fell by 32% whilst coal and mineral traffic fell only 8%. This decline, prophesied in 1938, was due to Government refusing to grasp the nettle and give equal commercial and legislative freedom to railways.

Gratitude for railways' Herculean wartime efforts were forgotten. Having milked them during the war and praised them for their vital role, with the war still a recent memory, railways were treated like an enemy of the State, and used to save inefficient industry, which still needed to be subsidised and protected against foreign competition, including European countries, whose industries suffered more devastation in two major Wars. Other countries introduced new techniques whilst our industrial magnates persevered with methods which predated the railways! [Barnett[1] Page 94, contains an interesting example].

Not content with imposing a more rigid post-war statutory control of railway charges, Ministers had to take it upon themselves to interfere in their appointed Court's decisions and superimpose Ministerial Directives. [see "Blueprints for Bankruptcy" Page 100].

In 1952, Sir Wm. Wood met the MoT after he interfered in the Tribunal's decision on fares with costly consequences. The Minutes of the BTC refer to that meeting, and the

Memorandum which he circulated to members of the BTC, but the relevant PRO file which contained other Memoranda and papers for that BTC meeting, did not contain this vital document. [see "Blueprints for Bankruptcy", Page 100]

In 1952, Tories abandoned their long proclaimed policy of transport co-ordination in the public interest - their pre-war excuse for blocking the Square Deal and reverted precisely to the 1938 situation of unfair competition - the Unsquare Deal. Statutory railway freedom was - up to a point - implemented in 1962, when UK heavy industry was in terminal decline, leaving railways with surplus assets which had been required to service inefficient heavy industry. By this time, road transport had secured a stranglehold on the more profitable traffics. Having milked the railways for many years to enable them to compete with foreign industry, instead of resolving costly demarcation problems and implementing modern methods, heavy UK industry eventually gave up the ghost and dragged railways down with them. When Churchill told the Cabinet in April 1952 that railways need not cover all costs from revenue, he was effectively removing the need for Equality. Perversely, his 1953 Act required the BTC to "Pay its Way"!

In 1956, in another twist, the MoT blocked BR from making an Application to the Court of the Transport Tribunal to increase fares and freight charges, which were trailing behind inflation indices. No control was exercised over shipping, canal or road charges. The Government "appealed" to industry to help to reverse inflationary trends by voluntarily holding price levels. The responses included : "We have an uncontrollable element in manufacturing costs", [National Union of Manufacturers], and "Will make every effort to avoid increasing prices", [Employers' Federation]*. Both gave plenty of latitude. A similar Directive was given to railways again in 1972. Again, industrial commitments gave them latitude. Despite frozen railway prices, inflation indices rose, clearly indicating the irrelevance of railway charges upon inflationary trends. The media was strongly critical of these policies. Ministers' ingenuous policy, which clearly acknowledged these measures would create losses, was to provide interest bearing loans! No industry would have accepted such an offer. These developments were not unlike the Government's wartime policy, when they froze railway charges for six years whilst other prices rocketed. Interestingly, the wartime file on rail prices was examined in 1956, but those concerned ignored its warnings that bankruptcy would ensue. [*Keesing 14807]

Had Government taken the obvious line of giving BR commercial freedom, in 1951, if not before, equal to that enjoyed by other nationalised industries and other transport, and enacted equal legislation and safety regulations on road transport, BR could have achieved solvency. However, that was unlikely whilst electoral implications remained. It would have demonstrated beyond doubt that Government policies had dragged railways down, and no politician would have taken that risk.

Instead of giving BR full commercial freedom, railways were privatised. This will enable them to demonstrate "how the private sector can do a better job" albeit operating in a freer environment than railways have enjoyed since 1830. The roles of the Franchise Director and Regulator pale into insignificance against the control exercised for 40 years by a public Court of Law, and Directions issued by Ministers, both of which caused horrendous losses. (see "Blueprints for Bankruptcy" for details).

The privatised companies are practising policies which would have led to a public reprimand and Ministerial Directives for BR - shorter trains, trains not making advertised calls to enhance punctuality, broken connections, overcrowded trains, refusal to provide buses in lieu of cancelled trains, the cessation of passenger freedom to use alternative routes, conveying locos and coaches by road to reduce costs, stabling coaches for which operators do not wish to pay, accidents involving contractors.

Ministers spoke of creating competition between different railway companies - something they decided to eliminate in 1921! Sections of the media took this at face value and began to speak of West Coast and East Coast competition! Those with a better grasp of geography will be puzzled by the scope for competition for passengers travelling on the one hand to Peterborough, Grantham, Doncaster, Leeds, York, Darlington, Newcastle & Edinburgh, with those wishing to travel to Northampton, Rugby, Coventry, Birmingham, Crewe, Warrington, Liverpool, Manchester, Preston, Carlisle & Glasgow.

Unsurprisingly, it did not take incoming management long to discover that railways' main competitor was road transport - public and private. It is pertinent to note the remarks made by the American Chairman of the privatised UK rail freight business, in a lecture to the Chartered Institute of Transport on 14th January 1997, when he called for a "level playing field between rail and road transport". As a newcomer to the UK scene, he can hardly be accused of being indoctrinated by historical railway opinions.

It is to be hoped that Government will take steps to create a level playing field, before history repeats itself and plunges the country into another war. When the Channel Tunnel opened, Ministers spoke of its potential for moving military equipment and manpower to the mainland. Simultaneous use of UK railways will be essential. Government will have to find funds to pay for railway vehicles, as they did for road vehicles 80 years ago, since their policies of the last 80 years have progressively reduced the rolling stock fleet and infrastructure.

It is tragic that Minister's aspirations to get freight back onto rail from road came so late in the day. Today's problems could all have been avoided had their predecessors, particularly in the period 1920-1953, ensured that railways were not denied equality of treatment, and that laws of 1871 and 1921 were not swept so blatantly aside after railways had responded so magnificently in two World Wars. This beating of the political chest carries all the confusing hallmarks of Whitehall farce and Greek tragedy.

Those who denied equal rights to railways cannot be protected from the consequences of their actions and inactions by the usual response that today's critics have the benefit of 20-20 hindsight. Government papers show quite clearly that they were fully aware that their actions would lead to railway insolvency - but they still pursued policies which would produce that result. They did not even need to be the visionaries that so many of them believed they were.

Former Ministers who pat themselves on the back because passenger volume is increasing have not studied history. Every recession has been marked by a reduction in leisure and business travel. Conversely, the end of a recession is marked by its return.

It defies belief that a democracy can have treated substantial taxpayers and ratepayers so cavalierly, and to have swept aside inconvenient laws. Gandhi's response to the question: "What do you think of democracy in Britain?" - that "it would be a good idea", can be seen in another light.

INDEX